D. H. Lawrence in His Time

D. H. Lawrence in His Time:
1908–1915

Kim A. Herzinger

Lewisburg
Bucknell University Press
London and Toronto: Associated University Presses

Associated University Presses, Inc.
4 Cornwall Drive
East Brunswick, N.J. 08816

Associated University Presses Ltd
27 Chancery Lane
London WC2A 1NF, England

Associated University Presses
Toronto M5E 1A7, Canada

Library of Congress Cataloging in Publication Data

Herzinger, Kim A., 1946–
    D. H. Lawrence in his time, 1908–1915.

    Bibliography: p.
    Includes index.
    1. Lawrence, D. H. (David Herbert), 1885–
1930—Criticism and interpretation.   2. English literature—20th century—History and
criticism.   I. Title.
PR6023.A93Z63127   823′.912   81-65863
ISBN 0-8387-5028-1   AACR2

PRINTED IN THE UNITED STATES OF AMERICA

For Kerry, Jessica, and Caitlin

Contents

Abbreviations Used in the Text and Notes   9

Acknowledgments   11

1   Introduction   15
     The Problem of "Placing" Lawrence   15
     The Problem of the Cultural Context   18

2   Lawrence and the Edwardians: 1908–1912   24
     The Edwardian Cultural Milieu: "Not So Far from the
         Crystal Palace"   24
     Lawrence among the Edwardian Uncles   27

3   Lawrence and the Georgians: Significant Affinities   39
     The "New World" and English Culture   40
     The Influence of the Continent   43
     Georgians in the "New World"   46
     The Uncles' Response to Georgianism   48
     Lawrence and *Georgian Poetry 1911–1912*   50
     Lawrence and the Georgians: Significant Affinities   52
     Georgians and Moderns   59
     Georgians and the Public   62

4   Landscape and Community: *The White Peacock* and *The
   Rainbow*   66
     The Attraction of Optimism: Rupert Brooke and E. M.
         Forster   66
     Howards End as Georgian Archetype   68
     Georgians and the Landscape   71
     The White Peacock   76
     Community and Isolation: Lawrence's Ambivalence   86
     The Rainbow as Georgian and Anti-Georgian Novel   92

5   Lawrence's Break with the Georgians   100
     The Evidence of Unrest   100
     The Dispute with Edward Marsh   106
     Georgian Failures   115

6 "Another Language Almost": The Impact of Futurism,
   Imagism, and Vorticism   120
      Lawrence's "Transition Stage" and the Vortex   121
      Lawrence and Futurism   127
      Lawrence, Imagism, and "Amygism"   140

7 Good-bye to All That: The Georgians, the War, and
   "England, My England"   158
      Georgians and War: The Example of Rupert Brooke   158
      "England, My England"   162

8 Extensions and Conclusions   172
      Extensions: Cambridge and Bloomsbury   172
      Conclusions   179

APPENDIX A: The Night Pound Ate the Tulips   183

APPENDIX B: The *English Review* "England, My England"   186

Notes   188

Selected Bibliography   212

Index   231

Abbreviations Used in the Text and Notes

CL *The Collected Letters of D. H. Lawrence*. 2 vols. Edited by Harry T. Moore. New York: Viking, 1962.

CP *The Complete Poems of D. H. Lawrence*. Collected and Edited with an Introduction and Notes by Vivian de Sola Pinto and Warren Roberts. New York: Viking, 1973.

Phoenix *Phoenix: The Posthumous Papers of D. H. Lawrence* (1936). Edited and with an Introduction by Edward McDonald. New York: Viking, 1972.

Phoenix II *Phoenix II: Uncollected, Unpublished, and Other Prose Works by D. H. Lawrence*. Collected and Edited with an Introduction and Notes by Warren Roberts and Harry T. Moore. New York: Viking, 1971.

CSS *The Complete Short Stories of D. H. Lawrence*. 3 vols. New York: Viking, 1968.

Acknowledgments

I would like to thank the following for permission to quote from published works:

From "Snap Dragon," "The North Country," "Baby Movements," "Night Songs," and "Wedding Morn" in *The Complete Poems of D. H. Lawrence*. Copyright 1964 by Angelo Ravagli and C. M. Weekley, Executors of the Estate of Frieda Lawrence Ravagli. Reprinted by permission of Viking Penguin Inc. and Laurence Pollinger Ltd.

From *Sons and Lovers* by D. H. Lawrence. Copyright 1913 by Thomas Seltzer Inc. Reprinted by permission of Viking Penguin Inc., Laurence Pollinger Ltd., and the Estate of the late Mrs. Frieda Lawrence Ravagli.

From *The Rainbow* by D. H. Lawrence. Copyright 1915 by D. H. Lawrence, copyright renewed 1943 by Frieda Lawrence Ravagli. Reprinted by permission of Viking Penguin Inc., Laurence Pollinger Ltd., and the Estate of the late Mrs. Frieda Lawrence Ravagli.

From *Women in Love* by D. H. Lawrence. Copyright 1920, 1922 by D. H. Lawrence, copyright renewed 1947, 1949 by Frieda Lawrence. Reprinted by permission of Viking Penguin Inc., Laurence Pollinger Ltd., and the Estate of the late Mrs. Frieda Lawrence Ravagli.

From *Phoenix* by D. H. Lawrence. Copyright 1936 by Frieda Lawrence, renewed 1964 the Estate of Frieda Lawrence Ravagli. Reprinted by permission of Viking Penguin Inc., Laurence Pollinger Ltd., and the Estate of the late Mrs. Frieda Lawrence Ravagli.

From *The Collected Letters of D. H. Lawrence*, edited by Harry T. Moore. Copyright 1962 by Angelo Ravagli and C. M. Weekley, Executors of the Estate of Frieda Lawrence Ravagli. Reprinted by permission of Viking Penguin Inc., Laurence Pollinger Ltd., and the Estate of the late Mrs. Frieda Lawrence Ravagli.

From "England, My England" in *The Complete Short Stories of D. H. Lawrence*, vol. 2. Copyright 1922 by Thomas Seltzer Inc., copyright renewed 1949 by Frieda Lawrence. Reprinted by permission of Viking Penguin Inc., Laurence Pollinger Ltd., and the Estate of the late Mrs. Frieda Lawrence Ravagli.

From *Lady Chatterley's Lover* by D. H. Lawrence. Reprinted by permission of Grove Press, Inc.

From "The Crystal Palace" by John Davidson in *John Davidson: a Selection of His Poems*. Reprinted by permission of Hutchinson Publishing Group Ltd.

From "A Greeting" by W. H. Davies in *The Complete Poems of W. H. Davies*. Copyright 1963 by Jonathan Cape Ltd. Reprinted by permission of Wesleyan University Press.

From "Town and Country" and "The Old Vicarage, Grantchester" by Rupert Brooke in *The Collected Poems of Rupert Brooke*. Reprinted by permission of Dodd, Mead and Company; McClelland and Stewart Limited, Toronto; and Sidgwick and Jackson.

From "Iron Founders and Others" and "From the Viaduct" by Gordon Bottomley in *Chambers of Imagery 1st and 2nd Series*. Reprinted by permission of George Allen and Unwin (Publishers) Ltd.

From *The Summing Up* by W. Somerset Maugham. Copyright 1938 by W. Somerset Maugham. Reprinted by permission of Doubleday and Company, Inc. and A. P. Watt and Son.

From *A Nest of Tigers: The Sitwells in Their Times* by John Lehmann, copyright 1968. Reprinted by permission of Little, Brown and Co., Inc.

Acknowledgment is made to the *Journal of Modern Literature* for permission to reprint "The Night Pound Ate the Tulips," which appeared in slightly altered form in *JML* 8 (1980).

I would also like to thank the University of Southern Mississippi for its support of this project, as well as a large number of friends and colleagues—Noel Polk, Gary Stringer, Tony Brinkley, Rick Barthelme, David Wheeler, Angela Ball, Philip Kolin, Tom Richardson, Rex Stamper, Ramona Quave, Bill Holman, Andrew Ruth, Russell Brubaker, Ray Hilliard, Herbert Shapiro, George H. Ford, and Bruce Johnson—for their invaluable aid and advice.

D. H. Lawrence in His Time

1 Introduction

"I do write because I want folk—
English folk—to alter, and have
more sense."

LAWRENCE, 1913

The Problem of "Placing" Lawrence

John Lehmann, in his book on the Sitwells, has painted a verbal portrait of the literary milieu of the first decades of the twentieth century. Naturally, in his portrait, the Sitwells dominate the foreground, but

immediately behind them, to the left, would appear the leading lights of Bloomsbury, now in the heyday of their influence, E. M. Forster (a little detached), Virginia and Leonard Woolf, Maynard Keynes, Lytton Strachey, Roger Fry, Desmond MacCarthy (with his back turned to them), Clive and Vanessa Bell, Aldous Huxley, T. S. Eliot with the diffident smile of the guest, and, gambolling at their feet such ardent youthful figures as Raymond Mortimer, Duncan Grant and David Garnett. . . .

On the right side of the picture, at a slightly further distance, would be depicted that group of poets, novelists and critics who came to be known as the Georgians, with the elegant, slightly affected but genial figure of Sir Edward Marsh as the focal point. . . . Arranged round Eddie Marsh would be such figures as Harold Monro, W. H. Davies, Lascelles Abercrombie, Gordon Bottomley, Edward Shanks, Edmund Blunden, Robert Nichols, John Drinkwater and Sir John (then plain Jack) Squire; Hugh Walpole casting ardent glances in the direction of Bloomsbury; and a chubby Yorkshire boy, Jack Priestley, at their feet. Separate, but nearer to the Bloomsbury group, would be a small cluster of Irish bards and dreamers, W. B. Yeats, James Joyce, "A. E." and James Stephens. Away in the background would be the seated Olympian figures of Joseph Conrad, Rudyard Kipling, H. G. Wells, Bernard

Shaw and Arnold Bennett; and somewhere between them all, thumbing his nose in most directions, a bearded young Nottinghamshire faun in gamekeeper's costume, D. H. Lawrence. [1]

Lehmann's portrait is not without accuracy. But the portrayal of Lawrence sitting "somewhere between them all" suggests the difficulty of firmly "placing" Lawrence in the context of early-twentieth-century British culture. Unlike that of almost all of his literary contemporaries, Lawrence's position has never been adequately defined and, consequently, we are left with the conventional notion of Lawrence as a snarling outsider to the cultural milieu of his time.

Establishing Lawrence's relationship to his cultural context has never been a major concern of Lawrentians. This might have surprised and disappointed Lawrence, who once said of his work that it should not "be judged as if it existed in the absolute, in the vacuum of the absolute. Even the best poetry, when it is at all personal, needs the penumbra of its own time and place and circumstance to make it full and whole."[2]

Even the indefatigable work of Harry T. Moore, Edward Nehls, Emile Delavenay, and Paul Delany, to name just four Lawrentians who have dealt with the relations between Lawrence and his literary and intellectual peers, has not excavated much below the biographical surface of those relationships. Scholars who do go below such surfaces, such as Martin Green in his work on the von Richthofen sisters, seem to choose to dwell upon intellectual relationships which, if important, remain tangential to the central concerns of this study.

Some important Lawrence critics—F. R. Leavis, Mark Schorer, George H. Ford, Eugene Goodheart, and Scott Sanders, for example—have certainly made significant suggestions in the way of establishing Lawrence's relationship to his period. But their major contributions, quite justifiably, lie elsewhere. It has been more important for these critics to illuminate what happens in the novels rather than to discuss how the novels came to happen. It still is, but the latter approach can surely shed light on the former.

Earlier Lawrentians were busy elsewhere. For many years, Lawrence's literary "place" was obscured by the writings of his friends, from which more recent criticism has, fortunately, almost completely rescued him. Of the fifty-two years since his death, fully twenty-five were devoted to, as Aldous Huxley called it, "destructive hagiography,"[3] and it was not until interest in the Lawrence myth was superseded by interest in his work that Lawrence became more accessible to ordinary modes of judgment and analysis. In the past three decades, then, Lawrentians have justifiably concentrated on the large body of work that he produced during his lifetime. The cluster of memoirs and biographies, which once determined Lawrence's artistic and personal reputation, has by now been demoted from historical Truth to the less rarefied atmosphere of more or less interesting personal testament; "destructive hagiography"—in the forms developed by Witter Bynner, Mabel Dodge Luhan, Jessie Chambers, Catherine Carswell, Dorothy Brett, Earl and Achsah Brewster, David Garnett, John Middleton Murry, Hugh Kingsmill, and others—has been left for those, such as Emily Hahn in *Lorenzo*, who still drag out savory aspects of the Lawrence myth for money.

Concentration on Lawrence as an artist or a myth is not the only reason that scholars have shied away from placing Lawrence inside his cultural context, however. Frank Kermode has suggested another reason in his admirable short study of Lawrence. "Lawrence," he says, "is always working alone. His relationship to the history of ideas in his time is so far below the surface that to write it would be to engage in very delicate and also very speculative excavations."[4] The difficulties of which Kermode warns, and they are difficulties indeed, are made even more perilous by the sheer complexity of the years between 1910 and 1920, years during which the frame of events persistently splintered into the literary picture, but the years nevertheless in which Lawrence fully entered the literary culture of England and wrote the works on which his reputation stands.

Lawrence's cultural "place," then, has often been the concern of scholars who are more devoted to cultural analysis, and for whom the complexity of the period achieves at least some kind of cohesion. But these scholars, including Raymond Williams, Malcolm Bradbury, J. A. V. Chapple, John Lester, and G. S. Fraser, although they have clearly pictured Lawrence in relation to the ideas and obsessions of his time, have done so while working on a much larger canvas. Their scope prevents them from concentrating solely upon Lawrence.

Lawrence is not always treated even this well, however, and sometimes he is not treated at all. Hugh Kenner, who in *The Pound Era* has written what is probably the single most stimulating book on the modern era, a book in which he develops continually fascinating connections between the modern *Zeitgeist* and almost every writer who contributed to it, mentions Lawrence only once. Kenner, of course, might dislike Lawrence, even ignore him; but a book which in every other way appears to be a comprehensive examination of the major literary and intellectual currents of the period seems unnecessarily restricted when Lawrence, alone among major modern writers, is almost completely excluded from discussion.

The Problem of the Cultural Context

This book, then, will attempt to approach Lawrence by "placing" him inside the cultural matrix of his time; it assumes that an understanding of Lawrence's cultural context, and his responses and reactions to it, is essential to a fuller comprehension of the meaning of his work. This study is not intended to be a search for sources, nor is it meant to be taken as an examination of direct influences. Lawrence, it is generally agreed, is rarely emulative in his work. When he is, it is usually in an idiosyncratic way; one might point to the affinities between H. G. Wells's *Ann Veronica* and Lawrence's *The Lost Girl*, or those between *A Passage to India* and *St. Mawr*, as examples. But Lawrence was to a great degree assimilative—not only of those books which he read, but also of the currents of thought which continually circulated around him. No young writer living in England in the years before 1914, and especially one so serious about his role as Lawrence, could have remained untouched by the electrified atmosphere which characterized the cultural milieu of the time. A study such as this, therefore, requires an examination of that background and atmosphere in the hope that it will help to define the preoccupations that Lawrence shared with his contemporaries, as well as the impact that these common elements had on the hidden infrastructure of Lawrence's imagination.

The very concept of a modern literary "milieu" is, in itself, difficult to define adequately. Before 1910, one can speak with some assurance of a British cultural and literary milieu, but after 1910 one must begin to speak of milieus. The "little clans" feared by Edmund Gosse, which would "band together for mutual protection against the reasonable world,"[5] had by then taken on their preliminary forms. In 1915, Richard Aldington could say, "The arts are now divided between popular charlatans and men of talent, who, of necessity, write, think and paint only for each other, since there is no one else to understand them."[6] By 1920, Harold Monro could rightly declare that the "common claim of the modern group is to differ by the possession of a secret unknown to those outside its circle."[7] The coterie spirit had so hardened by the end of the decade that attack and retaliation between differing cultural groups became habitual and expected. London had become a place of "specialized artistic enclaves, cosmopolitan villages with communications out into the world but with a localized, artistic hierarchy of values."[8]

Georgians, Imagists, "Amygists," Vorticists, and Futurists marshaled their considerable energies and set upon each other with venom; the Sitwells looked askance at Bloomsbury, Bloomsbury stared right back; Georgians disliked Imagists, Imagists disliked Georgians; everyone attacked the Edwardians, Wyndham Lewis attacked everyone. Paul Fussell attributes this literary warfare to the "paranoid melodrama" which had been produced by the prolonged trench warfare of 1914–18, and claims that "the most indispensable concept underlying the energies of modern writing is that of 'the enemy.'"[9] But the impulse toward the coterie—an enclave of sympathetic souls banded together not only for mutual protection, but also for the maintenance of whatever they considered preservable or desirable in their culture—existed before the war ever began. As Samuel Hynes has noted, "Though the war dramatized and speeded the changes from Victorian to modern England, it did not make them. Virtually everything that is thought of as characteristically modern already existed in England by 1914"[10]—not the least of which was the first stirring of the coterie spirit.

The coteries were, in part, an artistic extension of a problem with much wider implications—the problem of the survival of English civilization in the modern world. If the more intelligent among the Edwardians had seen that, to survive, their civilization would have to "transcend the limitations of class and nationality and build up a Great Society led by an *elite*,"[11] the more intelligent young writers of the years immediately preceding the war began to feel that civilization could "only survive in small islands of culture" that had to be "fashioned anew by a self-chosen *elite* that managed to escape the spiritual degradation of a commercialized world."[12] One is reminded of Ezra Pound's view of the reading public: "So far as I personally am concerned the public can go to the devil. It is the function of the public to prevent the artist's expression by hook or by crook."[13] In such a context, then, one can usefully compare the Edwardian H. G. Wells's desire for a "planetary community," or his claim that the Great War was fought to save civilization, with the modern man-about-Bloomsbury who, when asked why he wasn't fighting to save civilization, replied,"Madam, *I* am the civilization they are fighting for."[14]

Stephen Spender, discussing this movement away from full-scale cultural community and toward a literary culture dominated by isolated cultural enclaves, reveals the unlikely figure of E. M. Forster as one who was early attuned to the shift. Spender calls it the "Forsterian idyll."[15]

> Forster can both face the destruction of the England which he loves and yet create spaces in his novels (cellars) for the limited survival of personal relations. . . . The idyll rests on the faith that despite the general debased conditions of the world, people can create among themselves small societies apart.[16]

For confirmation of Spender's statement, one might point to *The Longest Journey*, Forster's own favorite among his novels. For Ansell, who carries many of Forster's authorial sympathies, "There is no great world at all . . . the earth is full of tiny societies . . . some are good and some are bad."[17] The "good" tiny society is exclusive; Ricky's wife Agnes, for one, is "not saved."[18] In fact, according to Ansell, she "has no real existence."[19] Ricky himself is provided the comfort of his own personal enclave for psychic restoration; characteristically, for Forster, it is a small clearing in the woods, a "jolly place"[20] which is hidden from the road.

What is particularly interesting here is that Forster, probably the most generous and tolerant of all the major modern writers, and one who remained particularly cautious of associating himself too closely with any of the existing coteries, exhibits the impulse toward the isolated, if "saved," group with a vigor equal to that of any of the later Georgians, Imagists, Vorticists, or Bloomsburians. His novels are finely wrought bottles with messages in them—and one of the messages is the desirability, perhaps even the inevitability, of cultural enclaves.

Much of the coterie warfare that characterizes these years seems to have emerged from the confrontation of two mutually exclusive ideals: first, the central Edwardian belief in the desirability and possibility of English civilization's being made whole and healthy through social and political reform; and second, the modern belief that mere reform would be inadequate and that an entirely new vision, a "new world," was both necessary and imminent. The modern writer, by rejecting Edwardian notions of reform—and unable to imagine any kind of full-scale cultural coherence—was forced to try to establish at least his particular group as the only one pointing the direction toward a viable future. Moderns after Forster would not be so gentle with the Edwardian "Heartbreak House" as he had been. Like Pound, they would throw "bricks through the front window," or, like Eliot, "go in at the back door and take out the swag."[21]

The method of this study derives from the development of Lawrence's own interactions with these various cultural milieus, and from the developing preoccupations of mind which were defined and explored through those interactions. Between 1908 and 1915, and for as long as he continued to maintain a reasonably close contact with the British literary and cultural world, Lawrence would associate himself with these small enclaves which, between them, determined so much of England's cultural life. Such associations followed a particular pattern. His connection with any specific group was usually brief, at first characterized by a period of intense interest and expressed hopes, which would be followed by a period of doubt and reaction; his original optimism would then recede into disillusion and, finally, utter disgust. Always, however, Lawrence would continue to assimilate methods and approaches which were generative to his own work, while rejecting those aspects which were not, or which he found repugnant.

This process of attraction and recoil was one that he would repeat throughout the years spanning World War I, and one through which Lawrence apparently had to pass in order to define his goals as an artist and as a prophet. And it is a process which becomes more important when we sufficiently recognize the seriousness with which Lawrence took both roles. Lawrence never completely abandoned his early intention: the regeneration of the English people and of English culture. This was the animating impulse behind all of his work. "I do write," he said in 1913, "because I want folk—English folk—to alter, and have more sense."[22] In 1929, Lawrence told Brewster Ghiselin, "If it weren't for all the lies in the world, I wouldn't write at all."[23]

As he once declared, Englishness *was* his very vision; even when he wrote of Italy, Australia, Mexico, or New Mexico, his purposive imagination was directed toward England. Lawrence retained the Victorian impulse to take responsibility for the total texture of his society, and he desired, like so many of his Victorian predecessors, to newly define the possibilities for community. It is this, as much as anything, which separated him from most of his contemporaries. Because of his faith in, and desire for, a living, vital society, Lawrence was in many ways the only significant modern writer consistently to choose nineteenth-century options to solve twentieth-century problems. Although Lawrence dabbled in most of the well-known twentieth-century modes of confronting experience—aestheticism titillated him for a short time early in his career, the notions of quasi-Nietzschean politics interested him during the middle years, and the construction of an auxiliary religion became more evident in the later years—he never wholly or finally gave himself to any of them. Lawrence never confused his aesthetic sense with his ethical sense; he did not, in other words, fall into that confusion which swallowed so many of his contemporaries: attributing social, ethical, and religious significance to preoccupations that were in fact aesthetic. Lawrence, to paraphrase G. K. Chesterton, would not treat taste as if it were a matter of morality, and could not treat morality as if it were a matter of taste.[24]

In contrast to his Victorian predecessors, however, Lawrence fully recognized that he lived in a time when there was no longer an active sense of community in progress; the artist could no longer function close to the center of society—because there was no center, no stable matrix, out of which he could work.

Consequently, Lawrence's work during this period displays both the impulse toward community as well as a profound corollary impulse of reaction away from the community and toward the enclave. These two opposing movements of Lawrence's imagination are apparent in all his work throughout the decade between 1910 and 1920.

Lawrence's earliest work either assumes community (*The White Peacock, Sons and Lovers*) or envisions it as a goal still achievable after radical individual and societal regeneration (*The Rainbow*). This side of his mind could declare: "Men are free when they belong to a living, organic, *believing* community, active in fulfilling some unfulfilled, perhaps unrealized purpose."[25]

But most of Lawrence's work during the war and after, including his ideas about the utopian Rananim, rejects the possibility of total cultural regeneration and focuses on the necessity of beginning anew, from a separate and often isolated enclave opposed to the wider society around it. Those, such as Paul Delany in his *D. H. Lawrence's Nightmare*, who see Rananim as simply the utopian fantasy of a hopelessly messianic and embittered Lawrence, do not sufficiently take into account the powerful attraction, and general success, of the small enclave-community in early twentieth-century cultural life. With few exceptions, every significant British writer between 1910 and 1930 attached himself more or less intimately to an actual enclave-community (like Bloomsbury or Cambridge or the Kensington Imagists) or to a de facto enclave-community of kindred spirits (like the Georgians). Lawrence's recoil from the notion of a full community can be felt most keenly in the "end-of-the-world"[26] atmosphere of *Women in Love*. "We must stand aside," claims this aspect of Lawrence, because "when many men stand aside, they stand in a new world; a new world of man has come to pass."[27] Still, as Raymond Williams reminds us, "if in his own life he 'rejected the claims of society,' it was not because he did not understand the importance of community, but because, in industrial England, he could find none."[28]

Lawrence, then, continued to search for a central community which would give direction to his animating purpose: the regeneration of England and English folk. His search for it, carried out for the most part among small, contained enclaves, almost always resulted in the process of attraction and recoil previously described. And if this process often resulted in significant work, it was because Lawrence's creative energies were best focused when he wrote out of a sense of fierce opposition to the coterie-societies with which he became entangled, and also because he could never completely relinquish his faith in the possibility of a living society. His optimism might grow dim, but "instead of staring, coldly and resignedly, at the figures of loss, he sets out to find how . . . the flame can be kept alive in an ugly and divided and rootless society," while continuing his search for "what is irreducible, substantial, life-bearing in others and in another."[29]

This study, then, will examine Lawrence's development in relation to those cultural entanglements in which he so often involved himself. It will focus on one particular involvement, with the Georgians, partially because of its relative, if undeserved, obscurity, but for the most part because of the powerful impact which the Georgian sensibility had on Lawrence; because his attraction to, and rejection of, this sensibility generated much of his most significant work; and because his connection with the Georgians led him into equally interesting associations with other groups and other sensibilities.

Still, though the Georgians were one of the first recognizable group manifestations of what has come to be thought of as modern British literature, this study must necessarily begin where Lawrence himself began—with the last remnant of the preceding era, the Edwardians.

2   Lawrence and the Edwardians: 1908–1912

The Edwardian Cultural Milieu: "Not So Far from The Crystal Palace"

In 1908, after he moved from Eastwood to Croydon, Lawrence lived physically where official British culture lived spiritually— "not so far from the Crystal Palace."[1] But for many Edwardians this was a rather uncomfortable juxtaposition; English past and English present were uneasy dwellers in the same cultural space. Although long since removed, significantly, from the center of London to the periphery, the Crystal Palace remained as a symbol of Victorian hope and accomplishment, an incontestable reminder of the immediate English past—too defiantly there to be ignored, but already too alien to be totally reverenced.

The new English mood was not a happy one. The Edwardians felt inferior, almost abandoned by the grand sweep of the culture which had preceded them. They found themselves having to dispense with social and cultural fixity and facing, instead, radical uncertainty. They found that the culture into which they fitted had been replaced by a culture which they had to fit into. The monuments of the Victorians were an affront to a national dignity which the Edwardians themselves felt had already been significantly diminished.

The future for what the Crystal Palace symbolized was being called into question, and there was no uniquely Edwardian voice authoritative enough to give the necessary guidance. Almost all of the long-lived Victorian greats were dead, and their tradition had been reduced to the size of William Watson, Alfred Noyes, and Stephen Phillips, poets so obviously inferior to their robust predecessors that comparisons could only be absurdly meaningless. The poet laureate was Alfred Austin, of whom perhaps the best that

24

could be said was that "he had all the qualifications of a really great poet except a sustained faculty for writing really good poetry."[2]

To be sure, Swinburne, Meredith, Hardy, and Kipling were still alive. But Swinburne and Meredith would die in 1909, Hardy remained a man apart, and Kipling remained apart from men—at least those who did not share his increasingly shrill imperialist convictions and his championship of men of action. In Kipling, Victorian assumptions began to sound curiously remote and, worse than that, simply inapplicable to the times. The Crystal Palace had clearly become a problem. It was, like Kipling himself, an anachronism. John Davidson, a late Victorian who desperately wanted to be a modern, saw the Crystal Palace—that symbol of the halcyon future, erected to "suggest all the unlimited outer world by the space within"[3]—as "The fossil of a giant myriapod," a "place/ Phantasmal like a beach in hell where souls/ Are ground together by an unseen sea."[4]

Davidson's lines point the direction for Samuel Hynes's contention that there was, in Edwardian England, an "ossification of authority that encased and cramped the new: the *forms* of values had become the values; institutions had become more important than the ideas they embodied."[5] For Lawrence, this would become one of the guiding obsessions of his work: England was dying because it could no longer accommodate vitality; the forms, the hard shells which encased so much of what was still living in English life, would have to be broken.

The Boer War, which had ended in 1902, had opened British eyes to the fragility of the empire, and had left its mark on the Edwardian attitude toward Britain's recent past. "Our Empire," claimed H. G. Wells, "was nearly beaten by a handful of farmers amidst the jeering contempt of the whole world—and we felt it acutely for several years."[6] Ford Madox Ford (then Ford Madox Hueffer) attributed the decline of arts and letters to the Boer War.

> That was the end of everything, of the pre-Raphaelites, the Henley gang, of the New Humour, of the Victorian great figures, of the last traces of the medieval superstition that man might save his soul by the reading of good books.[7]

The nation's unhappy experience in South Africa elicited a reaction which contributed to its suspicion of its Victorian predecessors. Britain had had enough of foreign involvements, and for the first years of the new century the nation felt that it needed to look to itself and lick its wounds. There was a turn away from the Continent, a self-communing which distrusted foreign influence. Samuel Hynes, in *The Edwardian Turn of Mind*, has pointed out the large number of imaginative versions of an invasion, often German, which were spawned during these years—including books such as H. G. Wells's *The War of the Worlds*. General Baden-Powell's fears that the English were becoming physically and morally attenuated (like Wells's "Eloi" in *The Time Machine*) and consequently unable to defend Britain's shores in case of a German attack, provoked him to organize the Boy Scouts. But if Germany was an actual physical threat, France was a spiritual threat. Early in the twentieth century, anything smelling faintly of France inspired suspicion in many quarters, and it was precisely the most recently interred corpses of the Victorian era which seemed most odious to the Edwardians. In Wilde, Beardsley, Dowson, Johnson, and the rest, Edwardians saw their worst fears for themselves. If Victoria's reign had produced Tennyson, it had also produced Wilde—and if a man like Tennyson might never again be seen, a man like Wilde would never again be countenanced. W. B. Yeats, in 1936, remembered the beginning of the new century by comparing it with the end of the old:

> Then in 1900 everybody got down off his stilts; henceforth, nobody drank absinthe with his black coffee; nobody went mad; nobody committed suicide; nobody joined the Catholic Church; or if they did I have forgotten.
> Victorianism had been defeated.[8]

C. F. G. Masterman, one of the most interesting liberal imaginations of the period, wrote what is perhaps the best single expression of the Edwardian mood:

> Expectancy and surprise are the notes of the age. Expectancy belongs by nature to a time balanced uneasily between two great periods of change. On the one hand is a past still showing faint survivals of vitality; on the other is the future but hardly coming to birth. The years as they pass still appear as years of preparation, a time of waiting rather than a time of action. . . . Here is a civilization becoming ever more divorced from Nature and the ancient sanities, protesting through its literature a kind of cosmic weariness. Society which had started on its mechanical advance and the aggrandisement of material goods with the buoyancy of an impetuous life confronts a poverty which it can neither ameliorate nor destroy, and an organized discontent which may yet

prove the end of the Western civilisation. Faith in the invisible seems dying, and faith in the visible is proving inadequate to the hunger of the Soul.[9]

Lawrence among the Edwardian Uncles

The writers who actually spoke with a voice which most closely resembled the accent of their age were H. G. Wells, George Bernard Shaw, John Galsworthy, and Arnold Bennett.* They were, as Rebecca West recalls them, "the Big Four." "All our youth," she goes on, "they hung about the houses of our minds like uncles. . . . They had the generosity, the charm, the loquacity of visiting uncles."[10] These avuncular Edwardians seemed to speak for their period because all of them were, in the main, interested in literature as social and cultural therapy. The "Uncles" differed in important ways, of course; Bennett lacked the sense of mission that burns behind so much of the work of Shaw and Wells; Galsworthy lacked their talent and intelligence. Still, as Samuel Hynes has pointed out, "the fundamental fact about the Edwardian decade, understood as a literary period," was that it was "concerned with the state of society, and acknowledged the force and urgency of social change, but it was *not* concerned to effect a *literary* revolution."[11]

Vivian de Sola Pinto has noted that the more intelligent of the Edwardians had seen that, to survive, their civilization would have to "transcend the limitations of class and nationality and build up a Great Society led by an *elite*."[12] It would be an elite which was well aware that English society, as it had existed for 400 years, and which had reached its apotheosis during the preceding century,

---

*The important literary voices of the period all expressed what Masterman calls "a kind of cosmic weariness," but not all of them spoke authoritatively for their period. Joseph Conrad is the most significant British novelist of the period, but it is his very scope and complexity—his artistry—that make him less than an authoritative voice for Edwardian England. E. M. Forster wrote his greatest work in 1924 and, in any case, seems to have shared the sensibility of the succeeding period; he was a Georgian, not an Edwardian. Then there were G. K. Chesterton and Hilaire Belloc, the "Chesterbelloc," who apparently felt that in themselves, "for the first time since the Reformation, there was a growing counterpoise to the deceptive fallacies of humanitarian positivism" (Douglas Jerrold, "Hilaire Belloc and the Counter-Revolution," in Douglas Woodruff, ed., *For Hilaire Belloc*, p. 7). Their position would be taken up later by another set of modern writers—Hulme, Eliot, Lewis, and in some ways, Lawrence—but not necessarily from the stance of Catholicism. Unlike most of the Edwardians, who are often blunt to the point of dullness, Chesterton and Belloc are writers from whom it is almost impossible to get a straight answer. They are never as serious as one wants them to be, and always more serious than one takes them to be.

was now in a state of disintegration. The only hope of these critics was in an educated minority which would lead the rest of England into conformity with their own advanced opinions. Their litera- ture, then, sprang from a new anxiety. If one hopes that a nation will conform to a new set of opinions and assumptions, one must, then, "be assured he is normal. Thus the need for freedom is re- placed by a need for therapy."[13] The majority of the English people could no longer afford to be ordinary, to hold stock opinions of reality; they could no longer, in their most dizzying fantasies of themselves, simply want to become a nation of Forsytes. The Ed- wardian "Uncles" persisted in putting their hands in their readers' pockets, either by presenting eloquently irresistible arguments or by arguing that their view of reality could be disregarded only at the cost of national failure.

It was the insistently pressing social purpose of the Edwardian novelists which made Henry James ask, "Yes, yes; but is this *all?*"[14] and which gave Virginia Woolf "so strange a feeling of incompleteness and dissatisfaction," a feeling that made her want to "do something—to join a society, or, more desperately, to write a cheque."[15] In 1909, years before Woolf was to write (in "Mr. Bennett and Mrs. Brown") what is perhaps the most famous con- demnation of Edwardian fiction, she wrote to Lytton Strachey: "I wish (as usual) that earth would open her womb and let some new creature out."[16] In fact, with the publication of Lawrence's first stories and poems in Ford Madox Ford's *English Review*, Woolf's "new creature" had already arrived. But, as Woolf would later discover, he did not at all arrive in the form that she most desired.

Although their "social-realist" view of the world, as well as an often overt interest in reform, is often the dominant feature of their work, it must be said here that Shaw, Wells, Galsworthy, and Bennett were not concerned with social therapy in the shape of social reform to the exclusion of everything else. As William Bel- lamy has noted, their work also involves a "transference from tele- ologies to direct remedial action undertaken on behalf of the self."[17] The Edwardian "Uncles" persistently invite responses to the situa- tion of the self amid cultural crisis. Their most completely realized characters—Soames Forsyte, George Ponderevo, Major Barbara, Sophia Baines—are invariably placed in situations in which their individual consciousnesses are forced to reconstitute themselves in the context of a fragmented culture, a culture suffering the "loss of traditions and distinctions and assured reactions."[18]

Lawrence, too, assumes this atmosphere of cultural breakdown, and it serves as a background to almost all of his important work from *The White Peacock* to *Lady Chatterley's Lover*. Insofar as Lawrence's work can be seen as pointing toward a kind of cultural, social, and individual therapy (predominantly cultural in *Women in Love* and *The Plumed Serpent*, social in *Aaron's Rod* and *Kangaroo*, individual in *Sons and Lovers* and *The Rainbow*, but always inclusive of all three) Lawrence can be seen to have inherited the tradition of the Edwardian "Uncles."

It was in this intellectual climate, then—a climate dominated by a limited yet forceful revolt against Victorianism, distraught by the tensions created by old ideas juxtaposed against the new, and activated by the therapeutic intentions of its most authoritative spokesmen—that Lawrence first entered the English cultural milieu.

Lawrence's entry into the Edwardian literary circle is well known: his "discovery" by Ford Madox Ford; his early excitement about meeting literary London; the help he received from established literary guides such as Ford and Edward Garnett; his profound disenchantment with teaching and his growing belief that he could give up teaching for writing and make a living as well.

The response of the Edwardian milieu to Lawrence's work followed, for the most part, Ford's strictures on *The Trespasser:* "'The book,' he said, 'is a rotten work of genius.'"[19] Ford's claim was one that met with such general agreement that Richard Aldington later used the title *Portrait of a Genius, But* . . . for his biography of Lawrence. In any case, what the Edwardians had to say about Lawrence was usually said years after they had first become aware of him as another clever young man, another of Ford's discoveries, writing masterpieces in London.

H. G. Wells, who was at first vaguely impressed by Lawrence, later compared Lawrence to himself during the writing of *Ann Veronica*.

> The craving, in a body that was gathering health and strength, for a complete loveliness of bodily response, was creeping up into my imagination and growing more and more powerful. This craving dominated the work of D. H. Lawrence altogether. For my own part, I could never yield it that importance. [As for the reaction to *Ann Veronica*], if I had been a D. H. Lawrence, with every fig leaf pinned aside, I could not have been considered more improper than I was.[20]

Wells was never to see what later became increasingly apparent: in comparison with the other writers of the younger generation, Lawrence was perhaps the closest to Wells in his notions of the novel's purpose and its power. Their novels, says one critic, "have exactly the same subject . . . they are about matrimony, about the mysteries and difficulties and agonies and tragedies and—rarely—the joys of the search for a true 'life of dialogue.'"[21] But Wells's obtuseness about who his actual literary allies were is something that has since become quite evident to literary historians.

In 1914, John Galsworthy wrote to Edward Garnett about *Sons and Lovers:*

> I've nothing but praise for all the part that deals with the Mother, the Father and the sons; but I've a lot besides praise for the love part. Neither of the women, Miriam nor Clara, convince me a bit; they are only material out of which to run wild on the thesis that this kind of man does not want *the* woman, only *a* woman. And that kind of reveling in the shades of sex emotions seems to me anaemic. . . . There's genius in the book, but not in that part of the book. The body's never worth while, and the sooner Lawrence recognizes that, the better.[22]

And, in 1915, he wrote to J. B. Pinker about *The Rainbow:*

> Frankly—I think it's aesthetically detestable. Its perfervid futuristic style revolts me. Its reiterations bore me to death. And—worse than all—at the back of its amazing fecundity—what is there? What real discovery, what of the spirit, what that is touching, or even true? There is a spurious creativeness about it all, as of countless bodies made with tremendous gusto, and not an ounce of soul within them, in spite of incredible assertions and pretence of sounding life to its core. It's a kind of portent; a paean of the undisciplined shallow fervour that passes with the young in these days for art. It has no time-resisting quality whatever. Brittle as glass, and with something of its brilliance.
>
> As to the sexual aspect. The writer forgets—as no great artist does— that by dwelling on the sexual side of life so lovingly he falsifies all the values of his work. . . .
>
> I much prefer a frankly pornographic book to one like this. That at all events achieves what it sets out to do; and does not leave on one the painful impression of a man tragically obsessed to the ruin of his gifts.
>
> I am a pagan; but this is not paganism, it is fever. A grievous pity—so much power, & vision (up to a point) run so young to seed. I don't see him getting back now—he will go on, & become more and more perfervid, seeing less and less the wood for the trees. And the worst of it is he will lead away those who think that what glitters must be gold.[23]

Lawrence, in his equally hostile essay on Galsworthy (1928),

certainly gets his own back. If there has been a seminal statement
made about Galsworthy, Lawrence's is it. Lawrence's criticism
prefigures almost everything important that has been said about
Galsworthy since.

> Galsworthy had not quite enough of the superb courage of his satire.
> He faltered, and gave in to the Forsytes. It is a thousand pities. He
> might have been the surgeon the modern soul needs so badly, to cut
> away the proud flesh of our Forsytes from the living body of men who
> are fully alive. Instead, he put down the knife and laid on a soft,
> sentimental poultice, and helped to make the corruption worse.[24]

The earlier generation, with the exception of Yeats—who read
Lawrence "with excitement"[25] in the 1930s—echoed much of what
Galsworthy had to say. George Moore, for instance, found "no
beginning, middle, or end"[26] in Lawrence.

> It is just the same as if I was to go into the garden and say, "I will have a
> spoonful of jam," and then after a while, liking it, decide to have
> another spoonful and then perhaps another. A man running after a
> woman all day long, and a woman he doesn't even like.[27]

W. H. Hudson's reaction is quite similar to Galsworthy's. In 1913,
he wrote to Garnett about *Sons and Lovers:*

> A very good book indeed except in that portion where he relapses into
> the old sty—the neck-sucking and wallowing-in-the-sweating flesh. It is
> like an obsession, a madness, but he may outlive it as so many other
> writers have done.[28]

But by 1916, Lawrence remained for Hudson "a small minor poet,"
whose "lyrical biting and gnawing at the breasts of his mistress till
his mouth is full of blood and foam,"[29] Hudson continued to abhor.

Perhaps the most decisive comment on Lawrence from a member
of the pre-Edwardian generation came from Henry James in his
article "The Younger Generation," published in early 1914. James
actually says almost nothing about Lawrence here (most of his
words are devoted to Conrad, Wells, and Bennett), but he does
announce that, among the younger generation of novelists such as
Compton Mackenzie, Hugh Walpole, and Gilbert Cannan, Lawrence hangs "in the dusty rear."[30] James's particular point of
reference was *Sons and Lovers,* which had been recommended to him
by Hugh Walpole in August 1913. But it was not so much what

James said about it, but what he didn't say, that constituted his criticism.

Compton Mackenzie, who probably received the most praise that James's article was willing to give, has declared that Lawrence "never recovered from what he fancied was Henry James's opinion of him, and not all the appreciation he received from critics in every country ever succeeded in making him forget the slighting of his genius by Henry James."[31] However much it might have pained Lawrence, and he was sensitive to criticism during these years, Mackenzie's claim is surely an overstatement, one that comes from one writer's identifying himself too strongly with another who has been summarily dismissed by a recognizably great critic.

Lawrence certainly did recover, although James's article might have indicated to Lawrence just how little help he would receive from that direction in subsequent years, especially during the *Rainbow* censorship case in 1915. Lawrence, by then, did not expect much—but he at least hoped that he would be supported on the grounds of being a fellow artist, if not (in James's eyes) a good one.

That James found so little to admire in *Sons and Lovers* is not difficult to understand. If we compare the arguments about the purpose of the novel that took place between James and Wells during these years (arguments which are in many ways still representative of distinctly opposite notions of the novelist's practice), it becomes evident that Lawrence, though he belongs "to the English tradition in the sense that James deplored as well as in the sense which he admired,"[32] stands in a closer relationship to Wells's conception than to James's. James, Lawrence once wrote, "was always on a different line—subtle conventional design was his aim."[33]

Lawrence had defenders, too, among the Edwardians, although most of the excitement generated by his early novels came from the sons and daughters of Edwardian parents, such as David Garnett and Ivy Low, many of whom were already reacting in opposition to their fathers' modes of seriousness, responsibility, and maturity. Violet Hunt's remark that *The White Peacock* "took the town"[34] is exaggerated insofar as she fails to note precisely what part of town it took—mainly the community of the young and, as far as literary respectability was concerned, the powerless. In any case, as Helen Corke has noted, being taken up by the young was in many ways as disturbing to Lawrence as being dismissed by the old.

The book [*The White Peacock*] brought him, indeed, to the notice of the

London *literati*, but it did not achieve any striking success. The patronage of the *literati* made him wince, and he became aware of the social gulf dividing an elementary schoolmaster from young artists who might be penniless themselves, but lived in touch with a charmed circle of influence and wealth.[35]

Of the official Edwardians, Edward Garnett was one of Lawrence's staunchest early defenders. In an article published in 1916, which Garnett's biographer calls the beginning of "authentic criticism of Lawrence,"[36] Garnett declares that Lawrence's "talent is one of the most interesting and uncompromising literary forces of the recent years."[37] Garnett goes on to express his admiration for *The White Peacock* and *The Trespasser* and asserts that *Sons and Lovers* "is really the only [novel] of any breadth of vision in contemporary English fiction that lifts working-class life out of middle-class hands, and restores it to its native atmosphere of hard veracity."[38] But more importantly, at least for Lawrence in 1916, Garnett defends him against attacks like those of Galsworthy in the letters quoted above.

> Mr. Lawrence, by his psychological penetration into love's self-regarding impulses and passionate moods, supplements our "idealistic" valuations of its activities and corrects their exaggeration by conventionalized sentiment.[39]

Richard Middleton and W. L. George both admired Lawrence's earliest work, although George feared that Lawrence might "develop his illusion of culture among the vulgar until it is incredible."[40] J. M. Barrie, although writing much later, was alive to Lawrence's power but also had some reservations.

> There are power and poetry in him as in few. He quite misrepresents the feeling of this country in wartime [in *Kangaroo*], but perhaps no wonder. A very happy man, with such a passionate interest in himself, roaming the world in search of that self and finding it everywhere. But he is big, and I should think in some ways lovable.[41]

But it was Arnold Bennett, at least by the 1920s, who was Lawrence's most exuberant Edwardian admirer. In 1928, Bennett declared that Lawrence was, along with R. H. Mottram, one of "the two real geniuses of the new age!"[42] Bennett especially liked *The Virgin and the Gipsy* (1930): "Nothing else exists by the side of it. Believe me. It is marvellous, truly."[43] Even Bennett, however, had his reservations, most of which by now should be familiar.

D. H. Lawrence has his faults. He can be very morbid; he is obsessed by the sexual relation; he can be formidably unreadable; nearly
all his books have long passages of tiresomeness. But he is the strongest
novelist writing today . . . a rough, demonic giant.[44]

Lawrence's earliest responses to the work of his Edwardian contemporaries were varied, but they were based upon what appears to
be a reasonably thorough sampling of their wares. Until about
1908, Lawrence's reading consisted mainly of the standard Victorian authors, with particular concentration, significantly, on
George Eliot, Dickens, Carlyle, and Tolstoy. After his move to
Croydon and his entry into the wider circle of Edwardian literary
and intellectual life, however, Lawrence began to read his older
contemporaries. In 1908, we find references to his reading of Shaw
and Bennett, in particular, but also the shorter pieces to be found in
the *English Review* and *The New Age*. In 1909, Lawrence read Wells's
Kipps, *Love and Mr. Lewisham*, *Tono-Bungay*, and *The War of the
Worlds*, Bennett's *The Old Wives' Tale*, Ford's *A Call*, Galsworthy's
A Country House, Conrad's *Lord Jim*, Barrie's *Margaret Ogilvy*, and
poetry by John Davidson and W. B. Yeats. In 1910, he read Wells's
Ann Veronica (which he thought "rather trashy"[45]) and Barrie's *Sentimental Tommy* (which he thought rather good). In 1911, he read
Forster's *Howards End*, Edward Garnett's *The Breaking Point*, and
more Galsworthy. In 1913 and 1914, we again find references to his
reading of Shaw, Conrad, Garnett, Bennett, and Wells.[46]
    Wells's *Tono-Bungay* was the one Edwardian novel that particu-
larly excited Lawrence.

> It is the best novel Wells has written—it is the best novel I have read
> for—oh, how long? But it makes me so sad. If you knew what a weight
> of sadness Wells pours into your heart as you read him—Oh, *Mon Dieu!*
> He is a terrible pessimist. But, *Weh mir*, he is, on the whole, so true.[47]

The precise cause of Lawrence's excitement is unknown, but the
thematic thrust of the novel, the passing of the old order and its
uneasy replacement by the "windy, perplexing shoals and chan-
nels"[48] of modern experience, must certainly have made an impact
on Lawrence's rapidly developing imagination. In this, of course,
he was not alone; the Edwardian social critic C. F. G. Masterman
found *Tono-Bungay* to be the era's most profound evidence of "an
experience fragmentary and disconnected in a tumultuous
world,"[49] a world, in fact, which he thought was manifest proof of
"the coming universal wish not to live."[50]

Early in *Tono-Bungay* Wells rings the prophetic note which Law-rence must have found so terribly pessimistic, but "so true."

> The great houses stand in the parks still, the cottages cluster respect-fully on their borders, touching their eaves with their creepers, the English country-side—you can range through Kent from Bladesover northward and see—persists obstinately in looking what it was. It is like an early day in a fine October. The hand of change rests on it all, unfelt, unseen; resting for a while, as it were half reluctantly, before it grips and ends the thing forever. One frost and the whole face of things will be bare, links snap, patience end, our fine foliage of pretences lie glowing in the mire.[51]

The "divine order" of the countryside, which at least partially symbolizes England itself, is "already sapped."[52]

By the end of *Tono-Bungay* we have followed George Ponderevo, Wells's narrator and homeomorph, through the "crumbling and confusion . . . change and seemingly endless swelling"[53] of his passage from old England to modern England. In the last few pages of the novel, we find Ponderevo throbbing down the Thames on a destroyer of his own making, seeing in the panorama of London all the history of England inexorably falling away.

> England and the Kingdom, Britain and the Empire, the old prides and the old devotions, glide abeam, astern, sink down upon the horizon, pass—pass. The river passes—London passes, England passes.[54]

The tone of this passage, and of the novel itself, still stands as a forceful indication of the direction of the early-twentieth-century mind, and further suggests the extent to which Wells was attuned to the preliminary sensibilities of those moderns who succeeded him.

The vision that dominates *Tono-Bungay* is a strong undercurrent in Lawrence's early work, and becomes a murderous undertow by the time he writes *Women in Love*. One finds it in *The White Peacock*, though it is often camouflaged by the radiance of the natural world and the sentimentality of Lawrence's budding Georgian optimism; in *The Rainbow*, in which it is the reality which generates the radical urgency of Ursula's "destructive—consummating"[55] rainbow vi-sion; and in *Women in Love*, in which it provides the glowering atmosphere of the novel, and in which the impact of a real war had replaced what Wells's fictional destroyer had prophetically sym-bolized.

A number of Lawrence's letters of the war years can be read as extensions of Wells's vision in *Tono-Bungay*, made even more urgent by the physical reality of the war. As in Wells, too, the poignancy of such passages is undercut by their devastating pessimism.

> When I drive across this country, with autumn falling and rustling to pieces, I am so sad, for my country, for this great wave of civilisation, 2000 years, which is now collapsing, that it is hard to live. So much beauty and pathos of old things passing away and no new things coming: this house of the Ottoline's—it is England—my God, it breaks my soul—their England, these shafted windows, the elm-trees, the blue distance—the past, the great past, crumbling down, breaking down, not under the force of the coming birds, but under the weight of many exhausted lovely yellow leaves, that drift over the lawn, and over the pond, like the soldiers, passing away, into winter and the darkness of winter—no, I can't bear it. For the winter stretches ahead, where all vision is lost and all memory dies out. . . .
> It sounds very rhapsodic: it is this old house, the beautiful shafted windows, the grey gate-pillars under the elm-trees: really I can't bear it: the past, the past, the falling, perishing, crumbling past, so great, so magnificent.[56]

Ottoline Morrell's estate at Garsington, which generated these letters, served as the model for Breadalby in *Women in Love*, and Lawrence's descriptions of it in that novel announce feelings which duplicate those of Wells in his analysis of Bladesover in *Tono-Bungay*.

> Birkin, sitting up in bed, looked lazily and pleasantly out on the park, that was so green and deserted, romantic, belonging to the past. He was thinking how lovely, how sure, how formed, how final all the things of the past were—the lovely accomplished past—the house, so still and golden, the park slumbering its centuries of peace. And then, what a snare and a delusion, this beauty of static things—what a horrible, dead prison Breadalby really was, what an intolerable confinement, the peace![57]

Lawrence, if not necessarily "influenced" by Wells in this passage, undoubtedly shared with his older contemporary that double-edged sense of the beauty and the failure of the English past. It was the Edwardians, particularly Wells, and, in certain respects, Galsworthy, who most cogently opened this avenue of feeling for Lawrence.

As *Tono-Bungay* suggests, much of what was thought to be the essential England was located in the English countryside and country home. Their decline, then, was taken to be a definitive indication of England's decline. C. F. G. Masterman—who as late as 1923 pronounced *Tono-Bungay* to be "far the greatest novel of the century"[58] and who had once worried that Lawrence "was writing masterpieces and teaching in a fetid atmosphere"[59]—is perhaps the most resignedly pessimistic commentator on his time. In *The Condition of England* (1909), for instance, Masterman clearly feels that the decay of the countryside is simply another manifestation of an England which has lost contact with its traditional sources of strength. The tone of the book is somber and elegiac, sometimes tinctured with acute nostalgia, sometimes with sheer, blank disillusion. For Masterman, the countryside had been the essential England, but that countryside, in which "wandering machines travelling with an incredible rate of speed, scramble and smash and shriek along rural ways,"[60] was under the "visible shadow of the end."[61]

Masterman no doubt recalled his own words when he read Lawrence's *The White Peacock*.

> "Hark!" said Lettie, as I was drying my face. There was the quick patter of a motor-car coming downhill. The heavy cart was drawn across the road to rest, and the driver hurried to turn the horse back. It moved with painful slowness, and we stood in the road in suspense. Suddenly, before we knew it, the car was dropping down on us, coming at us in a curve, having rounded the horse and cart. Lettie stood faced with terror. Leslie saw her, and swung round the wheels on the sharp, curving hillside; looking only to see that he should miss her. The car slid sideways; the mud crackled under the wheels, and the machine went crashing into Nethermere.[62]

Lawrence's version of the intrusion of the mechanical into the natural world—which threatens not only that world, but also the people in it—is symbolically appropriate to the novel. Leslie, the driver of the car, brings a certain kind of destructive civilization to Nethermere when he marries Lettie, thus breaking up the continuity of the pastoral community and leaving behind its fullest embodiment, George Saxton, as a pitifully sodden reminder of the old yeoman tradition. E. M. Forster makes a similar indictment of the mechanical intrusion into the countryside in *Howards End*, in which the offenders are the motoring Wilcoxes. Both novels were published within two years of Masterman's influential analysis of the decline of the English countryside in *The Condition of England*.

Whether Lawrence and Forster were aware of Masterman's book when they were writing their own (although both probably were) is not decisively important; what is more significant is the extent to which they shared, and expressed, Masterman's anxiety about the problem.

The decay of the countryside and its corollary literary modes— the pastoral and the ballad—would become, by 1913 at the latest, the central preoccupations of the Georgian poets, including, for a matter of years, Lawrence himself. By their attempts to revive those traditional forms of English culture which Masterman had found in decline, the Georgians proposed a new identity for England, and a new meaning for being English. Masterman and Wells, especially in their roles as the prophets of decline and fall, can be described as the fullest embodiments of Edwardian culture's dominant temperament. In contrast, the Georgians set about to replace Edwardian "cosmic weariness" with offerings of possibility and promise. If the Georgians could not deny the evidence of England's decay, they could nevertheless reject any resigned acceptance of it.

3   Lawrence and the Georgians: Significant Affinities

In October 1912, Lawrence wrote: "I hate England and its hopelessness. I hate Bennett's resignation. Tragedy ought really to be a great kick at misery. But *Anna of the Five Towns* seems like an acceptance—so does all the modern stuff since Flaubert. I hate it. I want to wash again quickly, wash off England, the oldness and grubbiness and despair."[1] Conrad, too, could not be forgiven for "being so sad and for giving in."[2] As early as 1910, Lawrence felt that the Edwardian milieu as a whole was a "particularly hateful yet powerful one. The literary element, like a disagreeable substratum under a fair country, spreads under every inch of life, sticking to the roots of the growing things."[3] The Edwardians had become obstacles to Lawrence's development.

> These damned old stagers want to train up a child in the way it should grow, whereas if it's destined to have a snub nose, it's sheer waste of time to harass the poor brat into Roman-nosedness. They want me to have form: that means, they want me to have *their* pernicious ossiferous skin-and-grief form, and I won't.[4]

Clearly, Lawrence was in need of a new stage. By March 1913, he thought he had found it in the Georgians, a literary group which was expressing ideas and feelings more closely akin to his own. Reading them, he said, was like taking "a breath . . . after a night of oppressive dreams."[5] In 1913, the Georgians were not yet a coterie; they were more like a "happy clan"[6] loosely assembled around the patronage and judgment of Edward Marsh. They would reach the coterie stage later, under attack for being revolutionary by the poetic right, and for being reactionary by the poetic left. But in the early years of their association they presented to view a number of related notions that attracted not only Lawrence, but a significant portion of the British reading public.

Some of these notions are particularly crucial because they were shared by Lawrence, and because they were central for his work during the period: the location of an authentic English tradition in the organic connection between man and nature which, even as the landscape was rapidly disappearing, was still available as a symbol of an unchangeable basis for English cultural life; an interest in, and, more importantly, a belief in the possibility of establishing an audience which would enthusiastically attend to what they had to say; a sense that history had been revived, a sense that theirs was a completely new epoch that would supplant the exhausted values and obsessions of the "old world"; the idea of an intimate community which could develop after the "old-world" nihilism had finally been sloughed off and a new basis for human relationships had taken its place.

The interest of this chapter, and the following chapters, will not be to chart the influence of the Georgian poets on Lawrence; assuredly it is not to chart the influence of Lawrence on the Georgian poets. It will, however, develop some of the interconnections between Lawrence and the Georgian sensibility, of which the Georgian poets are the most expressive manifestation. In any case, the relationship between Lawrence and the Georgians seems to be a matter of assimilation rather than emulation or direct influence, and, at that, assimilation from the *Zeitgeist* rather than from direct contact. It is, then, necessary first to characterize the mental climate, the atmosphere, of the period from which the Georgians emerged and to which they contributed. It can then be demonstrated that the points of contact between Lawrence and the spirit of the Georgian milieu are both numerous and significant, that his work during the period owes much to that spirit, and finally that some of his best work after 1914 is written out of the energy of opposition to the same Georgian spirit that he had earlier embraced.

The "New World" and English Culture

"It is the sign of the times," wrote Allen Upward early in 1911, "that so many of us should be busy in studying the signs of the times. In no other age since the birth of Christianity has there been manifested the same devouring curiosity about the future, and the same disposition to expect a new earth, if not a new heaven."[7]

The rhetoric and imagery which inform Upward's statement—

that of spiritual regeneration and renewed wonder—are reflective of the enthusiasm felt by the British intelligentsia for the condition in which they then found themselves. Hope was in the air; such phrases as "the new age" and "the new era" became little magazine clichés during the first years of the second decade. Englishmen, and English writers especially, felt the stir of a new beginning. "What with modern science, modern philosophy, modern religion, modern politics, and modern business," wrote Lascelles Abercrombie,

> the present is a time fermenting with tremendous change; the most tremendous of all changes, a change in the idealistic interpretation of the universe. . . . To any man with brain and spirit active and alert in him, the present is a time wherein the world, and the destiny of man in the world, are ideas different from anything that has ever been before.[8]

Ezra Pound, who differed from Abercrombie in almost every other way, agreed with him in this: the enthusiastic belief in the coming of a distinctively "modern" era, a new awakening that would "make the Italian Renaissance look like a tempest in a teapot."[9] For Leonard Woolf, "it seemed as though human beings might really be on the brink of becoming civilized. It was partly the feeling of relief and release as we broke out of the fog of Victorianism. The forces of reaction and barbarism were still there, but they were in retreat."[10]

The reasons for such an upsurge in the tone of cultural expectations are complex; they can be comprehended only by a full examination of a series of related social, political, economic, and aesthetic factors. "Rarely, indeed," claims G. H. Bantock, "can there have been a time when 'background' more readily obtrudes as an essential part of foreground."[11] Two elements of this background seem particularly significant. First, the common belief that the Victorian hegemony (and especially its Edwardian phase) had ended; second, the reconnection of Britain with the Continent, after a decade of suspicion about foreign influences.

The Edwardian inferiority complex and its attendant concerns about the future of England had died, it was felt, with King Edward himself. "His death was . . . more than the end of a reign: it was the end of a conception of what it meant to be English"[12]—a conception, one must add, which was essentially Victorian.

As *The New Age* noted in May 1910:

> The last genuine link with the Victorian age has been broken with the

death of King Edward VII. Nobody who will reflect for a moment on
the circumstances of the Queen's death and on the historic as well as
family relationship in which the late King stood to the late Queen, will
fail to realise at once that King Edward was spiritually the mere ex-
ecutor of Queen Victoria. The impulse of her epoch flowed over, as it
were, and merged in his reign, begun actually before her death, colour-
ing it with the peculiar tones of the Victorian era. King Edward VII
was adored almost as much as the son and successor of his mother as for
his own qualities and merits.

This fact, indeed, puts the seal of difference on the two accessions to
the throne which the last ten years have witnessed. The accession of
Edward VII was neither felt to be, nor in fact was it, a leap in the dark
or a plunge into a new period. Everything that the late King did on the
throne had been anticipated and expected, both from the evidence of
his own public life and from the impetus given to his times by the long
reign that drew to a close in him. But the situation is strangely different
at this moment, and all the surrounding circumstances mark it off as
unique in English history for many a generation. For if it is felt, as it is
clearly felt, that the era of Victoria is indeed and at last over, who is so
bold as to dare forecast the nature of the epoch that is now opening?[13]

Swinburne and Meredith, the great Victorian figures who had
lingered on into the twentieth century, both died in 1909, leaving
the field wide open for new luminaries. The Edwardian Uncles—
Wells, Bennett, Galsworthy, and Shaw—were considered too
closely associated with the era just passed to be much help in the
"plunge into a new period." They, after all, "did not recoil from
[contemporary existence] in disgust; they freely criticised but did
not reject society."[14]

Late in 1910, *The New Age*, whose pages had long "centred
around the Shavian drama, realism in the novel and other staple
Edwardian themes,"[15] began to attack basic Edwardian assumptions. Arnold Bennett, who had written reviews for *The New Age* (as
"Jacob Tonson") since 1908, felt compelled to resign his position at
that magazine in 1911. In February of that year he had written,
"What above all else we want in this island of intellectual dishon-
esty is some one who will tell us the truth 'and chance it.' "[16] *The
New Age's* editor, A. R. Orage, "chanced it" in an editorial which
clearly anticipates Virginia Woolf's more famous attack on the Edwardians—and especially Bennett—fourteen years later. Of the
Edwardian novelists, Orage had this to say:

They imagine that by exhausting the details of a given character they
can seize the whole. But in truth they can no more exhaust the aspects
of a single character than they can number the sides of a sphere. . . .

Psychology is the science of the psyche or it is mere post-mortem analysis and people who concern themselves with detail are, you may be sure, ignorant of the nature of the whole. . . . Hence comes, too, the bewildering multeity of the personages. In truth they are not person- ages at all, but dummies stuffed with notebooks.[17]

Orage, and *The New Age*, had quite clearly let Bennett know that the Edwardian novel was no longer spiritually equipped to lead the way into the new era.

It was Virginia Woolf who, in 1924, declared that "in or about December 1910, human character changed."[18] The statement, dra- matically if not historically definitive, was made as part of a speech which attacked the Edwardians for looking "very powerfully, searchingly, and sympathetically out of the window; at factories, at Utopias, even at the decoration and upholstery of the carriage; but . . . never at life, never at human nature."[19] Woolf, like *The New Age*, attacks the Edwardians for their inability to create living characters; theirs are characters, she feels, who are like a "sack stuffed with straw"[20] and who populate books that "leave one with so strange a feeling of incompleteness and dissatisfaction. In order to complete them it seems necessary to do something—to join a society, or, more desperately, to write a cheque."[21] Woolf, looking back, reconfirms what the new generation of writers already knew:

that there was no English novelist living from whom they could learn their business.[22] . . . [Their] tools are not our tools, and that business is not our business. For us those conventions are ruin, those tools are death.[23]

Whatever qualifications one would like to make in Virginia Woolf's choice of month, 1910 has proven to be a particularly propitious choice of year. The historian George Dangerfield, for one, agrees with her. "The year 1910," he writes,

is not just a convenient starting point. It is actually a landmark in English history, which stands out against a peculiar background of flame. For it was in 1910 that fires long smoldering in the English spirit suddenly flared up.[24]

The Influence of the Continent

For the young English writers, the spark for these fires was provided by the Continent. What was a small Continental flicker in 1910 became a conflagration in the years before the war, one which would be engulfed only by that still greater conflagration which would embroil all of Europe in August 1914.

Late in 1910 the first postimpressionist exhibition was in full swing at Grafton Gallery in London, selected and overseen by two of Woolf's friends, Roger Fry and Desmond MacCarthy. According to Samuel Hynes, Virginia Woolf's choice of December 1910 was mainly dictated by the effect that the exhibition had on English sensibilities. "She chose that occasion," says Hynes,

> as an appropriate symbol of the way European ideas forced themselves upon the insular English consciousness during the Edwardian years and so joined England to the Continent.[25]

The English public as a whole was not quite ready to be joined to the Continent, however. The exhibition threw it into "paroxysms of rage and laughter."[26] "These are not works of art at all," decided one Edwardian worthy, "unless throwing a handful of mud against a wall may be called one. They are works of idleness and impotent stupidity, a pornographic show."[27] The London *Times* noted that, "like anarchism in politics, it is the rejection of all that civilisation has done, the good with the bad."[28]

But it was too late; the *Times* reviewer had said more than he knew. Civilization, at least as it was seen from that splendidly isolated and willfully narrow Edwardian perspective, was indeed under attack. For the British avant-garde—especially those coalescing around Bloomsbury—the exhibition served to reveal the Philistines. Battle lines were drawn; *The New Age*'s attack on the limitations of the Edwardian novel was just one symptom of those new lines.

Ironically enough, one of the first to demand a public apology from the Philistines was Arnold Bennett, who himself was soon to be counted among their number. "The attitude of the culture of London towards [the show]," he wrote,

> is of course merely humiliating to any Englishman who has made an effort to cure himself of insularity. . . . The mild tragedy of the thing is that . . . it is London and not the exhibition which is making itself ridiculous. . . . For the movement has not only got past the guffawing stage; it has got past the arguing stage. Its authenticity is admitted by all those who have kept themselves fully awake. And in twenty years London will be signing an apology for its guffaw.[29]

It did not take anywhere near twenty years for London to

apologize; the first stammering words were uttered by June 1911, on the occasion of the first performance of Diaghilev's Russian Ballet at Covent Garden. The newspapers, diaries, and memoirs of those years rarely fail to note the excitement generated by the Ballet. The reviewer for the London *Times* wrote:

> This summer of 1911 has brought more than an aesthetic revolution with it; in bringing the Russian Ballet to Covent Garden it has brought a positively new art, it has extended the realm of beauty for us, discovered a new continent, revealed new faculties and means of salvation in ourselves. Alas! many pleasant illusions have been shattered thereby, many idols tumbled from their pedestals; we have grown up terribly fast and lost the power of enjoying things that pleased our callow fancies only a month or two ago.[30]

Again, one notes the use of rhetoric and imagery which suggests spiritual conversion and wonder. The Ballet was felt to have extended the possibilities of cultural growth—perhaps even to have saved culture altogether. As Rupert Brooke wrote in 1911, the Ballet "if anything, can redeem our civilization."[31] Edward Marsh had earlier written to Brooke, declaring that the Ballet was "a Post-Impressionist picture put in motion . . . it has almost brought me round to Matisse's pictures!"[32] Marsh's conflation of the Ballet and postimpressionism serves to indicate a significant point; the separate forces of the Continent's artistic incursion into Britain had become blurred because of their speed and power. The sense of "something new," of new possibilities in the air, overwhelmed the distinctive features of the various movements which had made such possibilities manifest. Postimpressionism became a "careless but not uncommon synonym"[33] for the new spirit that was surfacing.

Two other, older but equally stimulating, Continental influences must be mentioned here. With Constance Garnett's translations in 1912, Dostoevsky almost immediately became part of the "powerful liberation of emotions that had been held in check by nineteenth-century Rationalism, and by over-rigid aesthetic theories."[34] Virginia Woolf, coming to write of Dostoevsky some years later, announces precisely the kind of reaction which surrounded him then:

> The novels of Dostoevsky are seething whirlpools, gyrating sandstorms, waterspouts which hiss and boil and suck us in. They are composed purely and wholly out of the stuff of the soul. Against our wills we are drawn in, whirled round, blinded, suffocated, and at the same time filled with a giddy rapture.[35]

Like Dostoevsky, Nietzsche was available as a convenient stick to beat the Victorians with. Their similarities were strikingly obvious to the moderns who read them; both were powerful spokesmen for anti-Victorianism. Nietzsche's inflence in England predated Dostoevsky's ("1902 marked the opening of the 'Nietzschean decade' in English literature,"[36] says one critic), but his impact was perhaps not so strong. He was a "tremor in the atmosphere rather than an earthquake,"[37] but one which can be felt in the works of W. B. Yeats, Wyndham Lewis, T. E. Hulme, James Joyce, Edward Thomas, Harold Monro, Rupert Brooke, *The New Age* circle, and, finally, D. H. Lawrence.

It was, of course, not necessary to be a legatee of Dostoevsky and Nietzsche to feel caught up in the "giddy rapture" of reaction to the "old world." Lawrence, for one, came to have severe doubts about both of them. They are significant, however, not simply because they were the centers of a great upswell of interest during the period, but also because they suggested to many modern writers a tone and a stance which could be taken toward the modern condition, and because they helped to provide an ethos in which a new generation of writers felt they had found a new direction for the imagination.

Georgians in the "New World"

If it is true that the new awareness of the Continent was "probably the most important of all the transformations that took place in England before the war,"[38] then it is perhaps ironic that the first truly organized revolt against what we are accustomed to call the Edwardian establishment was carried out by a group of English poets who were English to the bone, and who are now generally considered "traditional" in the worst sense of that word. To be a Georgian poet, says Samuel Hynes, "was to attach oneself self-consciously to the tradition of English poetry, and to be not simply a poet, but an *English* poet."[39] George Dangerfield finds the Georgians "truly representative, in some way, of pre-war England,"[40] in that "they were in whole what the youth of England was in part," a group whose "romantic unrealities came chiefly up from the immature soul of a doomed generation."[41] John Wain claims that, had they not been doomed, "there would have been no need of a modern poetic idiom imported from France via America. . . . [They] would have made a living tradition out of English materials, arising naturally from English life."[42]

Such speculations are, of course, unverifiable, but Hynes, Dangerfield, and Wain are surely correct in drawing attention to the adamant Englishness of the Georgian vision. The peculiar kind of Englishness that characterizes the Georgian poet was in part derived from the stark relief in which England was placed when juxtaposed with the restless cultural energies being generated across the Channel. In effect, the extraordinary changes occurring on the Continent intensified the Georgians' solicitude about what was still viable in their own culture. Although Marsh, Brooke, Harold Monro, and Lascelles Abercrombie were well aware of the movements on the Continent, and sometimes advocates of them, their major concern was for the inner condition of England: whether England, in fact, "in the sense in which it existed in Shakespeare, in the countryside, and in certain human beings, has the capacity to survive."[43] They recognized, of course, that Shakespeare and the countryside no longer existed in the same sense as they once did; but the new epoch, in which they found themselves at the forefront, would, it was hoped, reestablish the necessary relation between England as it was and England as it was now.

Although the Georgian movement was consciously unprogrammatic—it never, for instance, issued anything approaching a manifesto—it can be said to have had a community of aim. The very term *Georgian*, chosen by Edward Marsh ("Eras are always christened after Sovereigns"[44]) after much discussion and disagreement, was never intended to distinguish a coterie, but instead to

> distinguish his own poetic era from the Edwardian decade which had preceded it and, in its context, to suggest the widely held assumption that by 1912 poetry was beginning to strike out on new and exciting paths. It was intended to suggest, moreover, that the new age dawning would be somehow more vital, more stimulating, more "modern," than the Edwardian era.[45]

The term itself was conceived, as was the first volume of *Georgian Poetry*, on September 19, 1912, in a discussion between Marsh and Rupert Brooke in Marsh's spare room at Gray's Inn. Both were discussing the apparent fact that no one seemed to be aware of the poetic renaissance which was just then taking place. It was pointed out that, although Masefield's *The Everlasting Mercy* had become well known and well read (it was one of the two events of 1911 that, for Marsh, "put it past a doubt that a golden age was beginning"[46]), there were at least a dozen writers of comparable merit who had not yet reached the public. After Brooke suggested that he might write a book himself under twelve different pseudonyms and issue it as an anthology of twelve promising experimental poets, Marsh's cooler and more practical head prevailed. He saw in the idea a way of winning over an apathetic public by publishing "at least twelve flesh-and-blood poets whose work, if properly thrust under the public's nose,"[47] would achieve the desired result—the recognition of a "revolutionary dawn"[48] in poetry.

The Uncles' Response to Georgianism

Now, of course, the poetry of the Georgians seems very quietly revolutionary indeed; if it is revolt at all, it is revolt on tiptoe. Its predominant tone is perhaps best suggested in a statement by Rupert Brooke: "I seemed to see almost every hour golden and radiant, and always increasing in beauty,"[49] or in W. H. Davies's lines:

> Good morning, Life—and all
> Things glad and beautiful . . .[50]

or in these lines by John Drinkwater:

> We cherish every hour that strays
> Adown the cataract of days:
> We see the clear, untroubled skies—
> We see the glory of the rose. . . .[51]

In 1913, however, the Georgians, like the postimpressionists, appeared to many to be dangerous artistic extremists. The Georgian rejection of the prevailing poetic lushness, its use of language toned down to the level of conversation, its realism, and its insistence on "being modern," severely disturbed many early reviewers. For Sir Edmund Gosse, undisputably the most powerful figure in literary England at the time (Ezra Pound called it "the age of Gosse"[52]), Georgianism was "a violence, almost a rawness in the approach to life itself."[53] The *Times Literary Supplement* took the Georgians to task for their "affected and self-conscious brutality."[54] *The Spectator* noted that "if the Georgian poet wishes to say a plain thing, he takes care to say it with an emphatic boldness and crudity, which not only hit you in the eye, but lay you flat."[55] Arthur Waugh, the father of Evelyn and a man of letters in the school of Gosse, thought the Georgians to be "audacious and incompetent revolutionaries."[56] In his view, W. W. Gibson, for instance, "has evidently thrown aside in weariness the golden footrule of the Augustans" in favor of a "fuliginous thunderstorm."[57] Lascelles Abercrombie's verse is "yet more rough and unmelodious," written for "the young bloods of the twentieth century" with "incoherent violence."[58] Rupert Brooke has "the itch to say a thing in such an arresting fashion as to shock the literary purist into attention even against his will."[59] As for Lawrence, he "might well serve as a cautionary example of realism running riot in verse." His is an "experiment in perverted symbolism, casting a sombre shadow upon the wholesome impulses of passion and of natural sexual attraction."[60]

Clearly, Waugh's response is that of a man who feels that he has been in some way violated, intruded upon. He stands, in many ways, for the England that the Georgians—and Lawrence—were in the process of rejecting. Arthur Waugh is exemplary of what Wells's George Ponderevo means when he declares that, in England "all that is modern and different has come in as a thing intruded or as a gloss."[61]

As these statements suggest, what most disturbed the reviewers who disapproved of the first Georgian anthology was its realism. In fact, according to Robert Ross, the most comprehensive historian of the movement, Georgianism was originally "synonymous with realism."[62] Georgian realism must, of course, be viewed historically for it to make any sense at all to the contemporary reader, whose taste has almost inevitably been formed by the more demanding and desperate realism of Pound, Eliot, and Joyce. Georgian realism was essentially based on antisentimentalism, skepticism of the grandiose metaphysical and ethical assumptions of faith and progress, a desire for clarity and an abhorrence of abstraction, a careful attendance to the concrete particulars of their experience, and an attempt to find elemental, unchanging truths in the flux of exterior experience.[63]

Arthur Waugh, again useful as a representative of establishment resistance, saw Georgian realism as indicative of the "general discontent with all surviving traditions."[64] Waugh, unlike many later critics of the Georgians, was able to gauge the distance between the new poets and their predecessors. Speaking of their use of poetic language, he says:

"We write nothing that we might not speak," proclaims the new rebellion in effect: "we draw the thing as we see it for the God of things as they are. Every aspect of life shall be the subject of our art, and what we see we will describe in the language which we use every day. The result shall be the New Poetry, the vital expression of a new race."[65]

This comment is particularly striking when juxtaposed to Rupert Brooke's own comments about what was perhaps the most famous of his ventures into "realism." Of "Channel-Passage," in which the poem's seasick speaker, like Byron's Don Juan, alternatively muses romantically and retches uncontrollably, Brooke wrote: " 'Whatever,' I declare simply and rather nobly, 'a brother man has thrown up, is food for me.' "[66] Despite the rather unfortunate phrasing, Brooke's statement does indicate the extent to which "every aspect of life" could indeed become a subject of Georgian art. Although Ezra Pound and Ford Madox Ford must certainly have guffawed over Waugh's critical concerns—knowing them to be anachronistic in the extreme—the immediate critical response to Georgian poetry quite clearly indicates the grounds on which Georgianism can be called a poetic revolt; furthermore, it enables one to understand the attraction Lawrence felt for the Georgian poets.

Lawrence and *Georgian Poetry 1911–1912*

In a review of *Georgian Poetry 1911–1912*, published in Murry and Mansfield's *Rhythm* for March 1913, D. H. Lawrence became the most eloquent advocate that the Georgians had yet seen. In Drinkwater's lines quoted above, and in others which express similar sentiments, Lawrence finds "hope, and religious joy."[67] To be sure, Lawrence's association with the Georgians, and his wildly enthusiastic review of the first volume of *Georgian Poetry*, is generally looked upon by Lawrentians as an unfortunate case of misidentification, a mistake soon mended by a Lawrence who was growing by leaps and bounds while the Georgians were still studying the advisability of taking a step. But the Lawrence-Georgian connection is more complex than this.

As C. K. Stead has pointed out: "It is common, since the Georgians are out of favour, for critics to insist of any Georgian poet they admire that he did not really belong to the movement."[68] Lawrentians only confirm Stead's point. Lawrence's review of *Georgian Poetry 1911–1912* "makes you wince," says one critic. "What a good man Lawrence must have been. It is easy to understand how painful it was for him to learn what evil really was."[69] Indeed, as we shall see later, Lawrence's final response to the Georgians would seem to confirm the view that he had simply blundered into an association with them, either out of "goodness," or the need for money, or the desire for recognition. But during the years 1910–14, Lawrence had more in common with the Georgians than Lawrentians generally care to perceive; his review of *Georgian Poetry 1911–1912*, not to speak of his poems which appeared in this and subsequent volumes, probably *does* suggest the actual measure of Lawrence's enthusiasm for their work, and further suggests some important points of contact between him and the spirit of the period in which they were so prominent.

Lawrence's review of *Georgian Poetry 1911–1912* (hereafter *Georgian Poetry I*) works from two major premises. First, the "old world," the nihilistic "years of demolition"[70] where "nothing was, but was nothing"[71] are passed, irrevocably. Second, the "new world," where "nothing is really wrong,"[72] is imminent, and is given eager expression by the poets of the Georgian anthology.

The "old world," that which had died with King Edward VII, was a "prison,"[73] a "dream of demolition"[74] in which "we were falling through space into nothingness."[75] Those who represented this "black dream"[76] were "the nihilists, the intellectual, hopeless people—Ibsen, Flaubert, Thomas Hardy"[77]—who, because "faith and belief were getting pot-bound,"[78] had to create works of demolition in order to reestablish truth. Lawrence is well aware of the necessity of their work:

> Because faith and belief were getting pot-bound, and the Temple was made a place to barter sacrifices, therefore faith and belief and the Temple *must* be broken. This time art fought the battle, rather than science or any new religious faction. And art has been demolishing for us: Nietzsche, the Christian religion as it stood; Hardy, our faith in our own endeavour; Flaubert, our belief in love.[79] [Italics mine]

But the battle, necessary as it was, had succeeded as far as it needed to; the Temple "is all smashed."[80] The new poetry comes out of the ruins "like a big breath taken when we are waking up after a night of oppressive dreams . . . our lungs are full of new air, and our eyes see it is morning."[81] Lawrence, who consistently and intentionally identifies himself as one of the Georgians, finds an "exceeding keen relish and appreciation of life"[82] in his fellow Georgians.

In almost every poem in the book comes this note of exultation after

fear, the exultation in the vast freedom, the illimitable wealth that we
have suddenly got. . . . I think I could say every poem in the book is
romantic, tinged with a love of the marvellous, a joy of natural things,
as if the poet were a child for the first time on the seashore, finding
treasures.[83]

He cites Abercrombie, Bottomley, Brooke, Drinkwater, Gibson,
Davies, Sargent, even Masefield, for their "keen zest in life found
wonderful."[84] There is, in their poetry, "an overwhelming sense of
joy"[85] but "no *carpe diem* touch."[86]

For Lawrence, the main indications of the arrival of a new epoch,
insofar as the Georgian poets are exemplary of it, are that the
Georgians are passionate, personal, constructive, and joyful. The
"joy" is especially important to Lawrence because it derives from a
kind of authentic sense of "being ourselves,"[87] which is, finally, a
fulfillment of the life of the body.

What are the Georgian poets, nearly all, but just bursting into a thick
blaze of being? . . . The time to be impersonal has gone. We start from
the joy we have in being ourselves, and everything must take colour
from that joy. It is the return of the blood, that has been held back, as
when the heart's action is arrested by fear. Now the warmth of blood is
in everything, quick, healthy, passionate blood.[88]

Lawrence's review of *Georgian Poetry I* evinces the same group of
values which characterizes those others who were attempting to
define the spirit of the new age: spiritual conversion, a renewed
sense of wonder and joy, exultation over the relaxation of the grip
of the "old world." The review is, in fact, the first of his published
essays which looks forcefully ahead to a direction which his fiction
had heretofore only vaguely suggested. In tone and intention it is
anticipatory of *The Rainbow*, rather than a restatement of any of his
previous fictions. By aligning himself with the Georgian revolt,
Lawrence's profound recoil from the Edwardian vision was given
sustenance and focus.

Lawrence and the Georgians: Significant Affinities

If Lawrence's "Review of *Georgian Poetry 1911–1912*" clarifies
much of that which drew him to the Georgians, it is much less clear
what drew the Georgians to Lawrence. David Daiches has said that
Lawrence's inclusion in the Georgian anthology was "pure acci-

dent,"[89] but, quite clearly, this is not borne out by the facts. Edward Marsh, who was in the admirable position of being able to present a fait accompli to most of the poets he felt should be included, actively searched out Lawrence—then living in Italy—to offer him a place in the volume. Nor was Lawrence's place as a "younger poet" assured simply by his having published a volume of his own during the requisite two years preceding; Lawrence was the only poet included in *Georgian Poetry I* who had not yet published a volume of verse.

But by the middle of 1912, Marsh had read Lawrence's *The White Peacock* and *The Trespasser* and believed them to have "elements of great and rather strange power and beauty."[90] Upon reading "Snap-dragon" in the June *English Review*, Marsh felt it revealed the same qualities. It is perhaps true, as Herbert Palmer and other commentators have remarked, that even from the single example of "Snap-dragon," Marsh should have recognized that he was allowing "a black sheep into the fold."[91] The point is, of course, that Marsh was quite aware of the color of Lawrence's coat, and that his fold was larger and more accommodating than is usually acknowledged.

In his memoir, Marsh has explained that he

> liked poetry to be all three (or if not all three, at least two; or if the worst came to the worst, at least one) of the following things: intelligible, musical and racy; and was happier with it if it was written on some formal principle which I could discern, and from which it departed, if at all, only for the sake of some special effect, and not because the lazy or too impetuous writer had found observance difficult or irksome. I liked poetry that I wanted to know by heart, and *could* learn by heart if I had time. If Mr. Palmer had understood that this was my point of view, I think he would not have marvelled at my choice of D. H. Lawrence's *Snapdragon* or Flecker's *Gates of Damascus*.[92]

Lawrence's poem succeeded in fulfilling at least one of Marsh's qualifications—raciness. Marsh defined this as "intensity of thought or feeling" which rules out the "vapidity which is too often to be found, alas, in verse that is written with due regard to sense, sound and 'correctness.'"[93] "Snap-dragon," if it suffers from a rather desperately inconclusive conclusion, certainly does not suffer from vapidity.

Moreover, the sexually loaded imagery and the treatment of theme which dominates "Snap-dragon," although alien to most of the poetry of the period, was not alien to Marsh, even though the intensity of thought and feeling might have been greater than he was in the habit of encountering. In fact, as if to open the way for Lawrence's intensely erotic love poem, one finds the following lines in the first poem of *Georgian Poetry I:*

> . . . prudence, prudence is the deadly sin,
> And one that groweth deep into a life,
> With hardening roots that clutch about the breast.
> For this refuses faith in the unknown powers
> Within man's nature . . .[94]

In some ways, "prudence" and the "unknown powers within man's nature" are the two poles between which Lawrence's poem moves. As in the earlier "Cruelty and Love," "Snap-dragon" demonstrates Lawrence's "special sensitivity to an *emotional* universe pulsing with . . . violent ambivalence."[95] Lawrence insists on recognizing both sides of this "emotional universe"—passion and cruelty, the yearning to be both victor and victim, the sadism and masochism intimately involved with desire:

> She laughed, she reached her hand out to the flower
> Closing its crimson throat: my own throat in her power
> Strangled, my heart swelled up so full
> As if it would burst its wineskin in my throat,
> Choke me in my own crimson; I watched her pull
> The gorge of the gaping flower, till the blood did float
>
> Over my eyes and I was blind—
> . . . .
> She turned her flushed face to me for the glint
> Of a moment. "See," she laughed, "if you also
> Can make them yawn." I put my hand to the dint
> In the flower's throat, and the flower gaped wide with woe.
> She watched, she went of a sudden intensely still,
> She watched my hand, and I let her watch her fill.
>
> I pressed the wretched, throttled flower between
> My fingers, till its head lay back, its fangs
> Poised at her: like a weapon my hand stood white and keen,
> And I held the choked flower-serpent in its pangs
> Of mordant anguish till she ceased to laugh,
> Until her pride's flag, smitten, cleaved down to the staff.[96]

Sandra Gilbert has said of "Snap-dragon" that it "strikes the casual reader leafing through *Georgian Poetry 1911–1912* as something . . . very much out of the ordinary. . . . It is the more penetratingly realistic stanzas of the poem that are most striking when one comes upon them after a bout with Brooke or Abercrombie."[97] Indeed, it is "out of the ordinary," but the difference is one of degree, not of kind.

Sexual, or at least sensual, love is examined—with more sophistication, if less force—in other poems in the volume. In Rupert Brooke's "Town and Country," for instance, as in Lawrence's poem, the expression of love is endangered by exterior complications. Lawrence's passion/guilt and punishment dynamic is replaced by Brooke's more traditional town/country dynamic, but in both poems the fragility of fully explored passion is offered up for the reader's examination. In "Snap-dragon," the poem's speaker claims a willingness to suffer "the large hands of revenge," if only he can sometimes feel fully alive. He does not care if these "hands"

> Shall get my throat at last—shall get it soon,
> If the joy that they are lifted to avenge
> Have risen red on my night as a harvest moon,
> Which even Death can only put out for me,
> And death I know is better than not-to-be.[98]

But the very elements which control the poem, the sense of conflict, guilt, and cruelty—the sheer emotional difficulty of accepting a relationship which is fully and passionately alive, suggests that thoughts of guilt and shame are never far from the speaker's mind.

In Brooke's "Town and Country," we are told that the town is

> where love's stuff is body, arm and side
> Are stabbing-sweet 'gainst chair and lamp and wall.
> In every touch more intimate meanings hide;
> And flaming brains are the white heart of all.[99]

The walls of the town become emotional walls that confine lovers to intimacy. Here, in town

> Two can be drunk with solitude, and meet
> On the sheer point where sense with knowing's one.[100]

Here, too, the

> roar, and glare, and dust, and myriad white
> Undying passers, pinnacle and crown

> Intensest heavens between close-lying faces
>> By the lamp's airless fierce ecstatic fire;
> And we've found love in little hidden places,
>> Under great shades, between the mist and mire.[101]

In the quiet and remoteness of the country, however, "be-neath/Unheeding stars and unfamiliar moons,"[102] the lovers find themselves placed against the vast, disinterested backdrop of nature, and their love is reduced to inconsequence:

> And gradually along the stranger hill
>> Our unwalled loves thin out on vacuous air,
>
> And suddenly there's no meaning in our kiss,
>> And your lit upward face grows, where we lie,
> Lonelier and dreadfuller than sunlight is,
>> And dumb and mad and eyeless like the sky.[103]

In these poems, Lawrence and Brooke are preoccupied with the disposition of *being*, and insist that passion is dependent on one's ability to overcome those forces which would deny it full and satisfactory expression. Passion is fragile, they say, and easily reduced to meaninglessness by the cruelty of indifference or the indifference of cruelty.

Brooke's "Town and Country" illustrates the extent to which modern pastoral—even, sometimes, Georgian pastoral—has, in Edwin Muir's phrase, only "one foot in Eden."[104] And by offering the city as a protection against an indifferent nature, Brooke has suggested that the Georgian vision is not always simperingly bucolic.

Nevertheless, the pastoral emphasis in Lawrence's poetry of this time was surely an aspect of his work which inclined Marsh to include him among the Georgians. But beyond the mere use of nature as a central subject, the more important similarities between Lawrence and the Georgians rest in the *treatment* of the subject; it is their equal interest in *how* rather than *what* the poet sees that indicates the most significant points of contact in their work. The immediacy of the self's encounter with the external world and the use of the external world as features of psychic landscape are approaches to poetry which directly link Lawrence with the Georgians. That Lawrence succeeded more often than they did is not at issue here; what is more to the point is the similarity of their desire to achieve an "unmediated, naked vision"[105] of reality.

Other significant affinities exist. "Snap-dragon," as well as other Lawrence poems that Marsh might have read in the *English Review* or *The Westminister Gazette*, reveal a world view that is "highly Wordsworthian in its emphasis on organic relatedness to nature."[106] R. G. N. Selgādo, like almost all readers of Lawrence's poetry, finds that it combines a "Wordsworthian pietas for the thing itself with a universe permeated through and through with the subjectivity of the seeing I."[107] Wordsworth was, of course, the most notable influence on Georgian poetry; like him (and perhaps because of him) nature and the countryside "though intensely and exquisitely appreciated for their own sake" in Georgian verse, "are mainly . . . an occasion for exploring and presenting [the poet's] mood and character and a whole mode of experiencing."[108] This impulse, to explore "the whole physical and mental engagement of the self with [the external] world"[109] in language that is "nearer the checks of intimate talk than those of regular prosody,"[110] was a goal of both Lawrence and the Georgians, the common source for which was Wordsworth. The mark of Wordsworth, which is sometimes too inflamed in Georgian work, would have been evident to Marsh, and was certainly a factor in his decision to bring Lawrence into the fold, as well as a reason for Lawrence's enthusiasm about entering it.

Lawrence's poetry of this period also relies, to a great extent, on dramatic narrative told by a speaker experiencing a moment of crisis, a technique which one finds again and again in Georgian verse, sometimes extended into poetic drama. *Georgian Poetry I* includes narrative poems such as Abercrombie's "The Sale of Saint Thomas," Brooke's "Dining-Room Tea," Davies's "The Child and the Mariner," de la Mare's "Winter Dusk," Drinkwater's "The Fires of God," T. Sturge Moore's "A Sicilian Idyll," and W. W. Gibson's "The Hare." Lawrence's "Snap-dragon," "Cruelty and Love" (published in both *Love Poems* and *Georgian Poetry 1913–1915*), "The Schoolmaster" (first published in *The Westminster Gazette* in 1912), and "Dreams Old and Nascent: Old" (first published in the *English Review* in 1909), all use this technique. One need only recall the impact on Marsh of John Masefield's dramatic narrative *The Everlasting Mercy* to imagine the extent to which Marsh was drawn to this form.

Finally, Lawrence's growing concern with what Jessie Chambers called "the leprosy of industrialism"[111] was confirmed and given further impetus by the Georgians. "The North Country" (first published in *New Poems*, 1918, but written by 1911) was, according to Tom Marshall, the first time Lawrence addressed himself to the "vision of the man-made nightmare of the dominance of the machine."[112] Lawrence's characteristic critique of industrial society was only later to be expanded into a position of centrality in his work; it had not yet become explicit in *Sons and Lovers* and was for the most part ignored in *The White Peacock* and *The Trespasser*. In "The North Country," however, Lawrence's fear that the "mechanical existence imposed by the machine was related to mechanical behaviour in human relations"[113] was given aroused, if awkward, expression.

In the first stanza of the poem, nature is described in a condition of unnatural disturbance:

> . . . black poplars shake themselves over a pond,
> And rooks and the rising smoke-waves scatter and wheel from the
>   works beyond:
> The air is dark with north and with sulphur, the grass is a darker
>   green,
> And people darkly invested with purple move palpable through the
>   scene.[114]

People, as always in Lawrence, are part of the natural order, and here they become passively imprisoned somnambulists by the mesmerizing hum of the machine. They are

> . . . shut in the hum of the purpled steel
> As it spins to sleep on its motion, drugged dense in the sleep of the
>   wheel.
>
> Out of the sleep, from the gloom of motion, soundlessly, somnambule
> Moans and booms the soul of a people imprisoned, asleep in the rule
> Of the strong machine that runs mesmeric, booming the spell of its
>   word
> Upon them and moving them helpless, mechanic, their will to its will
>   deferred.[115]

Almost all of the Georgian poets find a place for similar sentiments in their work, but Gordon Bottomley's *Chambers of Imagery I* and *II* (1907 and 1912) seem to provide particularly trenchant examples. In "The Viaduct" (1907), Bottomley expresses the same sense of human imprisonment by the machine that Lawrence had envisioned in "The North Country." A train from London crossing over a railway bridge makes the speaker

> . . . remember thus it must have been
> That Caesar's trampling Triumphing appeared—
> Elephants heaving, fuming flames upreared,
> Stacked waggons, slow unthinking slaves between.[116]

In "Iron-Founders and others" (1912), Bottomley warns against the destruction of the English landscape, and links this "poisoning" of England with the notion of man's worship of the machine:

> When you destroy a blade of grass
> You poison England at her roots:
> Remember no man's foot can pass
> Where evermore no green life shoots . . .
> . . . .
> Your worship is your furnaces,
> Which, like old idols, lost obscenes,
> Have molten bowels; your vision is
> Machines for making more machines.[117]

But beyond the apparent affinities of influence, technique, and preoccupation that undoubtedly exist in Lawrence's early work and in that of his Georgian contemporaries, there rests the reciprocal recognition by both parties of a shared sense of participation in the beginning of a "new world," where, in Lawrence's phrase, "nothing is really wrong"[118] and where one can feel a "keen zest in life found wonderful."[119] An unknown reviewer of Lawrence's first book of verse, *Love Poems and Others* (1913), took note of this "zest" when he wrote:

> The mood which is . . . beginning to stir poetry into new exertions may be summed up best, perhaps, in some Nietzschean phrase; if we call it, for instance, a mood of determined *yea-saying* to the actualities of existence, we shall get pretty close to it.[120]

Georgians and Moderns

It is of little use to expect to duplicate Lawrence's evident excitement by reading the text of *Georgian Poetry I;* the reasons for that excitement can only be found beneath the text, by attending to the spirit which stirs under its rather bland surface. The longer we stare at the poems which actually make up the Georgian revolt, the harder it is for us to remember that it was a revolt at all. Later readers have been more apt to call their work revolting—in its manifest preciousness, its sentimentality, its Disney version of the pastoral tradition. In fact, the amount of abuse heaped upon the Georgians since World War I is really unparalleled in modern literary history. Poets, literary historians, and critics alike can barely contain themselves when discussion turns to the Georgians; the mere invocation of their name brings tears of sardonic laughter to critical eyes. They are "vapid versifiers who sang the joys of country life from their desks in the city";[121] "non-recognizers" who "regard dreaming as an alternative to the nightmare of contemporary wakefulness";[122] "adolescent self-consciousness in an ironical disguise" that is "painfully embarrassing."[123] It is clear that when Edward Marsh, editor and patron of the early Georgians, wrote in his memoirs that "my proud ambiguous adjective 'Georgian' . . . became a term of derision,"[124] he was exhibiting a typically Georgian penchant for understatement.

Much of the critical derision leveled at the Georgians is misdirected; it usually either focuses on the late Georgian (Neo-Georgian) work of the postwar period, or uses the most vulnerable Georgian poems as easy targets for the entire movement.* The work of various contemporaries of the Georgians—particularly Pound, Eliot, and Hulme—is used as a convenient wedge to discriminate between true modernism and what has come to be thought of as merely the "last faint re-echo of the Great Tradition."[125] But if one is concerned with the image that the Georgians presented to the literary public at the onset of their influence, one must take note of the genial fraternity that existed between, for instance, the Pound-Hulme circle and the Georgians around 1911.

It has become quite easy to forget Pound's own narrow escape

---

*One poem which has come in for more than its share of criticism is Rupert Brooke's "The Old Vicarage, Grantchester." In "Inside the Whale," an essay which is, on the whole, long on wit and short on a sense of humor, George Orwell offers what has come to be the standard attack on the poem: "Rupert Brooke's 'Grantchester,' the star poem of 1913, is nothing but an enormous gush of 'country' sentiment, a sort of accumulated vomit from a stomach stuffed with place-names. Considered as a poem 'Grantchester' is something worse than worthless, but as an illustration of what the thinking middle-class young of that period *felt* it is a valuable document" (George Orwell, "Inside the Whale," in *A Collection of Essays*, p. 228). Orwell misreads the poem; as is so often the case with poets of less than major talent, we refuse to give them the credit for having any sense. "Grantchester" is a satire, the object of which—and this is what leads to the misreadings—is Brooke's own sentimentality, his half-repressed yearning for an England where "the dews/ Are soft beneath a morn of gold" and he can "get in touch/ With Nature there, or Earth, or such" (Rupert Brooke, "The Old Vicarage, Grantchester," in *The Collected Poems of Rupert Brooke*, pp. 155, 156).

from inclusion in the first *Georgian Poetry* volume. In September 1912, Edward Marsh wrote to Pound asking him if "The Ballad of the Goodly Fere" might be included in the anthology. Pound replied, "I'm sorry I can't let you have *that* poem as I'm just bringing it out in a volume of my own. Is there anything in the earlier books that you like?"[126] It is, of course, difficult to say whether or not Pound's reaction to the Georgians would have been the same if one of his poems *had* been included. Probably it wouldn't have, finding himself flanked—as he would have been—by T. Sturge Moore and Ronald Ross. Nevertheless, his rather cordial response to Marsh does indicate the extent to which even Pound, at this time, thought that the Georgians were representatives of a new, modern tendency in poetry, the first wave of the revolt against the Victorian and Edwardian backwaters.

T. E. Hulme, that other unflinching advocate of modern poetry, began meeting with Pound to discuss issues of modernism in April 1909. These meetings began not long after Hulme's "Poets Club" publication, *For Christmas MDCCCCVIII*, had graced London bookstands. The volume included Hulme, Selwyn Image, Lady Margaret Sackville, Henry Simpson, F. W. Tancred, Dermot Fryer, and Mrs. Marion Cran—"who later distinguished herself as an expert on flower gardens."[127] Such a gallery, perhaps, does not speak well for the strides that the new poetry had by then managed to take under Hulme's robust auspices. Despite the addition of Pound, and later F. S. Flint, Richard Aldington, H. D., and others who were to make *Imagism* a common poetic term, Hulme's attitude toward the Georgians remained cordial. His biographer, Alun R. Jones, reports that Hulme was on "friendly and even intimate terms with Harold Monro, Rupert Brooke, Edward Marsh and the poets of the *Georgian Anthology* [sic], even living for a time over the Poetry Bookshop . . . which was the headquarters for the whole Georgian movement."[128]

Hard as it is to imagine 200 pounds of T. E. Hulme living like a sword upstairs over Georgian heads, the implications are clear: during the years that constitute the genesis of what is generally considered to be "modern" in modern poetry, differences in aesthetic principles and poetic treatment were in no way as important as the generalized buoyancy over the act of being modern, of stepping full stride into the new epoch; both the Georgians and the Pound-Hulme circle were mainly marked by the instinct to dramatize their own modernity, and it was this buoyancy which attracted Lawrence.

Georgians and the Public

It can hardly be argued that Pound's and Hulme's critical considerations of the Georgians did not change radically between 1911 and the beginning of the war, nor that there came to be "two separate reactions against the ruling [Edwardian] convention, the 'Georgian' and the 'modern.' "[129] By 1914, their common enemy sufficiently dispatched, the differences between the Georgians and the Pound-Hulme circle had become clearly irreconcilable.

One of the crucial differences between them was their attitude toward their audience. Pound's attitude is well known, and it anticipates the relationship between writer and audience that would henceforth dominate modern literature. It suggests one of the reasons for the "singularly rootless character" of so much of modern literature, which seems to "exist in a vacuum, to spring from no particular society and to address no particular audience."[130] His opinion is comprehensive, but quite simply expressed, as some of his early letters show:

> As for the "eyes of too ruthless public": damn their eyes. No art ever yet grew by looking into the eyes of the public, ruthless or otherwise. You can obliterate yourself and mirror God, Nature, or Humanity but if you try to mirror yourself in the eyes of the public, woe be unto your art.[131]

> If one is going to print opinions that the public already agrees with, what is the use of printing 'em at all? Good art can't possibly be palatable all at once. . . .[132]

> . . . so far as I personally am concerned the public can go to the devil. It is the function of the public to prevent the artist's expression by hook or by crook.[133]

Pound's comments are indicative of what Graham Hough has described as "the temptation to exploit by snob-appeal a false assumption of common experience; or to exploit by a kind of bullying exoticism the absence of community."[134]

The Georgians, too, were suspicious of the public. It was, as far as the Georgians could tell, quite satisfied by Newbolt, Watson, Kipling, Noyes, and the like. Poetry and public seemed to have conspired together to deceive themselves about the nature of contemporary reality. To most readers, poetry was "acceptable when it effectively versified Imperialist sentiments, the public school spirit, or patriotic fervour: otherwise it was unlikely to be widely read."[135] So the poets of the "black dream behind us" expressed the rather saddeningly exhausted notions, and often the most pernicious notions, of their audience. Nevertheless, the Georgians, unlike Pound, refused to sever their art totally from their audience.

The Georgians believed, like Whitman, that to have great poets there must be great audiences too. They desired an audience with vitality equal to the poetry it read; but what they had in mind was not simply the old Victorian and Edwardian audience transformed. They were reaching for a new public, appropriate to the cultural rejuvenation they felt was at hand, and which seemed to them to have been the generative force behind the proven popularity of works like Masefield's *The Everlasting Mercy*. This was a public which was educable, and part of the poet's job was to educate. Edward Marsh, for instance, held strongly that

> poetry is communication, and that it is the poet's duty, to the best of his ability, to let the reader know what he is driving at. Some of the moderns seem to think that to be understood is to be damned . . . but this is an ungenerous attitude. . . . [it is] the doctrine of Privelege in its grossest and grimmest form. I am myself no democrat in literature, but I should never hold it against a poem that it appealed to all sorts and conditions.[136]

Indeed, as C. K. Stead has said of the Georgians, "Theirs was an attempt to educate public taste rather than to dismiss the reading public as too degenerate in taste to deserve consideration."[137] A public, it was felt, would respond enthusiastically if it were given good poetry, and poetry attuned to the temperament of the time.

The Georgian success was not, of course, simply a matter of tapping in to the predominant temperament; it was also a matter of hard work and excellent strategy. Marsh, with help from Rupert Brooke and Harold Monro, directed a particularly thorough prepublication campaign: potential reviewers were contacted; influential literary men were given prepublication copies of *Georgian Poetry I* and asked to mention the book publicly; Brooke, John Drinkwater, W. W. Gibson, and others of the more established younger poets stumped England pushing *Georgian Poetry I* "in season and out of season."[138]

The result was profound. "It was said that the Prime Minister's car was waiting outside Bumpus's shop in Oxford Street at opening-time on the day of publication,"[139] and the sales only went up from there. Seven months after publication it had gone through six editions, nine by the end of the year. Marsh's own reckoning in the late 1930s was that *Georgian Poetry I* had sold over 15,000 copies—a critic of that period called it "probably next to Palgrave's the most important and influential anthology ever published."[140]

W. H. Davies wrote Marsh soon after its initial publication, saying, "You have performed a wonder—made poetry pay!"[141] Walter de la Mare found that his contribution of five poems to *Georgian Poetry I* had brought in more money than all of his previously published poems together. He wrote his thanks to Marsh in appropriate form:

> Alas, these millstones round my neck—
> Another cheque! another cheque!
> Refrain, my soul; and keep thee steady:
> Strive to be—well—polite to Eddy . . .[142]

And in January 1914, writing from Italy, D. H. Lawrence confessed, "that *Georgian Poetry* book is a veritable Aladdin's lamp. I little thought my 'Snap dragon' would go on blooming and seeding in this prolific fashion. So many thanks for the cheque for four pounds, and long life to *G. P.*"[143]

The Georgians had fully believed that poetry could be assimilated into the existing social structure without disclaiming their own modernism, and the anthology's enormous sales seemed to prove them right. "Snap-dragon," Lawrence's first poem to be included in the *Georgian Poetry* volumes, *did* go on "blooming and seeding" long after Pound, Eliot, and others had made Georgianism a rear-guard action. The significant point here is that Lawrence both desired and needed a public at the time the anthology was published. Soon after accepting Marsh's offer of inclusion in *Georgian Poetry I*, Lawrence wrote to Edward Garnett: "Did I tell you about Marsh who is putting 'Snapdragon' in a vol. of contemporary poetry that is coming out just now? That'll help perhaps to advertise me."[144] To associate himself, or be associated, with a group that could reach a wide audience was essential to a writer who desired to alter the sensibilities of the English people.

Even partial assimilation into the Georgian milieu allowed Lawrence a range of creative options that he could not have otherwise expected. From a writer who hoped that "an audience might be found in England for some of my stuff,"[145] Lawrence could begin to write "bigger stuff than any man in England";[146] he could do so because his public was in the process of being educated "to know what they want"[147] ". . . not to just what they fancy they want."[148]

Reaching a public had always been a major consideration for Lawrence. One recalls the distress he felt about that subject in the years leading up to his association with the Georgians. Although the critical response to *The White Peacock* was generally favorable, Lawrence declared in 1911 that "the publishing of the book has brought me very little but bitterness. A good many folk have been hostile—practically all America."[149] As he wrote the first draft of what was to become *Sons and Lovers,* he felt that "the British public will stone me if it ever catches sight."[150] Upon its completion he declared, "It's quite a great work. I only hope the English nation won't rend me for having given them anything so good. Not that the English nation is likely to concern itself with me—but 'England, my England' is for me, I suppose, 'Critic, my Critic.' "[151]

Lawrence always harbored severe misgivings about his audience:

the blasted, jelly-boned swines, the slimy, the belly-wriggling inverte-brates, the miserable sodding rotters, the flaming sods, the snivelling, dribbling, dithering palsied pulse-less lot that make up England to-day.[152]

And after the suppression of *The Rainbow* in 1915, his attitude toward the literary public hardened considerably. But his lifelong intention—to help "English folk . . . to alter, and have more sense,"[153] always required that he believe that there would be, eventually, an audience for his work, even if it was only "a good public amongst the Meredithy public"[154] that he originally pro-jected as possible readers for *The Rainbow.* In 1913, the Georgians seemed to have located at least the rudiments of such an audience, located, one should say, an audience available for reconstruction into an effective community—not simply an essentially random and transitory group of readers.

4   Landscape and Community: *The White Peacock* and *The Rainbow*

The Attraction of Optimism: Rupert Brooke and E. M. Forster

The Edwardians had thought that a viable system was still possible through social and economic change; the Georgians did not necessarily reject this notion, but they clearly felt that cultural viability was to be found not so much through tampering with contemporary social and economic fashions, but through revived attention and reconnection with elemental, unchanging truths. "They wished," claims Myron Simon, "to cultivate and to receive a naked vision of the world's continuing revelation."[1]

As Lawrence had noticed in his review of *Georgian Poetry I*, such a revelation was essentially joyous. It is, perhaps, Rupert Brooke who best—or, at least, most often—expresses this joy. In his letters, Brooke declares that his joy

> consists in just looking at people and things as themselves—neither as useful nor moral nor ugly nor anything else, but just as being. . . . What happens is that I suddenly feel the extraordinary value and importance of everybody I meet, and almost everything I see. . . . And it's not only beauty, and beautiful things. In a flicker of sunlight on a blank wall, or a reach of muddy pavement, or smoke from an engine at night there's a sudden significance and importance and inspiration that makes the breath stop with a gulp of certainty and happiness.[2]

And again:

> But hurrah for the World! It's fairly bubbling and glittering round me! I'd do anything anywhere a million years.[3]

Brooke's letters are filled with like pronouncements; they are, to some, indicative of his naiveté and genteel prewar optimism; they seem, in some curious way, almost irresponsible. But they are also indicative of a way of vision which was of central significance in the years before the war, and one which meshed with Lawrence's long-standing desire to "study the living soul which is the essence of mankind"[4] by going beyond the obstructions of transient societal fashions. The Edwardians, like Wells, seemed in comparison to be "passionate declaimer[s] or reasoner[s]"[5] who looked at life "as a cold and hungry little boy in the street stares at a shop where there is hot pork."[6]

Between 1907 and 1914, E. M. Forster wrote a series of articles for *The Working Men's College Journal* which suggest a sensibility quite similar to Brooke's, and which, as Lawrence did, question the pessimistic tendencies of writers like Wells. In an article written in 1907, Forster stands in a middle position between the pessimistic convictions of the period and the optimistic impulse of his own temperament. In it, he understands the pessimist as one who has inherited "the modern idea of evolution, which teaches that all things alter,"[7] and "the modern tendency to see in everything some latent discomfort."[8]

> The older generation had a lightness of spirit, a robustness of outlook that is apparently denied to the younger. . . . In some way or another, nearly every modern writer lets us hear the note of sorrow. Take such a writer as Bernard Shaw. We call him a humorist, and no doubt he does make us laugh at the time. But when we come away, we don't know why we were laughing. We feel terribly depressed. There is none of the radiant afterglow that we feel when we have finished a novel of Dickens or seen a comedy of Shakespeare. In our literature there sounds that undernote, like the toll of a subterranean bell, "The world is a horrible place! The world is a horrible place!"[9]

Forster goes on to justify pessimism in modern literature as the inevitable outcome of the movements of modern thought. The modern author, "if he is conscientious and artistic,"[10] must sound the "subterranean bell" of pessimism because he knows too much to do otherwise. But Forster *does* insist on making a distinction between literature and life.

> In life we seek what is gracious and noble, even if it is transitory; in books we seek what is permanent, even when it is sad. I uphold optimism in life. I do not at present uphold optimism in literature. When the optimists fall on me in the discussion and rend me, as only optimists

can, let them remember that I am as anxious as anyone for cheerful books; but they must be cheerful with sincerity.[11]

By 1911, in another article for the same journal, Forster appears more inclined, or at least more determined, to present the case for optimism in *both* life and literature. Taking the "true optimist"[12] Walt Whitman as his source, Forster tells his audience that it is time to "stop grumbling."[13] And it is the poet who can show us the way. "We are absolutely certain," he said,

> though we cannot prove it, that life is beautiful. Fine weather—to take what may seem a small example; fine weather during the whole of a day; the whole city cheered by blue sky and sunshine. What a marvellous blessing that is! . . . Modern civilization does not lead us away from Romance, but it does try to lead us past it, and we have to keep awake. We must insist on going to look round the corner now and then, even if other people think us a little queer, for as likely as not something beautiful lies round the corner. And if we insist, we may have a reward that is even greater than we expected, and see for a moment with the eyes of a poet—may see the universe, not merely beautiful in scraps, but beautiful everywhere and for ever.[14]

Howards End as Georgian Archetype

The similarities between Forster's comments and those of Rupert Brooke do not necessarily indicate that one was influenced by the other, but they do suggest the extent to which both were breathing the atmosphere of the new Georgian era. In this context, Forster's *Howards End*, published in 1910, can be understood as both the best and the most typical twentieth-century novel to be thoroughly cast in the Georgian mold. Standing as it does at the gateway to the period, *Howards End* is a particularly important and imaginatively satisfying example of the kind of perception which dominated the work of the Georgians. Assuredly, it contains most of Georgianism's typical faults—a somewhat precious lyricism, an inability or unwillingness to come to grips with the harsher elements of existence, a sense that Forster (like Margaret Schlegel) "knew of life's seamy side as a theory" but was unable to "grasp it as a fact."[15] Perhaps because of these faults, *Howards End* may serve as a happy introduction to certain themes and issues that preoccupied all of the Georgians.

The most important of these themes and issues is man's relationship with nature; for Forster, as for the Georgians, the rural or organic image provides "almost *the* essential alternative myth for the era, the only outright model of community as opposed to crowd."[16] The characters in *Howards End* are consistently shown as being in sympathy or out of sympathy with nature, and from their abilities to "connect" with the landscape we learn a great deal about them. The Wilcox family's essential indifference to the landscape which surrounds them, their indifference to Howards End, and even their tendency to contract hay fever (with the significant exception of Ruth Wilcox) is indicative of the "panic and emptiness"[17] that characterizes the lives of those who have "no part with the earth and its emotions."[18]

With Howards End as its focal center, the landscape, threatened by the "red rust"[19] of London and the encroachment of automobiles which make it heave and merge "like porridge,"[20] remains the stable element of the novel—its potency is anterior to the changing fashions of the moment. For Forster, as for all the Georgians, nature (especially as it is localized in the English landscape) was the obvious choice of subject for the writer who is searching for a way to express "the world's continuing revelation," which persists despite historical and social ephemera.

One of the major issues in *Howards End* is whether or not the landscape will be inherited by those who can appreciate it or by those who cannot.

> England was alive, throbbing through all her estuaries, crying for joy through the mouths of all her gulls, and the north wind, with contrary motion, blew stronger against her rising seas. What did it mean? For what end are her fair complexities, her changes of soil, her sinuous coast? Does she belong to those who have moulded her and made her feared by other lands, or to those who have added nothing to her power, but have somehow seen her, seen the whole island at once, lying as a jewel in a silver sea, sailing as a ship of souls, with all the brave world's fleet accompanying her towards eternity?[21]

It is clear, of course, that although Margaret and Helen Schlegel know the spirit of Howards End, and by extension all of natural England, the Wilcoxes now own it. It is they who control the "ropes of life."[22] Nevertheless, through a supreme effort of wish fulfillment, Forster asserts by the end of the novel that the triumphant businessmen, "who saw life more steadily, though with the steadiness of the half-closed eye,"[23] will not triumph in the end. The final triumph rests with those, like the child Tom, who are ruled "by the movements of the crops and the sun."[24]

They are England's hope. Clumsily they carry forward the torch of the sun, until such time as the nation sees fit to take it up. Half clodhopper, half boardschool prig, they can still throw back to a nobler stock, and breed yeomen.[25]

The conflict over England's future is between yeoman stock and stocks and bonds, and the last word on it is Margaret Schlegel's. Although it is perhaps spoken with a greater degree of hope than belief, it does carry with it all of Forster's authorial weight. "All the signs are against it now," she says, "but I can't help hoping, and very early in the morning in the garden I feel that our house is the future as well as the past."[26]

In *Howards End*, Forster sees the landscape with a Georgian eye; although it often seems to be the view of a country weekender, it still exists in eternal counterpoint to the "continual flux"[27] of London. Such a view, the source for a "new pastoral in which the countryside stands for a lost organicism and the city for a new exposure,"[28] was one which was particularly agreeable to the "eyes of a poet," especially a Georgian poet. In some ways poetry was the only response adequate to the problem. Thus, the response of Margaret Schlegel, who, as tensions increase between herself and her businessman husband, becomes increasingly attentive to the countryside:

> Margaret was fascinated by Oniton. She had said that she loved it, but it was rather its romantic tension that held her. The rounded Druids of whom she had caught glimpses in her drive, the rivers hurrying down from them to England, the carelessly modelled masses of the lower hills, thrilled her with poetry.[29]

Margaret, of course, is not a poet—the forms and structures with which she works are invariably human. But she does think about poetry, she does see with the "eyes of a poet," and, when she does, it is in unmistakably Georgian terms.

> England still waits for the supreme moment of her literature—for the great poet who shall voice her, or, better still, for the thousand little poets whose voices shall pass into our common talk.[30]

The Georgians considered themselves, almost from the start, the "little poets" whose voices would pass into the English common talk. Harold Monro, for instance, felt that one of the most significant aspects of the poets of the period was that "a century hence, they may appear a kind of Composite Poet; there may be 500 excellent poems proceeding from 100 poets mostly not so very great, but well worth remembering a century hence."[31] F. R. Leavis, among others, points to this willful littleness of the Georgians as symptomatic of "an age in which there were no serious standards current, no live tradition of poetry, and no public capable of informed and serious interest."[32] Leavis's claim has the approval of literary history, yet it seems a more appropriate criticism of the years immediately before the Georgians than the years during and after them. Leavis disregards the close relations between the Georgians and the other modernists between 1910 and 1912, and declines to mention the "new bearings in English poetry" that they, together, first began to define. Furthermore, the "littleness" of most Georgian poetry, and of Georgian aspirations in general, is linked to the basic stance of Georgianism as a whole: the rejection of the grandiose claims, the political and poetic imperialism, of the preceding period; its desire for the attention of the common reader through the celebration of the common life in common language; and the desire to rediscover an existing state of cultural viability on English, not international, soil. Like one of the characters in *Howards End*, the Georgians seemingly felt that when "poets over here try to celebrate bigness they are dead at once, and naturally."[33]

Georgians and the Landscape

It was Forster who said, "The English countryside, its growth and its destruction, is a genuine and a tragic theme"[34] It was the Georgians, even if they were incapable of generating tragedy, who made the theme their own. It is certainly not true, as L. A. G. Strong has declared, that "the Georgians discovered the English countryside."[35] But they did, in some important ways, revive it. Harold Monro, in an article published in 1913, spoke for a number of Georgians when he said that the first principles of the new poetry were:

i. To forget God, Heaven, Hell, Personal Immortality, and to remember, always, the earth.
ii. To lift the eyes from a sentimental contemplation of the past, and through dwelling in the present, nevertheless, always, to *live* in the future of the earth.[36]

The reemergence of nature as a central subject for literature was commensurate with the Georgians' desire to express "the world's continuing revelation." Like Wordsworth, they were committed to the notion that imaginative perception creates value. And the imagination trained on the landscape suggests certain kinds of values in which they were particularly interested: "those elemental truths ineluctably resident . . . in nature, in the rhythm of the seasons, in love and birth and death, in the enigmas of personality, in the dependably certain and the dependably uncertain."[37] Gordon Bottomley, for instance, declared: "My business has seemed to be to look for the essentials of life, the part that does not change."[38] The well-known Georgian fondness for the pastoral, therefore, was a function of their realism—whatever exists essentially undistracted by transient social forms of experience—not as an "artistic mannerism or as a means of escape from personal responsibility or from the modern world."[39] If this led, as it often did, to quivering poetic-emotional gestures in which "authentic observation [is] overcome by a sub-intellectual fantasy,"[40] it also led to an image of the countryside presented as an authentically "gentle, just, and reasonable"[41] alternative to the existing condition of England.

The Georgians' concentration on nature as a subject for their verse was but one element in a general "back-to-nature" movement that had swelled slowly in the early years of the century.* Part of the fierce reaction to the garish artificialities of the 1890s and the "Moral Purposists Polonicisms"[42] of the Edwardian Uncles was the desire for a "restoration of confidence in the stoutness and reliability and essential healthiness of the things of the earth."[43]

Nevertheless, the Georgians, like so many others in England, were well aware that the center of English life had moved away

---

*One can point for confirmation to the continuing influence of writers such as A. E. Housman, Edward Carpenter, Richard Jefferies, and W. H. Hudson. Later came *Georgian Poetry* and *Howards End*, along with the immense popularity of such disparate things as Maurice Maeterlinck's *The Blue Bird* (1911), country songs as set forth by Cecil Sharp and Vaughan Williams, the books of George Bourne, and George Borrow's gypsies, all of which stand as manifestations of the tendency. It seems almost no accident that in December 1910, that most momentous month in a momentous year, Virginia Woolf herself was engaged in a search for a house in the country.

Here, too, one might mention the continued interest in the image of Pan, both as a simple representation of the countryside and as a symbol of a universal, transcendental Nature. Between 1908 (when Kenneth Grahame's *The Wind in the Willows* was published) and 1912 (which saw the publication of James Stephens's *The Crock of Gold*), there was a proliferation of benevolent Pan figures which suggests a desire on the part of English writers to reenlist the goat-god as an active force in English life (see Patricia Merivale, *Pan the Goat-God*).

from the rural, and toward the city. Much of their worst poetry comes from a kind of fragile nostalgia derived from their recognition that a whole, authentic way of life had been lost. Arcadia was gone, forever, and the Georgians knew it; but the landscape that persisted retained the power to evoke celebration.

Lawrence speaks to this in *The Trespasser*. In that novel, the Isle of Wight is celebrated in prose far lusher than modern taste ordinarily permits. Yet, even in *The Trespasser*, Lawrence is aware that Arcadia is unavailable except as a localization of certain impulses which yearn for expression. Looking down on a bucolic scene featuring a farmer's wife and her children, Siegmund declares:

> "Don't they seem a long way off?" he said, staring at the bucolic scene. "They are farther than Theocritus—down there is farther than Sicily, and more than twenty centuries from us. I wish it weren't."
> "Why do you?" she cried, with curious impatience.
> He laughed.[44]

Siegmund's laughter here, like the Brangwen women who laugh in church in *The Rainbow*, rises out of the recognition of his own sentimentality, and checks the impulse toward nostalgia. For Siegmund, as for Helena, the Isle of Wight is a "magic land,"[45] where "every fibre in his body was surprised with joy, as each tree in a forest at dawn utters astonished cries of delight."[46] But the magic is easily intruded upon; Caliban will have his day. Midway through the novel, Siegmund leans over the seawall to see that "in the bay were two battleships, uncouth monsters, lying as naive and curious as sea-lions strayed afar."[47] An onlooker comments:

> "They look rather incongruous, don't you think? We left the sea empty and shining, and when we come again, behold, these objects keeping their eye on us!"[48]

Lawrence's description of the battleships as "monsters" and "sea-lions" perhaps betrays an inability, in this novel at least, to come to grips with the nature of reality beyond the "magic land." One might, for comparison, remark the use H. G. Wells made of a symbolically similar situation at the end of *Tono-Bungay*. Nevertheless, the final point to be made about *The Trespasser* as a whole is its recognition of the limitations of the very thing it seems to love the most. It is, after all, Siegmund and Helena's inability to develop anything beyond an aesthetic relationship, to break open the magic casement of dream and fantasy which encloses them, that finally proves destructive and leads to Siegmund's suicide. Magic in the landscape or in human relations, like sentiment over what might have been, is not strong enough to withstand reality.

In its luscious description of the landscape, and its depiction—however unsuccessful—of an adulterous affair, *The Trespasser* quite clearly reveals itself as a Georgian novel. It is Georgian, too, in the recognition of its own limitations. Lawrence himself, writing of his distaste for both *The Trespasser* and *The White Peacock*, declared in 1910 that his next novel "will be a novel—not a florid prose poem, or a decorated idyll running to seed in realism."[49] Still, except for the fact that *The Trespasser* is indisputably Lawrence's worst novel, it is most memorable precisely because of its overripe prose and Wagnerian symbology. If one, perhaps, cannot continue to make battleships into sea-lions without being a genuine naïf, one need not be resigned to despair, either. "I am tired of life being so ugly and cruel," Lawrence wrote in 1911. "How I long for it to turn pleasant. It makes my soul heave with distaste to see it so harsh and brutal."[50] That the Georgians wrote pleasant poetry in and about a situation that *was* harsh and brutal almost perfectly satisfied Lawrence's needs and his mood.

Indeed, the harsh facts concerning the gradual disappearance of the English landscape were perceived as clearly by the Georgians as they had been by Masterman, but their recognition of this fact did not necessarily evince the sense of hopelessness that one feels, and is meant to feel, after reading Masterman's analysis. Masterman's discussion of the decline of the country is flavored with a kind of sad acceptance of the fact; it sounds the "subterranean bell" in precisely the way that Lawrence felt was hopeless and resigned. "No, I don't believe England need be so grubby," Lawrence wrote from Italy in 1912. "One *can* have the necessary things, life, and love, and clean warmth. Why is England so shabby?"[51]

If the Georgians did not have the insight to answer Lawrence's question fully, they were, when compared to the Edwardian alternative, clearly on the right track. "Life, and love, and clean warmth" was the very basis of their work. And in it, the disappearing English landscape became

a place of physical and spiritual regeneration. It was now the teeming life of an isolated nature, or the seasonal rhythm of the fundamental life processes. Neither of these feelings was new in itself. What was new was their fusion into a structure of feeling in which the earth and its creatures—animals and peasants almost alike—were an affirmation of vitality and of the possibility of rest in conscious contrast with the mechanical order, the artificial routines, of the cities.[52]

It should be noted here that the characteristic Georgian landscape is not only English, but English of a certain type. It is, for the most part, a supremely civilized landscape, clearly lived in; it has very little to do with those areas of the country which, because of their starkness or sublimity, confront the eye with natural forms that seem somehow fundamentally inimical to man. The geographical boundaries of Georgian poetry are safely within easy driving distance of London, an area of England characterized by what can only be called gentleness. The Lake District and the moors and dales of the north are all conspiciously absent from Georgian poetry; Cornwall, Wales, and Scotland certainly find no place there. What mysteries survive in Georgian landscapes are, to quote Forster, "quiet mysteries."[53] The Georgian Pan is best seen as the "little god Pan, who presides over social contretemps and unsuccessful picnics,"[54] and, as such, is indicative of the Georgian spirit, which continually emphasizes joy over panic. Georgian work, perhaps, suggests the truth of Aldous Huxley's remark that the "Wordsworthian adoration of Nature . . . is only possible in a country where Nature has been nearly or quite enslaved to man."[55]

Lawrence, having grown up in the Midlands, was better equipped to describe a nature "quite enslaved to man" than almost any of his contemporaries. When Lawrence chooses to give us his view of the famous "red rust" which sniffs and bustles toward the countryside in *Howards End,* he can give us a very close view indeed—a full, hard look at the worst—because he knows its source. But he did not really make that choice until later. Even though hints of Lawrence's alarm over the intrusion of industry into the countryside can be found in his early work—an alarm which was shared by the Georgians—it was not until his opposition to it stiffened and developed that we encounter the view which we now take to be characteristically Lawrentian. In his later work, Lawrence's rejection of industrialism is aggressive and indisputable, and his handling of the landscape—that which is found in *The Rainbow* or *Birds, Beasts and Flowers,* for instance—stands in distinct contrast to his earlier work. The landscape remains a "continuing revelation," but it is, finally, eternally incomprehensible to man. It stands in vital counterpoint not only to the "mechanical order" of the cities, but also to civilization itself. Such a landscape cannot, as Egbert discovers in "England, My England," be "re-created" or softened by simply filling it with flowers.[56] To attempt to do so is to deny its essential reality, its "otherness," by humanizing and therefore, given Lawrence's view of the human condition, mechanizing it. Toward the end of Lawrence's life, even the harshest areas of England appear to be too tainted with humanity. In *St. Mawr*, for instance, Lou Witt moves progressively away from the centers of civilization: from London, to Shropshire, to the border of Wales, and finally to the stark landscape of New Mexico, where man must constantly

> rouse himself afresh, to cleanse the new accumulations of refuse. To win from the crude wild nature the victory and the power to make another start, and to cleanse behind him the century-deep deposits of layer upon layer of refuse . . .[57]

The White Peacock

Lawrence's early work, however, is quite different. The "characteristically Lawrentian" view of nature becomes fully developed only after his contact with the harsher and more elemental landscapes of Germany and Italy, his attempt to discover basic principles by using the "exhaustive method"[58] in *The Rainbow*, his rereading of Hardy, and his brief but illuminating contact with the theories of the Futurists. But his early work like *The White Peacock* represents an earlier, Georgian phase of Lawrence's response to nature.

Claude M. Sinzelle has said of *The White Peacock* that "though the treatment of the human plot is pessimistic, the general impression left is one of brightness and hope. . . . This prevailing impression of brightness is not easy to account for, but it permeates subtly every description, and it is the out-of-doors scenes which impress the mind most in *The White Peacock*."[59] By comparing the two letters quoted earlier in this chapter (p. 74), one can perhaps begin to account for such a paradox. Lawrence was keenly aware of the "shabbiness" of England, its ugliness and cruelty, but he was empowered with an equally strong impulse to "turn life pleasant" and write of "life, and love, and clean warmth." In *The White Peacock*, knowledge and impulse mix together.

The White Peacock is a pastoral novel, although perhaps a "mutation of the pastoral genre,"[60] and, in many ways, a characteristically Georgian production. Even though it contains a number of realistic elements—it recognizes, for instance, that rural life is often coarse and harsh, as well as that industrial England is coming ever closer to intruding into the landscape—the dominant impression left by *The White Peacock* is made by its romantic-idyllic-pastoral strain. It would hardly seem to be a credit to Lawrence to applaud him for noticing things in his books that he could not possibly have failed to notice in his life; yet this is precisely what many critics have done. But despite heroic critical efforts to "save" the novel by emphasizing its naturalistic elements, and reducing the importance of the Georgian pastoral strain by finding its source in Lawrence's immaturity, one must finally recognize, as George H. Ford does, that, despite its displays of antipastoral sentiment and harsh realism, *The White Peacock*'s "action seems less important than the loving evocation of a pastoral setting,—the brooks, hayfields, and wild flowers which the characters observe in their walks."[61]

The main point to be observed here is that it is Lawrence's very recognition of realistic elements within the rural setting that makes *The White Peacock* "characteristically Georgian." Like the Georgians, Lawrence has only "one foot in Eden." Like theirs too, however, his other foot is so often smothered in a dense growth of primroses, violets, cowslips, forget-me-nots, snowdrops, dog mercury, wood anemones, and bluebells that its outline is obscured from view. At the risk of taking this metaphor too far, it can be said that, in reading *The White Peacock*, one either misses the flowers for the foot, or the foot for the flowers. By seeing both, the novel takes its decent place—as a characteristic production of the Georgian sensibility, as well as an immature novelistic effort which Lawrence would soon outgrow and reject, but one which nevertheless contains within it many of the central themes and preoccupations that dominate all of Lawrence's work.

One of the difficulties in discussing *The White Peacock* is that its primary ingredient does not easily lend itself to discussion. Warm, celebratory evocations of the landscape of Nethermere are the ligatures of the novel, and they have by far the greatest impact on the reader's imagination, but little can be learned by continuing to insist on their importance. One example should suggest the persistently warm glow of the landscape which permeates the book:

> Afternoon is all warm and golden. Oat sheaves are lighter; they whisper to each other as they freely embrace. The long, stout stubble tinkles as the foot brushes over it; the scent of the straw is sweet. When the poor, bleached sheaves are lifted out of the hedge, a spray of nodding wild raspberries is disclosed, with belated berries ready to drop;

among the damp grass lush blackberries may be discovered. Then one notices that the last bell hangs from the ragged spire of foxglove. . . . The mist steals over the face of the warm afternoon. The tying-up is all finished, and it only remains to rear up the fallen bundles into shocks. The sun sinks into a golden glow in the west. The gold turns to red, the red darkens, like a fire burning low, the sun disappears behind the bank of milky mist, purple like the pale bloom on blue plums, and we put on our coats and go home.[62]

In *The White Peacock* such descriptions become, despite our interest in the more pessimistic human action of the novel, the central focus of our attention. This is not to say, of course, that the landscape does not affect our grasp of the issues involved in *The White Peacock*—as the remainder of this section will demonstrate. It is to say, however, that for the most part these descriptions are simply *there*, and better left where they are.

As a pastoral novel, one might expect *The White Peacock* to manifest a powerful sense of correspondence between landscape and character. And so it does. Of *The White Peacock*, Baruch Hochman has noted:

Lawrence suggests a correspondence between outer scene and inner life, a correspondence made imaginatively viable by a more or less animistic view of nature. Scenes from nature are felt to be pervaded by life while Nature, metaphysically grasped, is identified with such life, as are the feelings of individual characters. . . . In such work, it is often not clear whether the reality being treated is a reality of the inner life or the outer world, and for Lawrence it does not ordinarily matter.[63]

Throughout the novel, often at the beginning of a chapter or at crucial points in the action, the countryside is made to take on the emotional atmosphere of the characters. Perhaps the most famous instance of this correspondence is the pastoral elegy which surrounds the funeral of Annable, which, according to Robert Gajdusek, ranks among the "great pastoral elegies in English."[64]

Rising and falling and circling round and round, the slow-waving peewits cry and complain, and lift their broad wings in sorrow. They stoop suddenly to the ground, the lapwings, then in another throb of anguish and protest, they swing up again, offering a glistening white breast to the sunlight, to deny it in black shadow, then a glisten of green, and all the time crying and crying in despair.

The pheasants are frightened into cover, they run and dart through the hedge. The cold cock must fly in his haste, spread himself on his streaming plumes, and sail into the wood's security.

There is a cry in answer to the peewits, echoing louder and stronger the lamentation of the lapwings, a wail which hushes the birds. The men come over the brow of the hill, slowly, with the old squire walking tall and straight in front; six bowed men bearing the coffin on their shoulders, treading heavily and cautiously, under the great weight of the glistening white coffin; six men following behind, ill at ease, waiting their turn for the burden. . . .

Again a loud cry from the hill-top. The woman has followed thus far, the big, shapeless woman, and she cries with loud cries after the white coffin as it descends the hill, and the children that cling to her skirts weep aloud, and are not to be hushed by the other woman, who bends over them, but does not form one of the group. How the crying frightens the birds, and the rabbits; and the lambs away there run to their mothers. But the peewits are not frightened, they add their notes to the sorrow; they circle after the white, retreating coffin, they circle round the woman; it is they who forever "keen" the sorrows of this world. They are like priests in their robes, more black than white, more grief than hope, driving endlessly round and round, turning, lifting, falling and crying always in mournful desolation, repeating their last syllables like the broken accents of despair.[65]

Such an elegy is appropriate to Annable in his role as pure animal; the explosion of mournful empathy is the response in the natural world of kind to kind. In his more sinister human aspect, however, the natural world is seen differently. Just before Cyril and George first meet Annable, they come upon a farmhouse:

The cow-yard startled me. It was a forest of the tallest nettles I have ever seen—nettles far taller than my six feet. The air was soddened with the dank scent of nettles. As I followed George along the obscure brick path, I felt my flesh creep. . . . Here and there we saw feathers, bits of animal wreckage, even the remnants of a cat, which we hastily examined by the light of a match. As we entered the stable there was an ugly noise, and three great rats half rushed at us and threatened us with their vicious teeth. I shuddered, and hurried back, stumbling over a bucket, rotten with rust, and so filled with weeds that I thought it part of the jungle. There was a silence made horrible by the faint noises that rats and flying bats give out. The place was bare of any vestige of corn or straw or hay, only choked with a growth of abnormal weeds. When I found myself free in the orchard I could not stop shivering. There were no apples to be seen overhead between us and the clear sky. Either the birds had caused them to fall, when the rabbits had devoured them, or someone had gathered the crop.[66]

Other scenes suggest similar correspondences: when George and Leslie, both threatening to declare their intentions simultaneously, are about to descend upon Lettie, who is meanwhile uncomfortably fending off the inquiries of a gossipy spinster, "the jet drops" of an approaching storm "twinkled ominously in the thunder light, as if declaring they would make something of it yet."[67] Similarly, after the death of their father, Lettie and Cyril discover "a new consciousness, a new carefulness"[68] in their relationship with the natural world. Where before the landscape was characterized by "water laughing, and the leaves tittering and giggling like young girls," now, Lettie finds:

> she had noticed again the cruel pitiful crying of a hedgehog caught in a gin, and she had noticed the traps for the fierce little murderers, traps walled in with a small fence of fir, and baited with the guts of a killed rabbit.[69]

As these passages suggest, all too often the animism which informs the correspondence between character and landscape is simple anthropomorphism. Passages abound:

> The lake was black like the open eyes of a corpse; the woods were black like the beard on the face of a corpse. A rabbit bobbed out, and floundered in much consternation.[70]

or again:

> I remember a day when the breast of the hills was heaving in a last quick waking sigh, and the blue eyes of the waters opened bright. Across the infinite skies of March great rounded masses of cloud had sailed stately all day, domed with a white radiance, softened with faint, fleeting shadows as if companies of angels were gently sweeping past; adorned with resting, silken shadows like those of a full white breast.[71]

Nevertheless, nature in *The White Peacock* is not always denied its proper processes. Nethermere is not always presented as an attractive, motherly, nurturing, and sustaining force, or as a mirror of the emotional states of the characters who live in it; Lawrence was too keenly aware of nature's quiddity to disregard totally its less pleasant aspects. Quite early in the novel we are confronted by a scene which disturbs the image of Nethermere as an idyllic, pastoral sanctuary:

> The bracken held out arms to me, and the bosom of the wood was full of sweetness, but I journeyed on, spurred by the attacks of an army of flies which kept up a guerrilla warfare round my head till I had passed the black rhododendron bushes in the garden.[72]

Pastoral sanctuaries do not usually support real flies in them; that they appear here, in the middle of a paragraph informed by the customary imagery and personification of the pastoral genre, indicates that a dual process is at work in the novel, and that pastoral and antipastoral elements will not always be clearly separated.

In a similar passage slightly later in the novel, George and Cyril wander through the woods in the "first hush" of twilight, when they come upon a disheveled man sleeping by a fallen tree. "Suddenly through the gloom of the twilight-haunted woods came the scream of a rabbit caught by a weasel."[73] Such a passage discloses the collision of Lawrence's methods in *The White Peacock*—not only do the little murders of the woodlands shatter the pastoral idyll, but nature, which had been presented in its blissful guise, changes to "gloom" and "twilight-haunted woods," corresponding to the experience of the characters.

Chapter 5 of the novel, "The Scent of Blood," is one of the few chapters of which it can be said that naturalistic, rather than pastoral, elements predominate. It fairly teems with animals—heifers, rabbits, mice, and rats—that appear in scenes which are unmistakably post-Darwinian in their natural violence. The chapter prepares us for similar, if less concentrated, scenes throughout the remainder of the novel, and we can no longer be surprised by the uneasy juxtaposition of idyllic and naturalistic images such as the following: "Under the groves of ash and oak a pale primrose still lingered, glimmering wanly beside the hidden water. Emily found a smear of blood on a beautiful trail of yellow convolvulus."[74] In any case, Kenneth Inniss's claim that *The White Peacock* is Lawrence's farewell to "the cherished Eden of his first affections"[75] must be tempered with the recognition that, even if Nethermere is predominantly Edenic, it nevertheless contains its serpents.

In *The White Peacock*, as in *Howards End*, the characters define themselves in part by their relationship with nature. All of the characters, in fact, can be arranged along a spectrum running from nature to civilization. One begins with Annable, whose motto is

"Be a good animal, true to your animal instinct,"[76] and who "was a man of one idea:—that all civilisation was the painted fungus of rottenness,"[77] and ends with Leslie, who becomes a mine owner and a Conservative M.P., and whose opinion of Annable is that the gamekeeper is merely a "splendidly built fellow, but callous—no soul."[78] Characters change by moving along the spectrum in one direction or the other. Annable fulfills his own axiom, "When a man's more than nature he's a devil,"[79] by moving completely off the spectrum in the direction of an animality too pure for his proper place as a human being. He comes to an appropriate end, crushed by stones and earth in a rock quarry with only his son, who "snuffed round him like a dog,"[80] to help him. George and Lettie, who occupy the center of the spectrum, both move toward civilization. Lettie finally outstrips even Leslie in her movement toward this end of the spectrum; we last see her dominating her husband among company in Hampstead, company which "overflowed with clever speeches and rapid, brilliant observations"[81] but whose conversation is nevertheless "like so much unreasonable rustling of pieces of paper, of leaves of books, and so on."[82] Lettie finally occupies one polar extreme in the novel; her experience is neutralized to such an extent that even Cyril notes "her shrinking, her shuffling of her life."[83] "Really!" says Lettie to the Hampstead crowd, "I don't see that one thing is worth doing any more than another. It's like dessert: you are equally indifferent whether you have grapes, or pears, or pineapple."[84]

As Lettie leaves Nethermere for her *Vita Nuova*[85] in the city, she meets George while wearing a sensuous cloak with the "silk splendour of a peacock's gorgeous blue."[86] Quite aware of her own splendor and triumph, she "talked on brightly about a thousand things. She touched on Paris, and pictures, and new music, with her quick chatter, sounding to George wonderful in her culture and facility."[87] The scene quite clearly connects Lettie with Annable's first wife, Lady Crystabel, the "white peacock"[88] of "vanity and screech and defilement."[89] Crystabel, we are meant to recall, enticed Annable by playing a role out of "a sloppy French novel,"[90] developed nothing beyond a purely aesthetic relationship with him ("she would have me in her bedroom while she drew Greek statues of me"),[91] and became intolerably "souly"[92] after mixing with a poet. "A poet got hold of her," Annable tells Cyril, "and she began to affect Burne-Jones—or Waterhouse—it was Waterhouse—she was a lot like one of his women—Lady of Shalott, I believe."[93] Although we should not accept as final the scale of values expressed by Annable, there can be little doubt that the connection made between Lettie and Crystabel is intended to suggest the extent to which Lettie has become alienated from those values implied by life at Nethermere.

George begins the novel as its most stable representative of man and nature in equilibrium—he is of that yeoman stock for which Forster had so much hope—but his awkward pursuit of Lettie and his "education" through Cyril push him irrevocably away from his natural instincts and toward a total dissolution. George is enchanted and fascinated by civilization, embodied here in Lettie, but he cannot assimilate it. Late in the novel, George complains to Cyril: "You and Lettie have made me conscious, and now I am at a dead loss."[94] His eventual marriage to Meg of "the Ram" is a stopgap measure, and it acts to sour him on the life he has lived, rather than to free him from the illusions of the life he might have lived. With Meg, George gets the "vanity and screech and defilement" of marriage without the accompanying fantasies of culture. The marriage becomes "more a duel than a duet"[95] and Meg becomes "a beautiful, unassailable tower of strength that may in its turn stand quietly dealing death."[96] George, in his own description, has become "just nothing, a vacuum . . . a little vacuum that's not dark, all loose in the middle of a space of darkness, that's pressing on you."[97]

By the end of the novel, Meg, wearing a "toque with opulent ostrich feathers . . . seemed to dominate everything, particularly her husband."[98] His decay complete, George is "like a tree that is falling, going soft and pale and rotten, clammy with small fungi"; we last see him "leaning against the gate, while the dim afternoon drifted with a flow of thick sweet sunshine past him, not touching him."[99]

Civilization, however, does not always destroy. If there is anything optimistic about the human action in *The White Peacock*, it comes from those who have left Nethermere, or those—like Tom Renshaw and Emily—who have returned and managed to achieve a kind of stability despite what it has become. If we are given the impression that Nethermere is being encroached upon by civilization, we should be equally aware that one of the most destructive forces at work there is the rapacious voracity of rabbits, both metaphorical and actual, from within Nethermere itself. The displacement of the original pastoral community in *The White Peacock* derives at least as much from the persistent nibbling of natural life as from any outside influence.

The traditional nineteenth- and twentieth-century "machine in the garden" mode of depicting the intrusion of civilization into the pastoral idyll does not function with much effect in *The White*

Peacock. The collieries and the cities of the novel are themselves "pastoralized," and are rarely invested with the overwhelming sense of foreboding that one would ordinarily expect of the pastoral genre, or indeed of Lawrence's later work. Although Lawrence maintains the traditional town-country contrast of the pastoral genre, it is for the most part blandly suggested rather than made descriptively explicit. If Cyril, that most shadowy of narrators, at first suffers from "the sickness of exile"[100] and the "bewildering pageant of modern life"[101] in London, he soon finds that London can satisfy him—especially in his mature role as a successful artist—in ways that Nethermere could not. There is a poetry of the city, he finds, just as there was a poetry of the country. London, too, is subject to "pastoralization":

> The spring came bravely, even in south London, and the town was filled with magic. I never knew the sumptuous purple of evening till I saw the round arc-lamps fill with light, and roll like golden bubbles along the purple dusk of the high road. Everywhere at night the city is filled with the magic of lamps: over the river they pour in golden patches their floating luminous oil on the restless darkness; the bright lamps float in and out of the cavern of London Bridge Station like round shining bees in and out of a black hive; in the suburbs the street lamps glimmer with the brightness of lemons among the trees. I began to love the town. . . .
>
> I did not know how time was hastening by on still bright wings, till I saw the scarlet hawthorn flaunting over the road, and the lime-buds lit up like wine drops in the sun, and the pink scarves of the lime-buds pretty as louse-wort a-blossom in the gutters and a silver-pink tangle of almond boughs against the blue sky. The lilacs came out, and in the pensive stillness of the suburb, at night, came the delicious tarry scent of lilac flowers, wakening a silent laughter of romance.[102]*

*In 1912 Compton Mackenzie, perhaps the most Georgian of the Georgian novelists, published *Carnival*. Here, too, London is "pastoralized," despite the fact that the novel itself presumes to examine realistically some of London's poor. *Carnival* opens:

> All day long over the grey Islington street, October casting pearly mists had turned the sun to silver and made London a city of meditation whose tumbled roofs and parapets and glancing spires appeared serene and baseless as in a lake's tranquility.
> The traffic, muted by the glory of a fine autumn day, marched, it seemed, more slowly and to a sound of heavier drums. Like mountain echoes street-cries haunted the burnished air, while a muffin-man, abroad too early for the season, swung his bell intermittently with a pastoral sound. [Compton Mackenzie, *Carnival*, p. 1]

That jolly curmudgeon, G. K. Chesterton, anticipated the notion of the poetry and the promise of the city in an early essay. In "The Poetry of Cities," he writes of the "exquisite purple of the distant chimney pots" and the "gem-like glitter of the evening lamps," and concludes that the city may even be "too fierce, too fascinating and too practical in its [poetic] demands" (G. K. Chesterton, "The Poetry of Cities," in *Lunacy and Letters*, p. 22, 23).

Late in the novel, when Cyril undertakes the traditional pastoral journey from the city to the country and returns to Nethermere, he finds that he "had done with the valley of Nethermere"[103] and that the "old symbols" now seem to him to be "trite and foolish."[104] Cyril's pastoral journey is unsuccessful because, now fully urbanized by his life as an artist in London and Paris, the pastoral world can no longer make anything more than an aesthetic claim upon him.

The landscape itself does not fail Cyril; Cyril fails the landscape—by failing to maintain his sympathetic (if intellectualized) connection with it. But his return home proves Nethermere to be just as beautiful as it ever was:

> I wandered around Nethermere, which had now forgotten me. The daffodils under the boathouse continued their golden laughter, and nodded to one another in gossip, as I watched them, never for a moment pausing to notice me. The yellow reflection of daffodils among the shadows of grey willow in the water trembled faintly as they told haunted tales in the gloom. I felt like a child left out of the group of my playmates. There was a wind running across Nethermere, and on the eager water blue and glistening grey shadows changed places swiftly.[105]

What has actually been reduced is the pastoral community of Nethermere, that "small nation with language and blood of our own,"[106] which has been replaced by isolated pockets of men and women who make Cyril feel that he is "a stranger, an intruder,"[107] and "a child left out of the group of my playmates."

> The brooks talked on just the same, just as gladly, just as boisterously as they had done when I had netted small, glittering fish in the rest-pools. At Strelley Mill a servant girl in a white cap, and white apron-bands, came running out of the house with purple prayer-books, which she gave the elder of two finicking girls who sat disconsolately with their black-silked mother in the governess cart at the gate, ready to go to church. Near Woodside there was barbed-wire along the path, and at the end of every riding it was tarred on the tree-trunks, "Private."[108]

The Saxton family of Strelley Mill has been replaced by "strangers from the north," one of whom speaks "Glasgow Scotch, and she had a hare lip."[109] Annable has been replaced by a "mouse-voiced"[110] couple, readers of the *Christian Herald*, who thoroughly disapprove of Lettie and George wandering onto their land. Annable's house, too, has changed. The kitchen reveals "wall pockets full of paper flowers," though "the wood outside was loaded with blossom."[111] The overripe naturalness of Annable has been succeeded by pale artificiality.

In *The White Peacock*, as Graham Hough has noted, "the human failures are almost absorbed in the quivering joy of earth, the vibration of the non-human world that surrounds them."[112] Indeed, it is Lawrence's loving evocation of the landscape, more than anything else, which exposes his Georgian impulse to invest nature with a quintessential importance that reverberates beyond the fuss of its human population. But even the natural becomes unnatural when the community, that "small nation with language and blood" of its own, entirely disappears. The landscape remains real, an alternative reality to the heterogeneous multiplicity of the urban world, even though it cannot necessarily support the characters who live in it. The city is, however, equally real, and is not without its redeeming features. Even in his romantic-idyllic-pastoral first novel, Lawrence recognized that beside the sense of vast indifference, distorted relationships, and atomized lives of the urban world, there went a "conviction of new possibilities—of independence, intellectual excitement, a new culture and civilization."[113]

In some ways, then, *The White Peacock* is a *Künstlerroman*, in which the city is shown to be capable of fulfilling the needs of the artist in ways that the country cannot. In this context, Cyril anticipates Paul Morel's significant turn "towards the faintly humming, glowing town"[114] at the end of *Sons and Lovers*. Here, too, in Lawrence's first novel, one finds what Eugene Goodheart has called "the coincidence of two impulses: the impulse toward *self-responsibility* . . . and the impulse toward true human community."[115] The collision of these two impulses becomes increasingly important, a thematic obsession in Lawrence's life as well as in his art. Before the war, this obsession nourishes Ursula in *The Rainbow*; during the war, it generates Lawrence's fantasy utopia, Rananim; and, finally, it will have its greatest impact in Lawrence's greatest novel, *Women in Love*.

Community and Isolation: Lawrence's Ambivalence

For Lawrence, the collision between "true human community" and self-responsibility is, in many ways, the collision between the Lawrence of Eastwood with the Lawrence of London and the Continent. So, too, it is the collision of the Georgian spirit with, for lack of a better phrase, the anti-Georgian spirit—that which eventually manifested itself in Futurism, Imagism, Vorticism, and Lawrence's own work during the war years. In *The White Peacock* Lawrence recognized the importance of the intimate community, as well as the necessity of moving away from the community in order to establish a responsible identity. He also recognized, from his own experience if from nothing else, the difficulty of doing so. All of Lawrence's work, even *The White Peacock* and *The Trespasser*, bears the evidence of this struggle.

The Georgians, as Lawrence was beginning to discover, rarely display the evidence of struggle in their work, because it was too vaguely felt by them. The Georgian warmth and radiance which Lawrence had praised in his "Review of *Georgian Poetry 1911–1912*" early in 1913, was often the kind of warmth induced by the Georgians' dreamy musing over the English landscape and the soothing notions of community that such landscapes are likely to suggest. The equally important impulse toward self-responsibility, both for themselves and for their culture, receded in the Georgians as their dreams became more facile and more fashionable.

The connection between the literary pastoral and the idea of community is both traditional and inevitable. One of the central impulses of the pastoral mode, and the Georgian pastoral is certainly no exception, is the impulse toward community. By presenting the image of the natural world in contrast to the processes of urban change, the pastoralist presents the image of authentic and fundamental life processes over against what he sees to be the artificial, atomizing flux of the city. In the image of the natural world there is revealed an "elementary link 'of man with all beings as beings.'"[116] The social order with its roots in the natural world is the *Gemeinschaft:* comparatively homogeneous, cohesive, with a shared culture and body of values—essentially, in a word, a community. At its center is the family, the unit which supplies the community with its matrix, and gives it definition. In the *Gemeinschaft*, everyone belongs to a group, a family group. "Everyone [has] his circle of affection: every relationship [can] be seen as a love-relationship."[117]

The extraordinary cohesion of such an order, where the most important experiences are lived out within the family, also creates incessant and unrelieved tensions which are incapable of release except in crisis. For if a family is a "circle of affection, it can also be a scene of hatred."[118] Lawrence's *Sons and Lovers* is perhaps the most powerful and most illuminating modern testament to the double movements of love and hate in the *Gemeinschaft*.

At the end of *Sons and Lovers*, after Mrs. Morel's death has shattered the family—and consequently eliminated the source of Paul's identity, which had been so closely bound to it—everything, even nature, loses its cohesion.

> Where was he?—one tiny upright speck of flesh, less than an ear of wheat lost in the field. He could not bear it. On every side the immense dark silence seemed pressing him, so tiny a spark, into extinction, and yet, almost nothing, he could not be extinct. Night, in which everything was lost, went reaching out, beyond stars and sun. Stars and sun, a few bright grains, went spinning round for terror, and holding each other in embrace, there in a darkness that outpassed them all, and left them tiny and daunted. So much, and himself, infinitesimal, at the core a nothingness, and yet not nothing.
> "Mother!" he whimpered—"mother!"
> She was the only thing that held him up, himself, amid all this. And she was gone, intermingled herself. He wanted her to touch him, have him alongside with her.
> But no, he would not give in. Turning sharply, he walked toward the city's gold phosphorescence. His fists were shut, his mouth set fast. He would not take that direction, to the darkness, to follow her. He walked towards the faintly humming, glowing town, quickly.[119]

Paul's movement toward the "faintly humming, glowing town" is representative of his need to move away from the web of the *Gemeinschaft*, and toward the new, if sharply different, promises suggested by the image of the city. The urban social order, the *Gesellschaft*, allows for independence, intellectual excitement, social and economic mobility, and a sense of identity less dependent on the web of family and social groups, even if it lacks the fundamental sense of intimate connection that the *Gemeinschaft* provides. The impulse toward both can exist simultaneously, as it often does in Lawrence, but it invariably creates a sense of dissatisfaction with things as they are.

As *Sons and Lovers* suggests, two significant poles of Lawrence's dualistic vision—the intimate, yet tortuous, ties of family and community, as well as the fragmented, but comparatively free, quality of the wider society and the city—were developed during Lawrence's early years in Eastwood. Raymond Williams has written of Lawrence that what his childhood gave him was not

> tranquillity or security; it did not even, in the ordinary sense, give happiness. But it gave what to Lawrence was more important than these things: the sense of close quick relationship, which came to matter more than anything else. . . . It is not that Lawrence, like any child, did

not suffer from these things. It is rather that, in such a life, the suffering and the giving of comfort, the common want and the common remedy, the open row and the open making-up, are all part of a continuous life which, in good and bad, makes for a whole attachment. Lawrence learned from this experience that sense of the continuous flow and recoil of sympathy which was always, in his writing, the essential process of living.[120]

Seventeen years after Lawrence wrote *Sons and Lovers,* he wrote of his return to Eastwood, and to the "extremely beautiful country-side"[121] in the English Midlands. In "Nottingham and the Mining Country" (1930) even the pit raises up warm memories—the memories, essentially, of community.

And the pit did not mechanize men. On the contrary. Under the butty system, the miners worked underground as a sort of intimate community, they knew each other practically naked, and with curious close intimacy, and the darkness and the underground remoteness of the pit "stall," and the continual presence of danger, made the physical, instinctive, and intuitional contact between men very highly developed, a contact almost as close as touch, very real and very powerful. This physical awareness and intimate *togetherness* was at its strongest down pit.[122]

Although Lawrence goes on to qualify his comments about mining life to a considerable extent, he does not retract his positive claims for the "intimate community" and "togetherness" of the colliers. Nevertheless, even if the sense of "curious close intimacy" mattered, to quote Williams again, "more than anything else," Lawrence still recognized that such intimacy was likely to be practically unattainable when forced to exist in a larger society that was unable or unwilling to accommodate it—a society, that is, which was no longer a community. In *The White Peacock* and *Sons and Lovers,* the binding webs of community and family, if not to be absolutely renounced, are certainly the social forms which most obstinately stand in the way of the self's fulfillment. But by the time of the writing of *The Rainbow,* Lawrence's experience in the "man's world"—in Croydon, in London, and on the Continent—had made clear that it was the wider society, not the community, that must be rejected. The open-ended quality found at the close of *Women in Love,* when Rupert and Ursula—having achieved "star-equilibrium"—end the book in the midst of an argument, stands as powerful and poignant evidence of the difficulty of attaining genuine togetherness in a fragmented, atomized society.

For Lawrence, a self-responsible identity is necessary before true intimacy, the "star-equilibrium," is possible; both of these qualities are necessary before true community is possible. At its best, community is the only social form which is able to absorb the claims of self and the claims of society; community is the buffer between self and society, fully satisfying neither, but smoothing the interface between the two. As long as community is absent, self and society must be in a state of continuous conflict. Lawrence's recognition of the inevitability of this conflict, and the position that the pressure of events and of his own life dictated that he take on it, both energized and vexed him.

Lawrence's belief that the "social passion"[123] had incapacitated Forster, and his feeling that the social-therapy novels of the Edwardians were wrong-headed and ultimately destructive, is only one side of his position. The other side is perhaps best stated in a letter to Trigant Burrow, in 1927:

> What ails me is the absolute frustration of my primeval societal instinct. The hero illusion starts with the individualist illusion, and all resistances ensue. I think societal instinct is much deeper than sex instinct—and societal repression much more devastating. There is no repression of the sexual individual comparable to the repression of the societal man in me, by the individual ego, my own and everybody else's. I am weary even of my own individuality, and simply nauseated by other people's.[124]

Still, society, when it is not community, must be either rejected or regenerated. In *Studies in Classic American Literature*, Lawrence writes that James Fenimore Cooper's tales of the friendship between Chingachgook and Natty Bumppo revealed a "nucleus of a new society."

> A stark, stripped human relationship of two men, deeper than the deeps of sex. Deeper than property, deeper than fatherhood, deeper than marriage, deeper than love. So deep that it is loveless. The stark, loveless, wordless unison of two men who have come to the bottom of themselves. This is the new nucleus of a new society, the clue to a new world-epoch. It asks for a great and cruel sloughing first of all. Then it finds a great release into a new world, a new moral, a new landscape.[125]

The "great and cruel sloughing" of society is necessary as long as society's claim is simply that of obligation, or "mere acquisition," having nothing vital to do with the spirit of the self or the human impulse toward meaningful community with others. Lawrence continually refuses to commit himself to such a society, in order that he might fulfill his own sense of responsibility toward his isolate self—a self that is "separate and proud as a lion or a hawk."[126]

In all of Lawrence's books after *Sons and Lovers*, says Eugene Goodheart, "Wherever society appears . . . as an external entity rather than as the fulfilment of man's need for community, it is rendered as *nullity*."[127] Goodheart observes passages in *The Rainbow* where this is clearly so. He notes, for instance, one description of Tom Brangwen's mine:

> The place had the strange desolation of a ruin. Colliers hanging about in gangs and groups, or passing along the asphalt pavements heavily to work, seemed not like living people, but like spectres. The rigidity of the blank streets, the homogeneous amorphous sterility of the whole suggested death rather than life. . . .
> The whole place was just unreal, just unreal. Even now, when he had been there for two years, Tom Brangwen did not believe in the actuality of the place. It was like some gruesome dream, some ugly, dead, amorphous mood become concrete.[128]

In this same context, one might also recall Lou Witt's growing recognition of the emptiness of her world, in *St. Mawr:*

> In such a world there was nothing even to conquer. It gave everything and gave nothing to everybody and anybody all the time. *Dio benedetto!* as Rico would say. A great complicated tangle of nonentities ravelled in nothingness. So it seemed to her.[129]

St. Mawr is perhaps Lawrence's most explicit fictive indictment of society; more than any other of his fictions, it insists on the necessity of completely rejecting the larger society and offering one's self up to the stark but restorative landscape of isolation. By the time of *St. Mawr* (1925), Lawrence's belief in the possibility of a living community had virtually died.

Ten years earlier, however, in *The Rainbow*, community *could* still be envisioned, albeit with the help of a rather strained Utopian rhetoric, while the claims of modern life were simultaneously rejected. Terry Eagleton, speaking of the last pages of *The Rainbow*, declares that Lawrence's intention was to insist that

society must be remade, with a completeness perceptible only to a man free from limiting investments in its present reality; yet it is *this* society which must be remade—these sordid, hard-scaled, separate people, known as they are from the inside. The form of contemporary culture is violently rejected, but within a continuing reverence for the still active energies of its people: and it is this fusion of uncompromising denial and persisting hope which is the passage's most striking quality.[130]

The Rainbow as Georgian and Anti-Georgian Novel

One of Lawrence's problems in *The Rainbow* was to locate a "place" for community. Mark Schorer has said:

> Husks, chiefly, Lawrence believed, were modern men, deprived of vital connections with life outside themselves, ensnared in their partial and divisive and mechanized "personalities." To discover a place where the vital connections could be maintained intact was the motive of Lawrence's life as it increasingly becomes the motive of his heroes and heroines.[131]

Although Schorer is no doubt thinking of Lawrence's later, more feverish, globe-trotting, his statement applies equally well to Lawrence's conception of *The Rainbow*. The obvious place to locate the image of community was also the traditional place—the natural world. But the natural world of late 1913 and early 1914 was essentially that which had been defined by the Georgian imagination. Although the Georgians had in some ways rescued the landscape by establishing it as an alternative to the sprawl and fragmentation of the city, Lawrence was coming to realize that they had also robbed it of much of its vitality.

The Georgian landscape, like the Georgian notion of community, was cozy, rather than intimate; attractive, rather than beautiful; engaging, rather than vital. The Georgians often seem to be profoundly disconnected from the landscape, simply external students of the pastoral community that they envision. The Georgian landscape still harbored the pastoral assumption, that nature provides the place in which man can be made whole, unified, gathered into the organic wholeness of community.

But, for Lawrence, the Georgians had forgotten the larger message of the natural world, the "primal morality greater than ever the human mind can grasp,"[132] in favor of the sentimental fantasies of twinkling streams and sylvan glens. In "Study of Thomas Hardy" and *The Rainbow*, Lawrence had to rethink man's relationship with nature; the natural world had to be differentiated from Georgian gentleness. The result was that Lawrence had to conceive of man's instincts and desires as being "radically continuous with the forces of generation and the processes of change in the natural world."[133]

The White Peacock, The Trespasser, and even *Sons and Lovers* are in many ways recognizable products of the Georgian ethos. In them, Lawrence, like the Georgians, "generally followed the dominant nineteenth-century literary tradition of viewing nature from the perspective of man."[134] *The Rainbow,* especially in its final vision of the "new world," by no means completely eliminates all Georgian qualities, but in it, "in part due to an increasing disgust with man's works, he came increasingly to view man from the perspective of nature."[135]

For the Georgians, the language of pastoral remained the language of community, which was, despite the evidence to the contrary, still devoutly to be wished; for Lawrence, the landscape becomes the symbol of resistance—persistently *there* in opposition to the obligations of "the cosy jam-pot of the State,"[136] where community has been made almost unachievable.

One of the major purposes of *The Rainbow,* then, is to suggest a way to reincorporate man into the landscape, to explore and reveal how man, or woman, can reabsorb the elemental vitality of nature in a way that supports, even creates, the sense of independent self, while at the same time revitalizing the possibility of regeneration for an entire culture. Such a realignment of nature and man, Lawrence feels, points the direction toward the revival of true human community.

The Rainbow begins with a statement of the conflict between self and society. In the first pages of the novel, we are told that the Brangwen men live on the Marsh Farm with life held "between the grip of their knees."[137]

They felt the rush of the sap in spring, they knew the wave which cannot halt, but every year throws forward the seed to begetting, and, falling back, leaves the young-born on the earth. They knew the intercourse between heaven and earth, sunshine drawn into the breast and bowels, the rain sucked up in the daytime, nakedness that comes under the wind in autumn, showing the birds' nests no longer worth hiding. Their life and interrelations were such; feeling the pulse and body of the soil, that opened to their furrow for the grain, and became smooth and supple after their ploughing, and clung to their feet with a weight that pulled like desire, lying hard and unresponsive when the crops were to be shorn away.[138]

But the Brangwen women "wanted another form of life than this, something that was not blood-intimacy."[139]

> Her house faced out from the farm-buildings and fields, looked out to the road and the village with church and Hall and the world beyond. She stood to see the far-off world of cities and governments and the active scope of man, the magic land to her, where secrets were made known and desires fulfilled. She faced outwards to where men moved dominant and creative, having turned their back on the pulsing heat of creation, and with this behind them, were set out to discover what was beyond, to enlarge their own scope and range and freedom; whereas the Brangwen men faced inwards to the teeming life of creation, which poured unresolved into their veins.[140]

The novel itself, moving through three generations of Brangwen men and women, attempts to resolve this conflict. At the beginning of the novel, Marsh Farm lies within the magic circle of organic community, the women must look *out* to the "world beyond." But by the time of Tom Brangwen, historically located in about the middle of the nineteenth century, "a canal was constructed across the meadows of the Marsh Farm, connecting the newly-opened collieries of the Erewash Valley."[141] And when the "Midland Railway came down the valley at the foot of Ilkeston hill, . . . the invasion was complete."[142] What has been invaded here is the "blood-intimacy" of the genuinely organic community, the unspoiled *Gemeinschaft*.

The magic circle has been intruded upon; even though the Brangwen home "was just on the safe side of civilisation,"[143] the intrusion makes the Brangwens "strangers in their own place."[144] Throughout the course of the novel the alternative "magic land," the "far off world of cities and governments" glimpsed originally by the Brangwen women, comes more and more to inhabit the boundaries of the magic circle, pushing the "cattle and earth and vegetation and the sky"[145] outside. What was originally beyond comes to be the reality, what was the reality comes to be beyond; outside has become inside.

Lawrence does not, of course, want to place the supreme value only on the unthinking, purely sensual, natural life of the early Brangwen men, as opposed to the Brangwen women's desire for the varied and vivid experiences of the wider social world. The Brangwen men, though in constant and intimate contact with the values of land and community, are also sluggish and far too acquiescent, much like the Marsh Farm geese, who have their food "pushed down their throttle."[146] *The Rainbow* insists upon a "dialectical polarity between the instinctual and the conscious requirements for life, and the struggle toward a synthesis of perfectly integrated humankind . . ."[147] If the values placed on the natural world seem almost naively positive, it is because Nature in *The Rainbow* is equated so powerfully with the emergence of self-responsible fulfillment, and because it was Nature, after all, which was most in need of reincorporation into the fundamental processes of human life. By the time of Ursula's generation, the social world, in its various manifestations, is clearly assumed to be the dominant force in each character's experience.

In fact, by the later stages of the novel the "widening circle" of the "man's world" [see chapters 10, 13, and 14] has become so dominant that contact with nature itself becomes threatening, or, at least, alien.

> This world in which she [Ursula] lived was like a circle lighted by a lamp. This lighted area, lit up by man's completest consciousness, she thought was all the world: that here all was disclosed for ever. Yet all the time, within the darkness she had been aware of points of light, like the eyes of wild beasts, gleaming, penetrating, vanishing. And her soul had acknowledged in a great heave of terror only the outer darkness. This inner circle of light in which she lived and moved, wherein the trains rushed and the factories ground out their machine-produce and the plants and the animals worked by the light of science and knowledge, suddenly it seemed like the area under an arc-lamp, wherein the moths and children played in the security of blinding light, not even knowing there was any darkness, because they stayed in the light.[148]

Ursula, the modern embodiment of the Brangwen struggle, carries with her the possibility of reincorporating the "vast darkness that wheeled round about"[149] and the "half-revealed shapes lurking on the edge"[150] back into the circle of modern experience. In the final chapter of the novel, Ursula, now firmly implanted in the "man's world," though intensely aware of its limitations, is confronted by a group of horses—symbolic, riderless fugitives from that time when life was held "between the grip of the knees"—whose hoofs flash "like circles of lightning,"[151] and who make a "wide circle"[152] around her, finally gathering "thunderously about her, enclosing her."[153]

> They stirred, they moved uneasily, they settled their uneasy flanks into one group, one purpose. They were up against her.

Her heart was gone, she had no more heart. She knew she dare not draw near. That concentrated, knitted flank of the horse-group had conquered. It stirred uneasily, awaiting her, knowing its triumph. It stirred uneasily, with the uneasiness of awaited triumph. Her heart was gone, her limbs were dissolved, she was dissolved like water. All the hardness and looming power was in the massive body of the horse-group.[154]

Before this confrontation, Ursula has been in a state of great agitation over her relationship with Skrebensky, the novel's major representative of society, whose social role is his sole developed identity. She knows only that she must "beat her way back through all this fluctuation, back to stability and security."[155] But after the confrontation with the horses, after these "half-revealed shapes" have intruded themselves into the lighted circle of her experience, Ursula is reconnected with a hitherto undiscovered region of her spirit.

As she sat there, spent, time and the flux of change passed away from her, she lay as if unconscious upon the bed of the stream, like a stone, unconscious, unchanging, unchangeable, whilst everything rolled by in transience, leaving her there, a stone at rest on the bed of the stream, inalterable and passive, sunk to the bottom of all change.[156]

This confrontation, then, symbolically the culmination of Ursula's movement toward self-realization and, ultimately, the possibility of true community, releases her from her bondage to Skrebensky and Skrebensky's world.

Why must she be bound, aching and ·cramped with bondage, to Skrebensky and Skrebensky's world? Anton's world: it became in her feverish brain a compression which enclosed her. If she could not get out of the compression she would go mad. The compression was Anton and Anton's world, not the Anton she possessed, but the Anton she did not possess, that which was owned by some other influence, by the world. . . .

And again, to her feverish brain, came the vivid reality of acorns in February lying on the floor of a wood with their shells burst and discarded and the kernel issued naked to put itself forth. She was the naked, clear kernel thrusting forth the clear, powerful shoot, and the world was a bygone winter, discarded, her mother and father and Anton, and college and all her friends, all cast off like a year that has gone by, whilst the kernel was free and naked and striving to take new root, to create a new knowledge of Eternity in the flux of Time. And the kernel was the only reality; the rest was cast off into oblivion.

This grew and grew upon her.[157]

Ursula has internalized the world symbolized by the horses, the outside has again become inside; one circle has become reincorporated into the other. The result is profound; Ursula's soul is "itself for ever," persisting in "a deep, inalterable knowledge."[158]

From this knowledge can come "a new day . . . on the earth."[159] And although Ursula must wait until *Women in Love* to complete her growth, by the end of *The Rainbow* she clearly embodies the kernel of the "new world" imagined by Lawrence and, although with a much different texture and emphasis, by his Georgian contemporaries.

> And the rainbow stood on the earth. She knew that the sordid people who crept hard-scaled and separate on the face of the world's corruption were living still, that the rainbow was arched in their blood and would quiver to life in their spirit, that they would cast off their horny covering of disintegration, that new, clean, naked bodies would issue to a new germination, to a new growth, rising to the light and the wind and the clean rain of heaven. She saw in the rainbow the earth's new architecture, the old, brittle corruption of houses and factories swept away, the world built up in a living fabric of Truth, fitting to the overarching heaven.[160]

Many critics have observed that the visionary, apocalyptic ending of *The Rainbow* seems incommensurate with the events that lead up to it. F. R. Leavis has said of *The Rainbow* that Lawrence mainly desired

> to get this book somehow finished and done with, in order that he might get on with the one he now wanted to write. There is something oddly desperate about that closing page and a half; the convalescent Ursula's horrified vision, from her windows, of the industrial world outside, and then that confident note of prophetic hope in the final paragraph—a note wholly unprepared and unsupported, defying the preceding pages. . . .
>
> The Lawrence of *Women in Love* could not have written that paragraph. And it was not really written by the Lawrence of the last part of *The Rainbow;* the note is one recaptured, momentarily, for the occasion.[161]

Leavis goes on to speculate that Lawrence must have left behind the

"spirit or radical mood" of the final symbol of *The Rainbow* "before
he had fully worked out the conception and seen his way to bring
the book to a close."[162]

George H. Ford, however, more accurately notes that the end of
The Rainbow is "ultimately appropriate even though the straining
crescendo is at times deafening."[163]

> One detects in the last paragraphs a sense of strain because the account
> of the final stages of her development has to be postponed and, as a
> substitute, we have to be content with a kind of prophecy of the future
> union of darkness and light when the heroine will encounter one of the
> sons of God, and society itself will be regenerated. . . .
>
> If this stage of the heroine's progress is celebrated too stridently, it is
> some compensation to recall the painful discords of scenes that pre-
> ceded her rebirth. And in *Women in Love*, the novel that followed *The
> Rainbow*, despite Ursula's final resolution of her own individual
> difficulties, the somber notes are much more persistently in evi-
> dence.[164]

Indeed, *Women in Love* continues the evolution of Ursula's
growth from a social and cultural perspective untouched by anything like the possibilities suggested by her final vision; *Women in
Love* presents a society most notable for its intractability, a society,
in fact, which seems incapable of achieving any kind of regeneration.

Of particular relevence to this study, however, is that the end of
The Rainbow is perhaps the period's most potent expression of the
Georgian "new world," that world which had seemed so imminent
in the years just following the death of Edward VII. Its tone and
imagery recalls the declarations of Allen Upward and Lascelles
Abercrombie, both of whom were quoted earlier in order to suggest
the buoyancy and enthusiasm which dominated the early Georgian
years. Such a connection perhaps begins to explain F. R. Leavis's
complaint that the vision of the last pages of *The Rainbow* was "one
recaptured, momentarily, for the occasion."

During the conception and early rendering of what was to become *The Rainbow*, the Georgian apprehension of a "new world"
had coalesced with Lawrence's own desperate hopes for a "new
germination" and a new universal community. And for the finish of
this, his most optimistic novel, Lawrence was able to recapture,
however momentarily, the same "radical mood" of hopeful and
visionary enthusiasm with which he had greeted what he found to

be the first manifestations of that spirit in *Georgian Poetry 1911–1912*.

But most of *The Rainbow*, of course, was generated out of ideas and obsessions which range in various degrees of opposition to the implications of the Georgian sensibility; *The Rainbow* is both a Georgian and an anti-Georgian novel. The very events which lead to Ursula's rebirth seem more characteristic of Lawrence's doubts about the efficacy of the Georgian spirit than they are expressive of his belief that such a spirit would someday triumph. His need to reestablish the connection between the natural world and the responsible self, a self in touch with its nonhuman and unchangeable core, owed more to his rereading of Hardy and his encounter with Futurism, Imagism, and Vorticism, than to anything the Georgians had to offer. Lawrence had to go beyond the Georgians, to transcend the small but joyful pleasures of hedgerows and streams, in order to confront the overwhelming problems of England in 1914.

Lawrence was never, in the full sense of the word, a Georgian—doubts, disagreements, and differences between his work and Georgian work are evident in all of the books that Lawrence wrote during the early Georgian years. Even though the Georgian impact on Lawrence was significant and never completely disappeared, the implications of his work after *The Rainbow*, and much of *The Rainbow* itself, clearly suggest that Lawrence had found that the Georgians could no longer help him. The Georgian poets as well as the spirit of which they were the most celebrated manifestation, had come to seem, at best, valueless, at worst, dangerous.

5   Lawrence's Break with the Georgians

The Evidence of Unrest

Horace Gregory has called D. H. Lawrence "a Georgian poet before the Georgians appeared,"[1] because of his "early desire to cleave to the earth, to select his materials at first hand, [and] to deal . . . with an immediate environment."[2] But, Gregory notes, by late 1913 Lawrence "saw *through* the Georgians, saw through them into something (he was not quite sure just what) beyond their purpose."[3] Their "purpose" had seemed evident during the period in which Lawrence wrote his "Review of *Georgian Poetry 1911–1912*"; not only did the Georgians manifest the principles noted by Gregory, but they also seemed to be advocates of a new, regenerated England, an England that would attend to the nature of human relations, unafraid to make contact with the "unknown powers /Within man's nature."[4] In 1909, Lawrence wrote that W. H. Davies's *Nature Poems*, "like those about rain—and leaves—and robins—are delightful—about cities, purblind and nonsensical."[5] By late 1924, all of Davies's work—and most of the Georgians' work—would seem "purblind and nonsensical."

By then, Lawrence's excavations into matters of form and character, the rich depth of his perceptions about the nature of English culture, and his growing belief that a society must be judged by the opportunities it offers for entering into genuine relationships, had coalesced in such a way that the shallowness of the Georgian spirit was made flagrantly apparent. The work of the Georgians began to seem radically incommensurate with the real problems and the real needs of the English people. The Georgian poet, that "child for the first time on the seashore, finding treasures,"[6] just never grew up, never came home to tell of the significance of what he had found. And, as Lawrence wrote later, to be children after a certain age was simply "a sign of arrested development, nothing else."[7]

100

The world for which the Georgians had been writing in 1913—that world where "nothing is really wrong"[8]—had become very wrong by mid-1914. There were, of course, some Georgians, notably Rupert Brooke, who began to show some strain under the burden of maintaining the characteristic Georgian optimism. As early as 1913, when he left England to visit America, and certainly in the months just preceding the outbreak of the war, Brooke evinced a profound sense of frustration and disappointment in what had been the promise of a new, exhilarating era. Like Gauguin and Robert Louis Stevenson before him, Brooke responded by turning away from the civilization he had earlier embraced, and found a new kind of vitality in the South Seas. Brooke, like Lawrence, had come to believe that the civilized ladies and gentlemen of England had become a "baleful influence."[9] By mid-1913 he was asking his friend Geoffrey Keynes to "spit at Bloomsbury from me,"[10] and describing the "subtle degradation of the collective atmosphere of the people in those regions [Bloomsbury]—people I find quite pleasant and remarkable as individuals."[11]

In the South Seas, however, Brooke found "beauty and courtesy and mirth. I think there is no gift of mind or body that the wise value which these people lack."[12] In his *Letters from America*, he goes on:

> It is part of the charm of these people that, while they are not so foolish as to "think," their intelligence is incredibly lively and subtle, their sense of humour and their intuitions of other people's feelings are very keen and living. They have built up, in the long centuries of their civilisation, a delicate and noble complexity of behaviour and of personal relationships. A white man living with them soon feels his mind as deplorably dull as his skin is pale and unhealthy among those glorious golden-brown bodies. But even he soon learns to *be* his body (and so his true mind), instead of using it as a stupid convenience for his personality, a moment's umbrella against this world. . . . That alone is life; all else is death.[13]

Brooke's work from 1913 until the beginning of the war reveals the context within which boredom with civilization and an interest in the primitive coincides with the impulse toward a new and more vital culture.

And Brooke was not alone. W. Somerset Maugham, a writer with a sensibility very different from Brooke's, has also described the malaise that followed hard upon the upsurge of expectations which had characterized the beginning of the Georgian period in 1911:

I was tired. I was tired not only of the people and thoughts that had
so long occupied me; I was tired of the people I lived with and the life I
was leading. I felt that I had got all that I was capable of getting out of
the world in which I had been moving; my success as a playwright and
the luxurious existence it had brought me; the social round, the grand
dinners at the houses of the great, the brilliant . . . people, writers,
painters, actors; the love affairs I had had and the easy companionship
of my friends; the comfortableness and security of life. It was stifling
me and I hankered after a different mode of existence and new experiences.[14]

Maugham's ennui led him to follow Brooke to the South Seas.
There he "found a new self."[15]

I stepped off my pedestal. It seemed to me that these men had more
vitality than those I had known hitherto. They did not burn with a
hard, gemlike flame, but with a hot, smoky, consuming fire. They had
their own narrownesses. They had their prejudices. They were often
dull and stupid. I did not care. . . . They seemed to me nearer to the
elementals of human nature than any of the people I had been living
with for so long.[16]

Brooke, then, who had achieved his reputation almost entirely
from his work as a Georgian, and Maugham, who had come up
through the Edwardian ranks in a most traditional fashion, were
both looking for a fundamental realness beneath what had come to
seem to them to be the artificial and meretricious veneer of British
culture. "In civilized communities," mused Maugham, "men's
idiosyncrasies are mitigated by the necessity of conforming to certain rules of behaviour. Culture is a mask that hides their faces.
Here [in Tahiti] people showed themselves bare."[17]
    The direction taken by Brooke and Maugham, by itself, does not
necessarily indicate the predilections of modern writers during the
second decade of the century. Their solution for cultural malaise
was both idiosyncratic and unoriginal; they were whoring after
gods which were all too familiar. Still, Brooke and Maugham become significant examples of a modern trend precisely because they
seem such unlikely spokesmen for anything that remotely approaches an espousal of primitivism. Both had made major investments in the life of their culture and in their perceptions of it.
Nevertheless, in Brooke and Maugham, one discovers the collision
of a pair of significant attitudes: first, the malaise which grows out
of the civilized suspicion of civilization; and second, the invocation

of the primitive as a potential cure for the mechanical dehumaniza-
tion of life. Both had come to recognize, however mincingly, what
Lawrence would argue aggressively in succeeding years: British
culture was dead or dying because it could no longer accommodate
vitality.

When Brooke and Maugham are bracketed with influential Continental works and movements in art and music (Picasso's *Les Demoiselles d'Avignon*, 1907; Stravinsky's *Le Sacre du printemps*, 1913;
the Fauves in France and der Blau Reiter in Germany), they begin to
appear more solidly exemplary of the kind of ennui that had surfaced all over prewar Europe, as well as the kind of solution for that
ennui toward which moderns were being attracted. "For a thing to
have a basis in ancient instinct," noted W. H. Hudson, was "to
have some kind of justification."[18] John Gould Fletcher, after seeing the famous first performance of *Le Sacre du printemps*, declared:

> There was but one lesson the modern artist must learn and ponder:
> the lesson already proclaimed by the Irish dramatist Synge, who had
> said that poetry, to be human again, must learn first to be brutal. In
> revolt against the elaborations of end-of-the-century aestheticism,
> against the romantic movement faltering in sentimental prettiness,
> against the genteel tradition in decay, artists everywhere were turning
> back to the primitively ugly, knowing that in primitiveness alone lay
> strength.[19]

As Fletcher's observation suggests, the modern's embrace of the
primitive was not only a criticism of modern civilization; it was also
an attempt to reincorporate a sense of vitality into a culture which
had become spiritually moribund. In some ways, it was an extension, verified, just in time, by anthropology, of the Romantic sensibility—a sense of irresponsible freedom which could undercut the
constructions of reason and civilization. "Passion and sensibility,"
says Octavio Paz, "belong to the world of origins—to the time
before and after history, always identical with itself."[20] The
primordial world, like nature, survives in immutable time, impervi-
ous to change; "it is not what happened once, but what always
happens."[21]

The modern impulse to reincorporate the view of the primitive
into the culture—a view which, if it lacks sophistication, retains the
power of taking sides—sprang inevitably from the belief that the
culture was failing. As E. M. Cioran has declared, "The nostalgia
for barbarism is the last word of a civilization."[22]

By 1913, the excitement over the coming of a new, post-

Victorian era had not completely perished, but the implication of much of modern art and literature was that the patient was dying fast, and in need of some drastic revitalization. "The soul needs its own mysterious nourishment," says Lawrence in *The Lost Girl*. "This nourishment lacking, nothing is well."[23]

Although Lawrence never visited Tahiti, and his known feelings about Polynesia (implied in the revised version of *Women in Love*, for instance) were a good deal more complex and critical than those of Brooke or Maugham, the central notions which animate their writings would have been quite familiar to Lawrence. In 1913, Lawrence's Tahiti was Italy, just as it would later become Mexico, New Mexico, some Etruscan places, and certain gamekeepers. For Lawrence, the "crude, strong, rather passionate" Italians were clear contrasts to his "shadowy and funny" countrymen; the Italian "special inner community"[24] was favorably compared with the "vile nature"[25] and artificial, mechanistic relationships of the English. Civilization, wrote Frieda in 1913 (with Lawrence's apparent agreement), was "only a top plaster."[26] Lawrence had begun to see England in the way that Alvina Houghton sees it in *The Lost Girl*; from a ship in the middle of the Channel, on its way to Italy, Alvina looks back at her homeland and sees a "long, ash-grey coffin, winter, slowly submerging in the sea."[27]

> For there behind, behind all the sunshine, was England. England, beyond the water, rising with ash-grey, corpse-grey cliffs, and streaks of snow on the downs above. England, like a long, ash-grey coffin slowly submerging. She watched it, fascinated and terrified. It seemed to repudiate the sunshine, to remain unilluminated, long and ash-grey and dead, with streaks of snow like cerements. That was England![28]

By the time Lawrence wrote "England, My England" in 1915 (at the same time he was working on *Women in Love*), the feeling that there was a "new world" to be made in England, or that the Georgians might in any way be useful or incisive advocates for it, was exhausted by the reality of the war and Lawrence's own bitter vision of the present and future condition of England. To be sure, something of the "old, brittle corruption of houses and factories"[29] was being swept away by the war, but Lawrence's culminating Georgian vision—the rainbow, fashioned from the "living fabric of Truth" and from which issued "the clean rain of heaven"[30]—was being swept away as well. The "destructive-consummating"[31] vision of the rainbow was replaced by a new luminary, a "new world in the heavens,"[32] which was "purely destructive."[33]

Last night when we were coming home the guns broke out, and there was a noise of bombs. Then we saw the Zeppelin above us, just ahead, amid a gleaming of clouds: high up, like a bright golden finger, quite small, among a fragile incandescence of clouds. And underneath it were splashes of fire as the shells fired from earth burst. . . . It seemed as if the cosmic order were gone, as if there had come a new order, a new heaven above us: and as if the world in anger were trying to revoke it. . . .

So it seems our cosmos has burst, burst at last, the stars and moon blown away, the envelope of the sky burst out, and a new cosmos appeared; with a long-ovate, gleaming central luminary, calm and drifting in a glow of light, like a new moon, with its light bursting in flashes on the earth, to burst away the earth also. So it is the end—our world is gone, and we are like dust in the air.[34]

The unrest that had begun to possess ordinarily sanguine figures like Brooke and Maugham in 1913 was, of course, rife by the time Lawrence finished *Women in Love*. The war meant the end of Georgian optimism, both for English culture as a whole and for Lawrence in particular. Henry James captured the mood of crisis in a letter written at the outbreak of the war:

The plunge of civilisation into this abyss of blood and darkness . . . is a thing that so gives away the whole long age in which we have supposed to be, with whatever abatement, gradually bettering, that to have to take it all now for what the treacherous years were all the while really making for and *meaning* is too tragic for any words.[35]

For English literary culture, the war was the ultimate confirmation of what Lionel Trilling has called "one of the shaping and controlling ideas of our epoch . . . the disenchantment of our culture with culture itself."[36] For Lawrence, the Edenic vision of *The Rainbow* could never again be recaptured, even momentarily.

With talk of the war, however, I get ahead of myself. As has already been suggested in the discussion of *The Rainbow*, Lawrence's suspicions about the Georgian sensibility had existed long in advance of 1914. In the previous chapters, much has been made of the significant points of contact between Lawrence and the Georgian milieu; these connections have been emphasized because they have been obscured or overlooked in the critical accentuation of other aspects of Lawrence's work, and because of the relative obscurity of the Georgians themselves. But if many of the manifest and latent notions of the Georgians were important to Lawrence, he had always had certain quarrels with them, too. In 1912, he found de la Mare one of a "generation of tender-feet!";[37] in 1913, he declared that John Masefield was "a horrible sentimentalist—the cheap Byron of the day";[38] James Stephens' *The Crock of Gold*, he felt, belittled "a great theme by a small handling":[39]

> Poor, poor Pan, he must be in his second childhood if he talks as he does via Stephens. . . . [Stephens is] a little man who has never entered into the fray, but sings "Buttercups and Daisies." Then for God's sake let him sing "Buttercups and Daisies," and leave the Great God Pan alone.[40]

And, during the later months of 1913, Lawrence carried on a vigorous dispute with Edward Marsh over matters of poetic form and technique.

Still, it was not until mid-1914 that Lawrence began to define himself in clear opposition to the Georgians. It was, of course, the war that confirmed his darkest suspicions about the inadequacy of the Georgian spirit, but even in the months just preceding the outbreak of the war Lawrence can be seen turning his back on the Georgians. There were a number of reasons for this, most of them personal: his new life with Frieda, his response to life on the Continent, the development of his own work, the recognition he was receiving (partly due to the Georgians) for his previous writing.

But other influences were also at work, and Lawrence, as usual, was assimilating them. The remainder of this section, as well as the following chapter, will deal with the impact of some of these influences, especially Imagism and Futurism, and also with the profound impact that the war had on Lawrence—all of which, one hardly needs to add, worked to the detriment of any further relations that Lawrence might have maintained with the spirit of Georgianism.

First, however, it would be useful to take up the controversy about poetic form between Lawrence and Edward Marsh, not so much because it thoroughly defines the growing differences in their respective *Weltanschauungen*, but because it points to some of the weak links in their association—links which events would eventually shatter forever.

The Dispute with Edward Marsh

The controversy over poetic technique that took place between Lawrence and Edward Marsh began in August 1913 and ended, for the most part, by December of the same year. It was never really a quarrel so much as it was a necessary exercise in self-examination for Lawrence and an attempt by Marsh to fulfill his role as Lawrence's poetic adviser, a role that Lawrence expressly wanted Marsh to fill as late as March 1914.[41] Neither man took the controversy as a breach of personal or literary relations; Lawrence continued to ask Marsh's advice and to send him poems, and Marsh continued to give advice and publish the poems that Lawrence sent.

Nor did the controversy signal an irrevocable break in Lawrence's loose association with the Georgians as a whole. Although Lawrence's enthusiasm for the spirit which they exhibited was waning during the period in which he and Marsh carried on their debate, the grounds on which he finally broke with the Georgians were not really the definitive grounds on which he argued with Marsh. Assuredly, during the five-month span of the dispute, Lawrence did find himself in the position of taking a closer look at the direction in which the Georgians were moving and, in doing so, sensed that their goals stopped somewhat short of his own hopes and capacities. What had earlier impressed Lawrence as the poetry of "hope, and religious joy,"[42] began to appear thin and artificial, full of "ridiculous imitation yokels,"[43] "the silly hash of . . . bucolics,"[44] and "the currency of poetry, not poetry itself."[45] Nevertheless, as Lawrence once wrote, "if an author rouses my deeper sympathy he can have as many faults as he likes, I don't care."[46] And the Georgians had, at least until mid-1914, generally been able to arouse that "deeper sympathy." When Lawrence finally makes his break with the Georgians, it is not over matters of poetic form, but because he feels, as he said of Abercrombie, "Something seems to be going bad in [their] soul."[47]

Eugene Goodheart has said that wherever Lawrence "finds a passion for form . . . he senses an animus against life."[48] This is not completely true, at least during the years now under discussion, as his somewhat passionate defenses of his own use of form (made to the criticism of Edward Garnett as well as to Marsh) quite definitely suggest. Although it is useless to deny that Lawrence was not suspicious of conspicuous technical displays, his suspicions of an "animus against life" were only aroused when such displays seemed to him evidence of an inability or an unwillingness to "pluck the very concentrated heart"[49] out of the thing at hand. Literature which was presented purely as an aesthetic event seemed to Lawrence to be a mere verbal camouflage for the void, and always generated his most ferocious criticism.

In his review of the work of Thomas Mann, for instance, written

soon after his review of *Georgian Poetry I*, Lawrence declares that
Mann's "craving for form is the outcome, not of artistic conscience,
but of a certain attitude to life."[50] Mann, he finds, can only connect
with life aesthetically, through careful attention to form, which is
"impersonal like logic."[51] Mann, says Lawrence, "has never found
any outlet for himself, save his art. He had never given himself to
anything but his art."[52] He suffers from a "soul-ailment,"[53] a profound "unbelief,"[54] which is "absolutely, almost intentionally, un-
wholesome."[55] Form is not really the center of the problem here;
the center, as Lawrence sees it, is Mann's soul. Form, if anything,
saves his work; as art, it is valuable—"and we give it its place as
such."[56] But even though Mann's "expression may be very fine . . .
by now what he expresses is stale. I think we have learned our
lesson, to be sufficiently aware of the fulsomeness of life."[57]

As early as 1909 Lawrence had written that he wanted only "to
write live things, if crude and half-formed, rather than beautiful,
dying, decadent things with sad odours."[58] The same notion is
expressed again in *Sons and Lovers*. Miriam, admiring one of Paul's
pictures, finds that she likes it because it "seems so true." Paul then
says:

> "It's because—it's because there is scarcely any shadow in it; it's
> more shimmery, as if I'd painted the shimmering protoplasm in the
> leaves and everywhere, and not the stiffness of the shape. That seems
> dead to me. Only this shimmeriness is the real living. The shape is a
> dead crust. The shimmer is inside really."[59]

Even though Lawrence's feelings about form were only beginning their struggle to emerge by the time of *Sons and Lovers*, the
kernel of his position can be found almost anywhere along the way.

In order to clarify his feelings, however, Lawrence needed an
adversary who, intentionally or unintentionally, would force Lawrence into self-examination and, finally, into a coherent statement
of his position. Edward Marsh was perfectly suited to such a task.
In April 1914 Marsh wrote to Rupert Brooke: "I'm glad you feel the
greatness of Lawrence—if he could arrive at 'form' he would be
splendid—but he doesn't seem even to try."[60] In all probability, this
was the basic position that Marsh took throughout his dispute with
Lawrence. One recalls that one of the determining factors in the
poetry that Marsh admired was that it be "written on some formal
principle which I could discern."[61] And in a 1923 letter to Robert
Nichols, who had written to declare himself in favor of a dynamic

spirit in poetry—as opposed to the "curse of Georgian easiness"[62]—Marsh clarified what was most probably the position he had taken with Lawrence in 1913.

> One of the many differences between us is that my first love has always been and always will be what you stigmatize as literature and poetizing, whereas you care first and foremost for "idea". You may very likely be right for here and now, because there must be times when the old kaleidoscope gets worn out, or at any rate when it has to be filled up with new bits of glass—still, in the long run I believe it is the "literary" side which is the important one. The "ideas" become common property, and unless they are beautifully arranged and expressed there is no reason why their first embodiment should continue to be sought after—whereas if they *are* beautifully arranged and expressed the work which contains them will keep its value long after they become not only common property but *exploded*.[63]

Marsh's position is certainly not a new one; still, it anticipates later critical responses, like those of R. P. Blackmur and Eliseo Vivas, to much of Lawrence's work. And in confronting it, and consequently developing his own sense of what form *is*, Lawrence was forced to work out his position both as a declaration of belief and as a defense against criticism.

Marsh had probably always felt, even as he published "Snapdragon" in *Georgian Poetry I*, that Lawrence was in need of instruction on poetic technique. But it was not until July 1913 that there was any evidence of Marsh's expressing such feelings to Lawrence. At a lunch in late July Marsh had, in order to impress Lawrence with a sense of poetic rhythm, read aloud a current favorite of his, James Elroy Flecker's "The Golden Journey to Samarkand." Lawrence was not impressed. In an August letter to Lady Cynthia Asquith, Lawrence wrote a particularly effusive and rhythmic description of the progress of a baker's bill, and then continued:

> Ask Mr. Marsh if that isn't perfect Flecker-rhythm. *The Golden Journey to Samarkand.* You knew it climbed Parnassus *en route*? I shall write a book called *The Poet's Geographer* one day. By the way Marsh will hold it as a personal favour if I will take more care of my rhythms. Poor things, they go cackling round like a poultry farm—but he told it me—I mean Eddie dear—in a letter. He thinks I'm too Rag-time!—not that he says so. But if you'll believe me, that *Golden Journey to Samarkand* only took place on paper—no matter who went to Asia Minor.[64]

Later in the month, after receiving a letter from Marsh which must have again expressed hesitations about Lawrence's technique, Lawrence wrote back a message which is at once conciliatory and also the beginning of his attempt to describe his own sense of rhythm.

> Dear Marsh: I was glad to get your letter. Here it does nothing but rain. It is enough to make one's verse as sloppy as Lamartine.
> I think you will find my verse smoother—not because I consciously attend to rhythms, but because I am no longer so criss-crossy in myself. I think, don't you know, that my rhythms fit my mood pretty well, in the verse. And if the mood is out of joint, the rhythm often is. I have always tried to get an emotion out in its own course, without altering it. It needs the finest instinct imaginable, much finer than the skill of the craftsmen. . . . Remember skilled verse is dead in fifty years—I am thinking of your admiration of Flecker.[65]

During this period Lawrence again began work on *The Sisters;* by 15 September he could write, "It is queer. It is rather fine, I think. I am in it now, deep."[66] This work, and his developing life with Frieda, further revealed to Lawrence the necessity of a commitment to pure *expression* and a rejection of restraint, both of which would affect his notion of form. In a letter to Henry Savage written at this time, he says:

> If we had any sense we should lift our hands to heaven and shriek, and tear our hair and our garments, when things hurt like mad. Instead of which, we behave with decent restraint, and smile, and crock our lungs.—Not that I've anything so tremendous and tragic in my life, any more than anybody else. Only I am so damnably violent, really, and self destructive. One sits so tight on the crater of one's passions and emotions. I am just learning—thanks to Frieda—to let go a bit. It is this sitting tight, this inability to let go, which is killing the modern England, I think.[67]

Later, he would call that ability to "let go," to express the "crater of one's passions and emotions" despite the threat of "self-destruction," his "demon," which "makes his own form, willy-nilly, and is unchangeable."[68]

Still, Marsh felt that Lawrence could use some healthy restraint, and again wrote Lawrence to tell him so. Lawrence's reply was again conciliatory.

> Dear Marsh: Don't think that it is because your last letter offended me at all, that I don't write. In reality, I quite agreed with what you said. I know my verse is often strained and mal-formed.[69]

Marsh wrote Brooke in reference to this that he had "got a most charming letter from Lawrence the other day. He has a real genius for letter-writing. I do hope he will go on."[70] A little over a week later, however, Lawrence apparently began to reconsider the neces- sity of conciliation. He wrote to Lady Cynthia Asquith: "I think I was wrong to feel injured because my verse wasn't well enough dished-up to please him."[71] Here, as is so often the case with Lawrence, his sense of the situation is located not so much in anger at Marsh, but in his own acquiescence to principles in which he does not fully believe.

Lawrence's next letter to Marsh disrupted the approach/retreat pattern of their dispute by taking on the work of W. H. Davies and Ralph Hodgson, Georgians who were both friends and favorites of Marsh. Davies, who Lawrence felt was trying too hard to be an artist,[72] had begun to make him "furious, and so sorry."

> He's really like a linnet that's got just a wee little sweet song, but it only sings when it's wild. And he's made himself a tame bird—poor little devil . . . I think one ought to be downright cruel to him, and drive him back: say to him, Davies, your work is getting like Birmingham tin- ware; Davies, you drop your h's, and everybody is tempering the wind to you, because you are a shorn lamb; Davies, your accent is intolerable in a carpeted room; Davies, you hang on like the mud on a lady's silk petticoat. Then he might leave his Sevenoaks room, where he is rigged up as a rural poet, proud of the gilt mirror and his romantic past: and he might grow his wings again, and chirrup a little sadder song.[73]

Lawrence's criticism of Hodgson's "Song of Honour" strikes even deeper. The poem, he finds, is

> banal in utterance. The feeling is there, right enough—but not in itself, only represented. . . . It is the currency of poetry, not poetry itself. Every single line of it is poetic currency—and a good deal of emotion handling it about. But it isn't really poetry. I hope to God you won't hate me and think me carping, for this. But look:
>
> > the ruby's and the rainbow's song
> > the nightingale's—all three.

> There's the emotion in the rhythm, but it's loose emotion, inarticulate, common—the words are mere currency. It is exactly like a man who feels very strongly for a beggar, and gives him a sovereign. The feeling is at either end, for the moment, but the sovereign is a dead bit of metal. And this poem is the sovereign. "Oh, I do want to give you this emo- tion," cries Hodgson, "I do." And so he takes out his poetic purse, and

gives you a handful of cash, and feels very strongly, even a bit senti-
mentally over it.[74]

The next letter from Lawrence to Marsh is perhaps the most
crucial of the controversy. It was written in response to Marsh's
criticism of certain of Lawrence's poems, evidently on the already
established ground of metrical pattern and form, but also on the un-
established ground of "Sloth," "Purity," and being "Drearisome."[75]
Lawrence wasted no time in answering Marsh:

> Dear Marsh: You *are* wrong. It makes me open my eyes. I think I read
> my poetry more by length than by stress—as a matter of movements in
> space than footsteps hitting the earth. . . . I think more of a bird with
> broad wings flying and lapsing through the air, than anything, when I
> think of metre. . . . It all depends on the *pause*—the natural pause, the
> natural *lingering* of the voice according to the feeling—it is the hidden
> *emotional* pattern that makes poetry, not the obvious form. . . . It is the
> lapse of feeling, something as indefinite as expression in the voice carry-
> ing emotion. It doesn't depend on the ear, particularly, but on the
> sensitive soul. And the ear gets a habit, and becomes master, when the
> ebbing and lifting emotion should be master, and the ear the transmit-
> ter. If your ear has got stiff and a bit mechanical, *don't* blame my
> poetry. That's why you like *Golden Journey to Samarkand*—it fits your
> habituated ear, and your feeling crouches subservient and a bit
> pathetic. "It satisfies my ear," you say. Well, I don't write for your ear.
> This is the constant war, I reckon, between new expression and the
> habituated, mechanical transmitters and receivers of the human con-
> stitution. . . . You are a bit of a policeman in poetry.[76]

If this letter seems the closest thing to an actual attack on Marsh,
it was considerably softened by one of Lawrence's typical disclaim-
ers:

> Don't mind me. I find it frightfully easy to theorise and say all the
> things I don't mean, and frightfully difficult to find out, even for my-
> self, what I do mean.
> I only *know* that the verse you quote against me is right, and you are
> wrong. And I am a poor, maligned, misunderstood, patronised and
> misread poet, and soon I shall burst into tears. . . .
> [P. S.] Your letter was jolly good to me really—I always thank God
> when a man will say straight out to me what he has to say. But it's rare
> when one will.[77]

Soon after, Marsh wrote to Brooke:

I've been having a vehement correspondence with Lawrence about what I consider the formal deficiencies of his poems. He tells me I am the policeman of poetry—just as Sturge Moore compared me to a schoolmaster—but I am impenitent.[78]

Lawrence's letter, Christopher Hassall reports, "gave Marsh peculiar pleasure."[79] In any case, Marsh continued to praise *Sons and Lovers* as the "gospel,"[80] receiving for his pains a severe scolding from Edith Wharton, who was "amazed that he could approve such bungled work."[81] But far from disinclining him to accept Lawrence's repeated offers to visit him in Italy, the letter seemed only to confirm Marsh's desire to meet Lawrence there, which he did in January 1914. In the meantime, Lawrence had been descended upon by three members of the Georgian brood—W. W. Gibson, R. C. Trevelyan, and Lascelles Abercrombie. Gibson and Trevelyan, he thought, were "really lovable fellow[s]"[82] and Abercrombie seemed to Lawrence "one of the sharpest men I have ever met."[83] Still, he felt that "they seemed so shadowy and funny, after the crude, strong, rather passionate men"[84] he saw in Italy. "Modern geniuses," he said, "are so tame, and so good, and so generous. I really do love Gibson, and Abercrombie. They make me feel ashamed of myself, as if my human manners were very bad."[85] This sense of tameness, of the "shadowy" quality of his visitors, would become increasingly important to Lawrence's vision: Gibson and Abercrombie would soon become more than representative Georgians, they would become representative of English culture as a whole. Lawrence would soon insist on linking tameness with acquiescence, and acquiescence with a dangerous inability to confront experience.

Lawrence's last letter of the year to Marsh suggests that Lawrence, at least, had become tired of the controversy. "About metres," he wrote, "I shall have to pray for grace from God. . . . I send you a poem which you ought to like. If you do, give it to somebody to publish, when you've got an easy, leisurely occasion."[86] The poem was "Grief," written in strict iambics, and dedicated "To Eddie Marsh, with much affection, this poem for a Christmas card, which, albeit a trifle lugubrious, pray God may go daintily to his ear." The poem was signed and dated, and ended *"Requiescat in pace."*[87] In effect, that is precisely what the controversy did.

The relationship between Lawrence and Marsh never developed much beyond this. And even though Marsh came more and more to represent the "dull and woolly"[88] England that Lawrence violently rejected, and Lawrence was soon to feel that "one might as well talk to a daisy by the path, as be one's further self with Marsh,"[89] Lawrence always maintained "a real gratitude . . . and a kindness, and an esteem of the genuine man"[90] for him. The coolness which grew up between them two years later developed for reasons other than the matters discussed above; it occurred as a result of Marsh's typically Georgian position on the war, his actual position in the war government, Marsh's feeling that "he was no longer needed"[91] by Lawrence, and Lawrence's growing disgust with that which the Georgians had come to represent. Marsh later admitted that his criticism of Lawrence's work had been an "overweening presumption," though he was "glad to feel that we were always on friendly terms."[92] In any case, Marsh summarized, Lawrence "was too great and strange for the likes of me."[93]

The main drift of Lawrence's comments to Marsh was "in the air" by 1913, principally because of the prodigious literary bellows of the Imagists and proto-Imagists. If Lawrence had known it, and it is unlikely that he did, he could have confirmed his feelings about the nature of form by appealing to a short essay by Edward Storer, appended to Storer's book of verse, *Mirrors of Illusion* (1908). Storer's essay not only "embodies the first coherent argument for free verse"[94] in English, but was also, in some ways, "a blueprint for subsequent Imagist formulation"[95] in matters of poetic form and technique. It is interesting not only because it codifies, however stumblingly, what were to become concepts held dear by subsequent literary schools, but because it serves to yoke together Lawrence and those schools in an illuminating way.

Storer's comments on the mechanical utilization of form correspond admirably with Lawrence's notions of the "constant war . . . between new expression and the habituated mechanical transmitters and receivers" of poetry, that he expressed in the letter to Marsh of 19 November 1913. "Form," claims Storer in his "Essay,"

> even stimulates thought, as Flaubert said, but form must not be allowed to domineer over thought. Form should take its shape from the vital inherent necessities of the matter, not be, as it were, a kind of rigid mould into which the poetry is to be poured, to accommodate itself as best it can. There is no absolute virtue in iambic pentameters as such. . . . Indeed, rhythm and rhyme are often destructive of thought, lulling the mind into a drowsy kind of stupor, with their everlasting regular cadence and stiff, mechanical lilts.[96]

Whether Storer's "Essay" directly influenced later and better-known theorists is unclear, but it does clearly suggest ideas which would later become the basis for much of what many of them had to say on such matters. In 1912, Ezra Pound wrote:

> I believe in an "absolute rhythm," a rhythm, that is, in poetry which corresponds exactly to the emotion or shade of emotion to be expressed. . . . Some poems may have form as a tree has form, some as water poured into a vase.[97]

Pound's statement, as well as Storer's, along with later expressions by T. E. Hulme, Ford Madox Ford, Wyndham Lewis, and T. S. Eliot, suggest significant connections between them and D. H. Lawrence. The notion that emotion is an organizer of form bloomed later into a wider, more comprehensive notion: since modern life had radically altered sensibilities, the new sensibilities had to be expressed in radically altered forms. The inability of the Georgians to accept this, and the speed with which their comfortable poetic mode became outmoded, shunted them from the advance-guard to the rear-guard in a space of only two years. By late 1913, art, like life, had lost its calm, and, to quote Edgar Wind, the artist had become "an agent in those developments of which he sees himself only as a victim."[98]

Georgian Failures

Three lines concerning the "deadly sin of prudence," from Lascelles Abercrombie's "The Sale of St. Thomas," were quoted earlier in order to introduce a central notion of Georgian peotry—that all forms of experience, including the erotic, were available for poetic examination and expression. Lawrence himself had directed attention to this poem and to these lines, declaring that prudence is deadly because it "will not risk to avail itself of the new freedom."[99] It is worthwhile now to note the lines which follow:

> . . . prudence, prudence is the deadly sin, . . .
> For this refuses faith in the unknown powers
> Within man's nature *shrewdly bringeth all*
> *Their inspiration of strange eagerness*
> *To a judgment bought by safe experience;*
> *Narrows desire into the scope of thought.*[100]
> [Italics mine]

Abercrombie's poem suggests both the roots of Georgian

strength and the seeds of its destruction. For Lawrence, by 1914, the poetry written by the "tame" and "shadowy" poets that he had greeted in Italy began to seem less the expression of a "strange eagerness" and more "a judgment bought by safe experience," written with desire which had, indeed, narrowed "into the scope of thought." Lawrence's comments on Davies's "wee little sweet song" and Hodgson's banal poetic currency suggest that he had glimpsed the nature of what would become universally recognized as the failure of Georgianism. He was, as Robert H. Ross has remarked, already a "Jonah in the Georgian boat."[101]

What happened to Georgianism, or, perhaps more importantly, what happened to Lawrence's and others' *perceptions* of Georgianism, was that it had become too conscious of itself. What had originally seemed to Lawrence to be a vital release of creative energies arising from direct contact with experience had become, finally, merely a formula. The Georgian rejection of the past had become mechanical; Georgian realism had become artificial and deliberate. Even J. C. Squire, who was generally very sympathetic to the Georgians, complained of Bottomley's "King Lear's Wife" that "one feels about the horror, not that it is a natural and inevitable growth, but that [Bottomley] is *putting* it there all the time."[102]

The Georgians had begun to display the first signs of hardening into a coterie. Their tone as a group, which became especially evident after harsh critical attacks on "King Lear's Wife," Abercrombie's "End of the World," and *Georgian Poetry 1913–1915*, began to suggest a certain defensive exclusivity, a homogeneity of attitude that had not existed earlier. The posture of defense denied the Georgians their original flexibility; they began to insist on the rightness of their own work, while looking only to themselves for confirmation and praise. John Drinkwater, for example, who had staged "King Lear's Wife" to small and sour audiences, wrote that he was "very proud . . . to have been the cause of it. . . . That Gordon [Bottomley] and Wilfred [Gibson] were delighted there is, I think, no doubt, and in work of this kind it is the opinion of the two or three that outweighs the world."[103] To use Lawrence's terms from his "Study of Thomas Hardy," the Georgians had discounted their impulse to extend human consciousness, and begun instead "the achieving of self-preservation."[104]

Georgian poetry had become a kind of industry. Innumerable poets clamored for a niche in the anthology, with the result that the characteristic Georgian subject matter was transformed not into poetry, but rather into poetic commonplace. Squire, for one, expressed the hope that the "poetical pursuit of insects and bachtrians will not become a habit."[105] The younger poets and critics— Imagists, Vorticists, and Futurists—began to look at Georgian poetry as being "not only un-modern, but positively anti-modern."[106]

In an essay called "The Serious Artist" (1913), Ezra Pound spoke for many ascending writers when he said:

> Bad art is inaccurate art. It is art that makes false reports. . . . If the artist falsifies his reports . . . in order that he may conform to the taste of his time, to the proprieties of a sovereign, to the conveniences of a preconceived code of ethics, then that artist lies. If he lies out of deliberate will to lie, if he lies out of carelessness, out of laziness, out of cowardice, out of any sort of negligence whatsoever, he nevertheless lies and should be punished or despised in proportion to the seriousness of his offence.[107]

In 1914, Pound acted on his convictions, with direct reference to the Georgians. He singled out Lascelles Abercrombie, apparently on the grounds of laziness, negligence, or carelessness, and, declaring with ear-ringed bravado that "stupidity carried beyond a certain point becomes a public menace,"[108] challenged him to a duel. If Pound's challenge seems to suffer from the preciousness of a French novelistic birth, it correctly denotes the degree of distaste felt by the literary left for the literary center. And if the Georgians later claimed that their attackers hit below the belt, it was because they all too often wore their belts as hatbands.

Georgian discrimination between conception and technique disallowed them from accepting a central tenet of poetry expressed by the newer schools: "that the rules of poetic form and prosody and the actual sensibility should change because life had changed."[109] Georgian poetry seemed to take on a kind of pallid inevitability— "falsified reports" issuing from preconceived ideas. The impulses which had originally celebrated the English countryside hardened into a rigid set of ideas about the "rural" and "pastoral," carrying with it an entire set of poetic conventions and techniques. The significance of nature, as developed by Lawrence in *The Rainbow* and the "Study of Thomas Hardy," had become radically different from the use that the Georgians continued to make of it. Instead of the "great background, vital and vivid, which matters more than the people who move upon it,"[110] the Georgians appeared to be more interested in the "little human morality play"[111] which goes on within it. The image of nature as a protective sanctuary, a place of pastoral repose where "men need only reach down toward their best impulses to do their duty by life,"[112] may have been available to the early Brangwens, but it could no longer bear the weight of change which had taken place upon it. For Lawrence, the Georgians had begun to replace natural vitality with an artificial, aesthetically induced facsimile of it. Their intense observation had been reduced, as Raymond Williams points out, to a "conjunction of the homely and colloquial with a kind of weak-willed fantasy . . . a working man becoming 'my ancient' and then the casual figure of a dream of England, in which rural labour and rural revolt, foreign wars and internal dynastic wars, history, legend and literature, are indiscriminately enfolded into a single emotional gesture."[113]

The most powerful and cohesive connection between Lawrence and the Georgian sensibility—the representation of natural life as an unchangeable standard of value—was dissolved by Lawrence's developing perception of what nature actually meant. Nature, he would say later, is "absolutely the safest thing to get your emotional reactions over."[114]

> This Nature-sweet-and-pure business is only another effort at intellectualizing. Just an attempt to make all nature succumb to a few laws of the human mind. . . .
> You can idealize or intellectualize. Or, on the contrary, you can let the dark soul in you see for itself.[115]

The emergence of Lawrence's "dark soul," that "demon" over which he and Edward Marsh had so vigorously disputed, had revealed that a large part of the "Pristine Nature and Paradisal Simplicity" evinced in so much Georgian work was merely part of "all that gorgeousness that flows out of the unsullied fount of the ink-bottle."[116]

In May 1914, Lawrence read Abercrombie's "End of the World" in an issue of *New Numbers*. His response to it, written to Marsh, brings his criticism of Abercrombie into a direct line with his criticism of the two other Georgians—Davies and Hodgson—and reechoes the same charges that he had leveled at Thomas Mann in 1913.

> The other day I got the second *New Numbers*. I was rather disappointed, because I expected Abercrombie's long poem to be great indeed. I can't write to Wilfred because I think I have never seen him to worse advantage than in this quarter. And it is no good your telling me Lascelles' "End of the World" is great, because it isn't. There are some

fine bits of rhetoric, as there always are in Abercrombie. But oh, the spirit of the thing altogether seems mean and rather vulgar. When I remember even H. G. Wells's "Country of the Blind," with which this poem of Abercrombie's had got associated beforehand in my mind, then I see how beautiful is Wells's conception, and how paltry this other. Why, why, in God's name, is Abercrombie messing about with Yokels and Cider and runaway wives? No, but it is *bitterly* disappointing. He who loves *Paradise Lost* must don the red nose and rough-spun cloak of Masefield and Wilfred [Gibson]. And you encourage it—it is too bad. Abercrombie, if he does anything, surely ought to work upon rather noble and rather chill subjects. I hate and detest his ridiculous imitation yokels and all the silly hash of his bucolics; I loathe his rather nasty efforts at cruelty, like the wrapping frogs in paper and putting them for cartwheels to crush; I detest his irony with its clap-trap solution of everything being that which it seemeth not; and I hate that way of making what Meredith called Cockney metaphors:—moons like a white cat and meteors like a pike fish. And nearly all of this seems to me an Abercrombie turning cheap and wicked? What is the matter with the man? There's something wrong with his soul. *Mary and the Bramble* and *Sale of St. Thomas* weren't like this. They had a certain beauty of soul, a certain highness which I loved:—though I didn't like the Indian horrors in the *St. Thomas*. But here everything is mean and rather sordid, and full of rancid hate. He talked of *Sons and Lovers* being all *odi et amo*. Well, I wish I could find the *"amo"* in this poem of his. It is sheer *"odi,"* and rather mean hatred at that. The best feeling in the thing is a certain bitter gloating over the coming destruction. What has happened to him? Something seems to be going bad in his soul. Even in the poem before this, the one of the "Shrivelled Zeus," there was a gloating over nasty perishing which was objectionable. But what is the matter with him? The feelings in these late things are corrupt and dirty. What has happened to the man? I wish to heaven he were writing the best poems that were ever written, and then he turns out this.[117]

"End of the World" appeared, along with "King Lear's Wife," as one of the two central pieces in *Georgian Poetry 1913–1915*. Marsh not only admired it, he thought it "a sublime work, in its fusion of poetry and comedy there has been nothing like it,"[118] and that its dedication to him would "in itself assure me of immortality."[119] The distance between Lawrence and Marsh, and, in effect, between Lawrence and the Georgians, was by now immense. Although Lawrence continued to publish in the Georgian anthologies (three poems in *Georgian Poetry II*), his contributions were offered more out of a tired sense of habit and a genuine gratitude to Marsh, than for any other reason.

6 "Another Language Almost": The Impact of Futurism, Imagism, and Vorticism

In Angus Wilson's novel *Anglo-Saxon Attitudes*, Professor Emeritus Gerald Middleton finds on his desk one day a letter from an unknown American Ph.D. candidate at the London University School of English Literature. The candidate's thesis subject, he reads, is "The Intellectual Climate of England at the Outbreak of the First World War." Middleton reads on:

> As you may imagine, I am anxious to concentrate on what posterity has shown to be really vital in that age rather than on the conventional aspect—Shaw, Wells, Galsworthy, etc. Whilst, therefore, paying some attention to the foundations of the Bloomsbury school in the Cambridge thought of the early years of the century, I am devoting the major part of my thesis to D. H. Lawrence and Wyndham Lewis.[1]

Unfortunately, the results of the candidate's investigations are never revealed, but the pairing of Lawrence and Lewis as the subjects of his thesis probably seems to us, as it no doubt did to Gerald Middleton, to be a mildly comical focus for a discussion of what was "really vital" during the first decades of the century. Still, as long as one takes Lewis as the embodiment, a culmination in extreme form, of certain attitudes taken up by a number of writers during the period, he and Lawrence *can* be seen as the twin, snarling lions of the early phase of modern literature—working independently, and sometimes antagonistically, to mount crucial attacks on the old values and assumptions, and to replace them with new ones.

As early as 1937, the German critic Max Wildi declared that between 1912 and 1915 Lawrence—like Lewis, Pound, Eliot, Joyce, and others usually located on the cutting edge of modernism—was forced to develop "an entirely new metaphysical outlook,

a fundamental change of attitude to the problems of human existence, which cut him off from the old modes of feeling and thinking
and made him reach out for new, not yet existing forms of expression."[2] Wildi calls this new form "expressionism," and uses it in its
widest possible sense—"reaching from Strindberg in the north to
Marinetti in the south and covering many 'isms.'"[3] One of the "old
modes" that Lawrence and the other "expressionists" discarded,
according to Wildi, was the traditional "joy in vivid scenes,"[4] the
lively representation of the exterior world, which was replaced by
"the impulse to present, directly and indirectly, states of the individual soul; to project a powerful, spontaneous, often explosive
inward life into universe, *deforming in that process the conventional
shape of things in the attempt to give them an essential one*"[5] (Italics mine).

The italicized lines of Wildi's analysis indicate, I hope, what
Angus Wilson's fictional Ph.D. candidate had in mind for his dis-
sertation. For it is surely the attempt to find the essential shape of
things in modern experience that justifies placing Lawrence and
Lewis in such a significant juxtaposition. During the years just
preceding the war, both men were involved in what Ford Madox
Ford declared to be his own unflinching aim—"to register my own
times in terms of my own time."[6]

By 1914, the transition from Edwardian to modern was in many
ways completed. The transition period itself was embodied in the
Georgians, and for Lawrence, who, as has been demonstrated, was
more closely connected with the Georgians than any other major
modern writer, a full acceptance of the modern, without Georgian
options, was particularly difficult—so difficult, in fact, that he often seemed to be fighting against it. But the impulse which drove
Lawrence toward an acceptance of modernism was, to use his own
phrase, "the wave which cannot halt."[7]

Lawrence's "Transition Stage" and the Vortex

In late January 1914, Lawrence wrote Edward Garnett that he
was in a "transition stage";[8] he was "changing, one way or the
other."[9] The letters Lawrence wrote between the beginning of the
year and the beginning of the war confirm his own sense of transition, and suggest that it basically had to do with discarding the
pleasures of the fine surface, the fine scene, and the "old forms and
sentimentalities,"[10] in favor of "the exhaustive method—"[11] a
search for the authentic core of his material and his life—"another

ego, according to whose action the individual is unrecognisable."[12] The new method was written out of "a deeper sense than any we've been used to exercise,"[13] and it was immensely difficult to achieve. "It is *hard* to express a new thing, in sincerity,"[14] Lawrence wrote to Garnett, hoping that his onetime mentor could find a way to understand and accept his new method.

> And you should understand, and help me to the new thing, not get angry and say it is *common*. . . . You see—you tell me I am half a Frenchman and one-eighth a Cockney. But that isn't it. I have very often the vulgarity and disagreeableness of the common people, as you say Cockney, and I may be a Frenchman. But primarily I am a passionately religious man, and my novels must be written from the depth of my religious experience. That I must keep to, because I can only work like that.[15]

Keeping to the "religious experience," the authentic core out of which his writing had to emerge, required persistence. In February 1914, Lawrence wrote to A. W. McLeod about his progress on what was finally to become *The Rainbow*:

> I have begun my novel again—for about the seventh time. I hope you are sympathising with me. I had nearly finished it. It was full of beautiful things, but it missed—I knew that it just missed being itself. So here I am, must sit down and write it out again. I know it is quite a lovely novel really—you know that the perfect statue is in the marble, the kernel of it. But the thing is the getting it out clean.[16]

Earlier, in 1913, Lawrence had written a letter to Henry Savage, also about *The Rainbow*, which further explores and elaborates the effect he desired—the "eternal and unchangeable"[17] that lies beyond personality, like "a Venus of Melos, still, unseeing, unchanging, and inexhaustible."[18]

> I have done 340 pages of my novel. It is very different from *Sons and Lovers*. The Laocoön writhing and shrieking have gone from my new work, and I think there is a bit of stillness, like the wide, still, unseeing eyes of a Venus of Melos. I am still fascinated by the Greek—more, perhaps, by the Greek sculpture than the plays, even, though I love the plays. There is something in the Greek sculpture that any soul is hungry for—something of the *eternal stillness that lies under all movement, under all life, like a source, incorruptible and inexhaustible. It is deeper than change. . . . And now I begin to feel something of the source, the great impersonal which never changes and out of which all change comes.*[19] [Italics mine]

From our current perspective, Lawrence's "transition stage" seems entirely of a piece with changes which were occurring in England, changes which are now inextricably connected with the names of Ezra Pound, T. E. Hulme, Wyndham Lewis, and T. S. Eliot. What was in the English air at the beginning of 1914 had been there in various manifestations since at least 1910, but in the months before the war what had been a mild disturbance in the atmosphere became an electrical storm. One could still run for cover, but one could not help but take notice. "The season of 1914," wrote Douglas Goldring, "was a positive frenzy of gaiety. Long before there was any shadow of war, I remember feeling that it couldn't go on, that something *had* to happen."[20] The mental climate disclosed, in Ezra Pound's words, "a sort of energy, something more or less like electricity or radio-activity, a force transfusing, welding, and unifying. A force rather like water when it spurts up through very bright sand and sets it in swift motion."[21] To Wyndham Lewis, these forces formed "a vertiginous but not exotic island, in the placid and respectable archipelago of English art. This formation is undeniably of volcanic matter, and even origin; for it appeared suddenly above the waves following certain seismic shakings beneath the surface. It is very closely-knit and admirably adapted to withstand the imperturbable Britannic breakers which roll pleasantly against its sides."[22]

These forces gathered names: Imagism, Vorticism, Futurism.

History allows us to see these important modern movements as being somehow expressive of a central modern preoccupation—a basic need that the modern "soul is hungry for"—which nourishes the roots of all three movements. As difficult as defining their similarities and differences may be, as well as their connection with Lawrence, it is worth recalling a dictum of Ezra Pound's here: "We advance by discriminations, by discerning that things hitherto deemed identical or similar are dissimilar; that things hitherto deemed dissimilar, mutually foreign, antagonistic, are similar and harmonic."[23]

Excluding, for the moment, Futurism (which was never really an English movement at all, and which could claim only one full-fledged English adherent, the painter C. R. W. Nevinson), the seed out of which so much of modernism seems to grow is the desire for an absolute stability, the desire for a stillness which comes from being caught out of the flux of time and history, beyond the ego, beyond the "messiness" of personality, of nature and natural rhythms. In Lawrence's phrase, it is "the eternal stillness that lies

under all life, like a source, incorruptible and inexhaustible." Hugh
Kenner has called this the "steady preoccupation with persistently
patterned energies,"[24] highly charged lines of force leading to a
point of maximum energy, a vortex, where though "time, place and
personnel alter; the pattern remains."[25] The Vortex, according to
Pound, was "a radiant node or cluster . . . from which, and through
which, and into which, ideas are constantly rushing."[26] Paradoxi-
cally, however, it was "topologically stable."[27] As Lewis explained:
"At the heart of the whirlpool is a great silent place where all the
energy is concentrated. And there at the point of concentration, is
the Vorticist. . . . The Vorticist is at his maximum point of energy
when stillest."[28] The Vortex exists; the artist's job is to make it
visible. It is a "patterned integrity accessible to the mind" which
the poet can bring "into the domain of the senses by a particular
interaction of words."[29]

If Vorticism was not the most important *movement* in modern
British literature, it was, nevertheless, a movement which more or
less directly apprehended a central notion—as much an image as a
notion—around which much of the most important work of the
time was constructed.

The Vortex was a typical form, perhaps the dominant form, of
Modernist thinking and feeling. Modalities such as the Vortex, to
use the terms of the French painter and theorist Amédée Ozenfant,
"find their expression in certain forms, colours, and, of course,
sounds or ideas. When a particular kind of feeling is dominant in
certain epochs, the general distribution of certain 'modes' creates
what is known as its 'style.' "[30] The Vorticist "style"—this sense of
things, this way of seeing—occurs and reoccurs throughout the
work of the most significant modern British writers. We find it, of
course, in Wyndham Lewis and Ezra Pound, but we find it as well
in Eliot's "still point of the turning world"; in Yeats's gyres and
tower; in Stephen Dedalus's walk on the strand; in Lily Briscoe's
finishing brushstroke in Woolf's *To the Lighthouse;* in Forster's
Marabar Caves. And, like the others, Lawrence displays his Vorticist imagination at crucial moments in his work.*

*Though he does not explicitly have Vorticism in mind, Leo Bersani has brilliantly
analyzed some of Lawrence's crucial texts—especially *Women in Love*—in such a way as to
suggest that the Vortex (my word, not Bersani's) appears in Lawrence as a structure of
desire, connected to the "ineffable riches" of successful lovemaking. In Bersani's view, "the
best Lawrentian sex seems to involve the least movement. Or, more exactly, the villain in sex
is frictional movement." He compares the failure of sex between Connie and Clifford in *Lady
Chatterley's Lover*, with the success of that between Connie and Mellors. "With Mellors,
Connie gets beyond the sharp pleasures of rubbing and rubbed skin; he initiates her into a

At the end of *The Rainbow*, for instance, at that crucial moment which is the symbolic culmination of Ursula's movement toward her "new self," we find the Vortex.

> As she sat there, spent, time and the flux of change passed away from her, she lay as if unconscious upon the bed of the stream, like a stone, unconscious, unchanging, unchangeable, whilst everything rolled by in transience, leaving her there, a stone at rest on the bed of the stream, inalterable and passive, sunk to the bottom of all change.[31]

In *The Rainbow*, Lawrence, like Lewis, Pound, and the rest of the Vorticists, wanted to invent, through art, a "pattern of hope,"[32] which would influence society as a whole. The Vorticist's "pattern of hope" was one that, to quote Wyndham Lewis, would "shatter the visible world to bits, and build it nearer to the heart's desire."[33] The "great silent place" of the Vortex would "revolutionize the world"[34] and ennoble its inhabitants; it was, then, like Lawrence's rainbow—"the earth's new architecture, the old, brittle corruption of houses and factories swept away, the world built up in a living fabric of Truth, fitting to the over-arching heaven."[35]

Lewis's "great silent place" had first been revealed, in different ways, by the discoveries of science and the revelations of Impressionism toward the end of the nineteenth century. As early as 1868, Walter Pater could declare that "experience, already reduced to a group of impressions, is ringed round for each one of us by that thick wall of personality through which no real voice has ever pierced on its way to us, or from us to that which we can only conjecture to be without."[36] The consequence, Pater claimed, was the isolation of the individual, "each mind keeping as a solitary prisoner its own dream of a world."[37] It had begun to appear to

kind of rippling, liquefying orgasm, into an 'unspeakable motion that was not really motion, but pure deepening whirlpools of sensation swirling deeper and deeper through all her tissue and consciousness, till she was one perfect concentric fluid of feeling'" (Leo Bersani, *A Future for Astyanax*, p. 161). That "concentric fluid of feeling," though certainly not what Lewis was interested in describing, is nevertheless a brilliant evocation of Vorticism outside the limited scope of *BLAST*.

Bersani also notes that in crucial moments of *Women in Love* "an enforced stillness on the stylistic level runs parallel to the characters' spiritual stillness," and that the entire novel "moves between the opposite poles of 'infinitely repeated motion' and Pharaoh-like stillness" (Bersani, p. 163). In Gerald, it appears, the stillness of the Vortex is arctic; it is death. It generates no vitality because Gerald is a corpse. In Rupert, the center of the vortex is still, impersonal, beyond the "old stable ego" that is mere personality. There are, then, "currents of life energy or currents of death energy" (Bersani, p. 164) in *Women in Love*. And both are modes of the Vortex.

many that there was no eternal or credible truth to be found behind the shimmering world of observable experience which was in any way consistent with traditional human aspirations; or that, if there was such a truth, it was radically inhuman. If some viewers were gratified by the impressionists' vivid strokes of paint, others were horrified by the empty spaces *between* the strokes. John Lester, in his study of the period, states that the "one thought that appalled the imagination of this time was that behind all the phenomena perceptible to human senses there might lie—NOTHING."[38] Lawrence's Gerald Crich and a whole host of his other characters, as well as Conrad's Kurtz, Eliot's Prufrock, and Forster's Mrs. Moore, would soon become the standard literary embodiments of such fears. Lawrence, like Conrad, Eliot, Forster, and the Vorticists, would attempt to refill and reenergize that "great silent place" where God once was but where now was nothing.

I want to insist, then, on two main ideas. First, that Vorticism is more central to twentieth-century thought than is generally supposed, insofar as it gathers within its scope many of the lines of thought put forward by other significant figures and schools—such as Imagism, Futurism, and Cubism—and insofar as it can be seen to insist on the image of stabilized energy as its symbolic matrix. Second, that Lawrence, by mid-1914 at the latest, through struggling with problems encountered in constructing *The Rainbow* to his satisfaction, arrived at a position which was similar in many respects to Lewis's and Pound's notion of the Vortex. Lawrence did so, of course, while maintaining both an artistic and physical independence from the Vorticist coterie's fiercely clever programmatic and propagandistic declarations, declarations which, in many ways, had a greater impact on contemporaries than did the group's aesthetic precepts. Lawrence's most cogent statements about the effect he was trying to achieve in his work must be found in his letters, and they were written to explain and examine his own intentions as an artist; consequently, they bear the evidence of his struggle to understand exactly *what* he was trying to achieve. The Vorticists, in contrast, sound absolutely sure of themselves; their tactics are those of the publicist, and even when their declarations cannot bear the weight of critical examination, they still maintain the flavor of certainty. Nevertheless, like the Vorticists, the statue that Lawrence was attempting to "get out clean from the marble" was the essential shape of modern life—but it was to be carved, as usual, entirely in his own image.

Lawrence and Futurism

Like the Vorticists, Lawrence arrived at his new aesthetic in
great part through a process of attraction to, and recoil from, Futurism. Except for Cubism, Futurism was, internationally, the most
widely recognized influence on the art of the prewar years. Its task
was nothing less than "mastering reality afresh,"[39] which it would
achieve by repudiating man's traditional relationship with the
world around him, his preoccupation with nature, and the conventions of the past. Futurism was, in Kenneth Burke's phrase (which
might more appropriately be applied to Vorticism), "a concentration point, a summing-up, of movements that occurred in less
'efficient' form"[40] all around it. Every writer and artist who was
committed to expressing the new way of feeling and seeing that
modern life demanded had to wrestle with the implications of
Futurism.

Futurism began in Milan in 1908 as a reaction, mainly by painters, against the Academy. In February 1909, F. T. Marinetti published the first Futurist manifesto, and it soon became clear that the
movement had developed pretensions to encompassing all of art,
perhaps even all of modern experience, within the scope of its
declarations. Although it originated in Italy, by Italians, there were
French Futurists almost as soon as there was a movement at all; the
first manifesto, in fact, was published in *Le Figaro*. From 1910 to
1914, Marinetti made frequent and flamboyant appearances in London, and by 1913 a collection of Futurist verse was translated and
collected in an anthology published by Harold Monro, which, according to him, sold 35,000 copies by the end of the year.

The fundamental premise of Futurism was that modern com-
munication and machinery had brought about a radical change in
the twentieth-century sensibility and that such a change had to be
registered in its art. To do otherwise was to be *"passéist,"* to maintain a sentimental attachment to a way of life that modern man had
made impossible. Henceforth, declared the Futurists, one must
begin to comprehend and celebrate the newfound beauties of life
which had been, quite literally, manufactured by modern inven-
tiveness. Marianne W. Martin, in her book *Futurist Art and Theory*,
states that the message of the first manifesto was based on three
major precepts: "(1) to seek inspiration in contemporary life; (2) to
be emancipated from the crushing weight of tradition, which to
Marinetti was synonymous with existing academies, museums, li-

braries and all similar institutions. Implicit in his repudiation of tradition was (3), contempt for prevalent values of society and its corresponding conceptions of art."[41]

Martin finds that these precepts were, in many ways, traditional. All of them had been used by earlier artistic revolutionaries. What was new, however, and what created the most unsettling effects on early readers, was that these notions were put forward in frenetic, self-assertive prose—featuring fierce language, abrupt tone, rapid changes in imagery, deliberate exaggeration and insult, all of which were permeated with a sense of dynamic vitality—which, if at least somewhat familiar to the French and Italians, was quite new to the English. Richard Aldington, an astute observer of literary movements during the period, wrote in 1913: "M. Marinetti has been reading his new poems to London. London is vaguely alarmed and wondering whether it ought to laugh or not."[42] Edward Marsh thought that Marinetti's performance was "about on the level of a very good farmyard imitation—a supreme music hall turn."[43] Aldington's and Marsh's comments about Futurism resemble quite closely what earlier critics had said about the Post-Impressionist exhibition (which was, in every way, a much milder assault on English sensibilities), and indicate the extent to which artistic change had escalated during the intervening three years; that the anthology of Futurist poetry sold 35,000 copies is indicative of the extent to which the English were open to, and seemingly desirous of, such changes. The popular press, perhaps primed by the uproar over the postimpressionists and the Ballet, was more than happy to translate the newest artistic shock waves into columns for its papers. The quality of life in England had heated up; the Futurists, as well as the press, reflected it. James Gibbons Huneker, who had a foot in both worlds, admonished his readers: "The very chaos you resented in the . . . Futurists is in the streets."[44]

The Futurists had thrown over the traditional British technique of graceful persuasion in favor of high-voltage shock treatments, and it was a technique which was not lost on the developing English movements. Marinetti was never hesitant to force the issues. The first Futurist manifesto serves as well as any to demonstrate the issues that he forced.

> We intend to sing the love of danger, the habit of energy and fearlessness.
> Courage, audacity, and revolt will be essential elements of our poetry.

Up to now literature has exalted a pensive immobility, ecstasy, and sleep. We intend to exalt aggressive action, a feverish insomnia, the racer's stride, the mortal leap, the punch and the slap.

We say that the world's magnificence has been enriched by a new beauty; the beauty of speed. A racing car whose hood is adorned with great pipes, like serpents of explosive breath—a roaring car that seems to ride on grapeshot—is more beautiful than the *Victory of Samothrace*.

We want to hymn the man at the wheel, who hurls the lance of his spirit across the Earth, along the circle of its orbit. . . .

Except in struggle, there is no more beauty. No work without an aggressive character can be a masterpiece. Poetry must be conceived as a violent attack on unknown forces, to reduce and prostrate them before man.[45]

The first manifesto was followed by a series of essays, manifestoes, and exhibitions—with contributions from Boccioni, Carra, Balla, Severini, Soffici, and Buzzi—which both elaborated upon the declamations of the first manifesto and developed new particulars on the foundations it had already established.

Although Lawrence was out of England during the peak years of Marinetti's fame there, he may well have known of some of the basic Futurist tenets as early as anyone else in England. The company that he kept certainly knew of them, and was never hesitant to discuss new forms of art when new forms surfaced. Nevertheless, there is no evidence of Lawrence's awareness of Futurism until 1914.

A little over a week after Lawrence wrote his dismissal of Abercrombie and, by extension, Georgianism, he wrote to A. W. McLeod.

I have been interested in the futurists. I got a book of their poetry—a very fat book too—and a book of pictures—and I read Marinetti's and Paolo Buzzi's manifestations and essays and Soffici's essays on cubism and futurism. It interests me very much. I like it because it is the applying to emotions of the purging of the old forms and sentimentalities. I like it for its saying—enough of this sickly cant, let us be honest and stick by what is in us. Only when folk say, "Let us be honest and stick by what is in us"—they always mean, stick by those things that have been thought horrid, and by those alone. They want to deny every scrap of tradition and experience, which is silly. They are very young, college-student and medical-student at his most blatant. But I like them. Only I don't believe in them. I agree with them about the weary sickness of pedantry and tradition and inertness, but I don't agree with them as to the cure and the escape. They will progress down the purely male or intellectual or scientific line. They will even use their intuition for intellectual and scientific purpose. The one thing about their art is that it *isn't* art, but ultra scientific attempts to make diagrams of certain physic or mental states. It is ultra-ultra intellectual, going beyond Maeterlinck and the Symbolistes, who are intellectual. There isn't one trace of naiveté in the works—though there's plenty of naiveté in the authors. It's the most self-conscious, intentional, pseudo-scientific stuff on the face of the earth. Marinetti begins: "Italy is like a great Dreadnought surrounded by her torpedo boats." That is it exactly—a great mechanism. Italy has got to go through the most mechanical and dead stage of all—everything is appraised according to its mechanic value—everything is subject to the laws of physics. This is the revolt against beastly sentiment and slavish adherence to tradition and the dead mind. For that I love it. I love them when they say to the child, "All right, if you want to drag nests and torment kittens, do it lustily." But I reserve the right to answer, "All right, try it on. But if I catch you at it you get a hiding."[46]

The effect Lawrence's interest in the Futurists had on his response to Abercrombie's "End of the World" is quite difficult to determine, but it seems evident that while Lawrence was going through his "transition stage," a transition *from* Georgianism and *to* something yet unclarified, the Futurists provided him with a new direction and a new language which helped him "be honest" and stick by what he felt was in him. In an article on the evolution of *The Rainbow* and *Women in Love* (appropriately entitled "The Marble and the Statue"), Mark Kinkead-Weekes proposes that during this time Lawrence was attempting to find "a language in which to conceive the impersonal forces he saw operating within and between human beings; involving a new clarification of what the novel he had been trying to write was really *about*; and the discovery of a 'structural skeleton' on which to re-found it in a new dimension."[47] Kinkead-Weekes claims that Lawrence discovered his new language and his new dimension by "studying Hardy's art and Hardy's people."[48] Indeed, Kinkead-Weekes is at least partially right, but Lawrence's letters—as well as the "Study of Thomas Hardy" itself—reveal that Futurism was an equally important ingredient in the evolution of his new style.

Quite clearly, however, from the start Lawrence insisted on qualifying the Futurist line, bending it in a direction which would accommodate his deepest feelings about himself, his art, and his notion of human relationships. Still, Lawrence, as he was to do so often, found in Futurism a central issue of interest which could not be ignored, even if it could be violated by what he recognized as the "silly" particulars of individual Futurists.

Lawrence's letter to McLeod is quite clear about what Futurism had to offer in the way of buttressing his own feelings about the necessity for a new dimension in his work: "it is the applying to emotions of the purging of the old forms and sentimentalities," a "revolt against beastly sentiment and slavish adherence to tradition and the dead mind." In a letter to Edward Garnett, written three days later, Lawrence elaborates upon these issues while disclosing a newer, more central, issue which he derives from Futurism—the "non-human" element in humanity.

> I don't agree with you about *The Wedding Ring*. You will find that in a while you will like the book as a whole. I don't think the psychology is wrong: it is only that I have a different attitude to my characters, and that necessitates a different attitude in you, which you are not prepared to give. As for its being my *cleverness* which would pull the thing through—that sounds odd to me, for I don't think I am so very clever, in that way. I think the book is a bit futuristic—quite unconsciously so. But when I read Marinetti—"the profound intuitions of life added one to the other, word by word, according to their illogical conception, will give us the general lines of an intuitive physiology of matter"—I see something of what I am after. I translate him clumsily, and his Italian is obfuscated—and I don't care about physiology of matter—but some-how—that which is physic—non-human, in humanity, is more inter-esting to me than the old-fashioned human element—which causes one to conceive a character in a certain moral scheme and make him consist-ent. The certain moral scheme is what I object to. In Turgenev, and in Tolstoi, and in Dostoievsky, the moral scheme into which all the characters fit—and it is nearly the same scheme—is, whatever the ex-traordinariness of the characters themselves, dull, old, dead. When Marinetti writes: "It is the solidity of a blade of steel that is interesting by itself, that is, the incomprehending and inhuman alliance of its molecules in resistance to, let us say, a bullet. The heat of a piece of wood or iron is in fact more passionate, for us, than the laughter or tears of a woman"—then I know what he means. He is stupid, as an artist, for contrasting the heat of the iron and the laugh of the woman. Because what is interesting in the laugh of the woman is the same as the binding of the molecules of steel or their action in heat; it is the inhuman will, call it physiology, or like Marinetti—physiology of matter, that fasci-nates me. I don't so much care about what the woman *feels*—in the ordinary usage of the word. That presumes an *ego* to feel with. I only care about what the woman *is*—what she IS—inhumanly, physiologi-cally, materially—according to the use of the word: but for me, what she *is* as a phenomenon (or as representing some greater, inhuman will),

instead of what she feels according to the human conception. That is where the futurists are stupid. Instead of looking for the new human phenomenon, they will only look for the phenomena of the science of physics to be found in human beings. They are crassly stupid. But if anyone would give them eyes, they would pull the right apples off the tree, for their stomachs are true in appetite. You mustn't look in my novel for the old stable *ego*—of the character. There is another *ego*, according to whose action the individual is unrecognisable, and passes through, as it were, allotropic states which it needs a deeper sense than any we've been used to exercise, to discover are states of the same single radically unchanged element. (Like as diamond and coal are the same pure single element of carbon. The ordinary novel would trace the history of the diamond—but I say, "Diamond, what! This is carbon." And my diamond might be coal or soot, and my theme is carbon.) You must not say my novel is shaky—it is not perfect, because I am not expert in what I want to do. But it is the real thing, say what you like. And I shall get my reception, if not now, then before long. Again I say, don't look for the development of the novel to follow the lines of certain characters: the characters fall into the form of some other rhythmic form, as when one draws a fiddle-bow across a fine tray delicately sanded, the sand takes lines unknown.[49]

The imprecision of the language in the letter to Garnett is attributable to the informality of the occasion and also because the rhetoric of Futurism—in Lawrence's own words, "pseudo-scientific"—was essentially alien to him. Nevertheless, writers on Lawrence have consistently taken the letter as the most important of his several theoretical statements on the nature of his technical innovations, and certainly the most important statement concerning the methods he was developing during the period just before the war. In any case, critics have generally agreed that the letter is Lawrence's declaration of intent: "He will now create more *essential* beings, will be concerned first of all not with the 'ego' that interests the traditional novelist, but with the 'primal forces' that are prior to 'character.' "[50] On the same evidence, R. E. Pritchard declares that "different characters are not important to Lawrence as independent individuals, but only as manifestations of the common principle with which he has imbued them"[51]; H. M. Daleski agrees, saying that "the abandonment of the 'certain moral scheme' means that a character is judged not by social or ethical criteria but by the degree to which he is true to his deepest being, to the 'carbon' of his nature."[52] Frank Kermode notes the letter's claim to an "affinity with the Futurists,"[53] and goes on to say that the position Lawrence was trying to enunciate "is about a change in the apprehension and representation of *character;* but its implications as to the relation between the novel and society, the novel and the world, are enormous."[54]

The necessity of maintaining a "metaphysic" that would serve as a solid foundation for the relation between the "novel and the world" became increasingly important to Lawrence. In *Fantasia of the Unconscious*, for instance, Lawrence claimed:

> It seems to me that even art is utterly dependent on philosophy: or if you prefer it, on a metaphysic. The metaphysic or philosophy may not be anywhere very accurately stated and may be quite unconscious, in the artist, yet it is a metaphysic that governs men at the time, and is by all men more or less comprehended, and lived. Men live and see according to some gradually developing and gradually withering vision. This vision exists also as a dynamic idea or metaphysic—exists first as such. Then it is unfolded into life and art.[55]

But it was in his "Study of Thomas Hardy," written only a few months after his declared interest in the Futurists, that Lawrence was to first state the need for such a foundation. In the Hardy study he says that "every novel must have the background or the structural skeleton of some theory of being, some metaphysic. But the metaphysic must always subserve the artistic purpose beyond the artist's conscious aim. Otherwise the novel becomes a treatise."[56] If the Futurists too often allowed their metaphysic to overwhelm their art, Lawrence still detected in their work at least two elements necessary to the construction of a "structural skeleton" for his own work. First, the notion that modern life demands a new perception, and that the artist must, consequently, slough off his sentimental adherence to the old forms. Elsewhere in "Study of Thomas Hardy," for instance, Lawrence insists that "each work of art has its own form, which has no relation to any other form,"[57] and, since the conjunction of the two basic principles of form (Love and Law) "always meet under fresh conditions, form must always be different."[58] Second, as the critics quoted above have suggested, Futurism spurred Lawrence's growing recognition of the necessity of portraying an essential, unchanging reality which lies beneath the varying moods and personalities of his characters.

If this second notion was made more evident by his reading of the Futurists, Lawrence was not hesitant to relate it to other discoveries—its relation to his "Study of Thomas Hardy" has already been suggested, and later he would find evidence for it in other forms. In September 1914, for instance, Lawrence writes:

Then the vision we're after, I don't know what it is—but it is something that contains awe and dread and submission, not pride or sensuous egotism and assertion. I went to the British Museum—and I know, from the Egyptian and Assyrian sculpture—what we are after. We want to realise the tremendous *non-human* quality of life—it is wonderful. It is not the emotions, nor the personal feelings and attachments, that matter. These are all only expressive, and expression has become mechanical. Behind in all are the tremendous unknown forces of life, coming unseen and unperceived as out of the desert to the Egyptians, and driving us, forcing us, destroying us if we do not submit to be swept away.[59]

Lawrence's recoil from "sensuous egotism and assertion," implied in this letter, again has roots in his response to Futurism, specifically to the Futurist declarations which Lawrence had actually read. The essay by Marinetti that Lawrence refers to in his letter to McLeod, and quotes in his letter to Garnett, was the "Technical Manifesto of Futurist Literature," first published in May 1912. The "Technical Manifesto of Futurist Literature" presents the case for the poetry of an "uninterrupted sequence of new images,"[60] which Marinetti contrasts to the "mere anemia and green-sickness"[61] of the poetry of the past. In order to approach the images "just as they are born,"[62] without preconception, the artist must "destroy the *I* in literature" and substitute "the lyric obsession with matter"[63]—a "matter whose essence must be grasped by strokes of intuition."[64] Marinetti's rejection of the projecting ego, the ego which says, to quote Lawrence, " '*I* am all. All other things are but a radiation out from me,' "[65] is a step that Lawrence quickly realized was necessary in order to discard the "certain moral scheme" into which all fictional characters seemingly had to fit.

The notion of the ego as a barrier to the full recognition of the "tremendous *non-human* quality of life"—what C. E. M. Joad calls " 'the object' "[66]—had occurred to Lawrence before. But he had earlier relied on "faith"[67] to counteract the demands of the ego. In a letter to J. M. Murry in April 1914, Lawrence wrote, "I am rather great on faith just now. I do believe in it. We are so egoistic, that we are ashamed of ourselves out of existence. One ought to have faith in what one ultimately is, then one can bear at last the hosts of unpleasant things which one is *en route*."[68] "Faith" here is, in fact, the ability to believe in an authentic, core self, an absolute and unchanging identity which, like Lawrence's "demon" and the "Venus of Melos," is "incorruptible and inexhaustible."[69] But "faith" was finally unacceptable as a meaningful term; it was too ambiguous and too much tainted by the associations of the past. The Futurists, by raising a new language into consciousness, and applying it to a new field, established new terms and a new basis on which Lawrence could build his "metaphysic." Marinetti's suggestion that the artist had to free himself from the "*I* in literature" before he could free his images and symbols from preconceptions was to be echoed in Lawrence's letter to Gordon Campbell a little later in 1914:

> I think there is the dual way of looking at things: our way, which is to say "*I* am all. All other things are but radiation out from me."—The other way is to try to conceive the whole . . . because symbolism avoids the I and puts aside the egotist; and, in the whole, to take our decent place.[70]

Mary Freeman, in her book on Lawrence's ideas, suggests one further connection between Lawrence and Futurism. "In *Women in Love*," she claims, "and in other works where Lawrence tries to raise death and pain to an ecstasy, he approached the attitude characteristic of literary futurism."[71] Freeman's claim couples Lawrence's interest in the often entangled relations between aggressor and victim, creation and decay, with the Futurists' acceptance of chaos, their deification of indiscriminate sensations, and their celebration of the beauty of "the sheer naked slidings of the elements."[72] Freeman relies heavily on what Kenneth Burke, in his *Attitudes toward History*, calls Futurism's passive "frame of 'acceptance.' "[73] By this, Burke means that the Futurists, in order to make peace with the modern *Zeitgeist*, optimistically accepted and even glorified those very aspects of experience which were generally held to be abhorrent by more traditional frames of reference. For instance, "The futurist, to praise war, needed only to recite its *horrors*, and call them *beautiful*."[74] Marinetti, says Burke, "contrived to attain 'yea-saying,' at whatever cost."[75]

Indeed, Lawrence's use of this dynamic becomes increasingly important about the same time as his confrontation with Futurism. Much of *The Rainbow* and all of *Women in Love* depend heavily on the reader's ability to accept Lawrence's notion that out of the decay of the old world a new world could emerge. Of *Women in Love*, for instance, Lawrence said, "The book frightens me: it is so end-of-the-world. But it is, it must be, the beginning of a new world too."[76] But Freeman's claim that Lawrence is like the Futurists in their "effort to accept pain as pleasure, ugliness as beauty,

death as life,"[77] surely misrepresents Lawrence's position, if not
theirs. From his earliest stories and poems, as well as *The White
Peacock* and *The Trespasser*, Lawrence had manifested an acute
awareness of the coexistence and necessary conflict of apparent
opposites. And his use of the collision of those opposites in his work
after 1914, and especially during and after the war, is hardly due to
a passive "frame of 'acceptance,'" or an attempt to "salute his times,
to be a 'yea-sayer,' an 'answerer,' to make his peace with the
Zeitgeist."[78] Instead, it is due to Lawrence's increased recognition
that "each opposite [is] kept in stable equilibrium by the opposition
of the other," and, as he says in his "Note to 'The Crown'":

> The whole great form of our era will have to go. And nothing will really
> send it down but the new shoots of life springing up and slowly burst-
> ing the foundations. And one can do nothing but fight tooth and nail to
> defend the new shoots of life from being crushed out, and let them
> grow. We can't make life. We can but fight for the life that grows in
> us.[79]

With Futurism as with other currents of thought, Lawrence assimilated what was useful to him and gave the remainder a "good
hiding." Consequently, Lawrence's disagreements with Futurism
are usually more evident than his debts. Lawrence's distaste for the
Futurists' "medical-student" rhetoric is quite clear in the letters,
and it is a distaste which takes on special importance insofar as the
rhetoric of Futurist theory was often as influential as its content.
What Lawrence had to say of D'Annunzio in *Twilight in Italy*,
written during the first flush of Lawrence's encounter with Futurism, is illuminating when related to that movement:

> It was the language which did it. It was the Italian passion for rhetoric,
> for the speech which appeals to the senses and makes no demand on the
> mind. When an Englishman listens to a speech he wants at least to
> imagine that he understands thoroughly and impersonally what is
> meant. But an Italian only cares about the emotion. It is the movement,
> the physical effect of the language upon the blood which gives him
> supreme satisfaction. His mind is scarcely engaged at all. He is like a
> child, hearing and feeling without understanding. It is the sensuous
> gratification he asks for. Which is why D'Annunzio is a god in Italy. He
> can control the current of the blood with his words, and although much
> of what he says is bosh, yet the hearer is satisfied, fulfilled.[80]

If Lawrence approved of the Futurists' ambition to disregard all traditional assumptions and preconceptions as a working basis for their art, he still thought it "silly" of them to "deny every scrap of tradition and experience"[81] from which, as his later works would continually argue, a great deal could still be learned. And if Lawrence applauded the Futurists' revolt against sentiment and the Romantic projecting ego, he could not agree with them as to a replacement; science, he felt, would not do. The extent to which Futurism insisted upon celebrating the achievements of science and the advancement of technology was proof to Lawrence of its progress along the curve of pure "male," or "intellectual," dissolution; by praising the flux represented by a speeding race car or the movement of the molecules of steel, the Futurists proved themselves to be heralds of "the most mechanical and dead stage of all," where "everything is appraised according to its mechanic value." "The attitude of the Futurists," Lawrence wrote in his study of Hardy, "is the scientific attitude, as the attitude of Italy is mainly scientific. It is the forgetting of the old, perfect Abstraction, it is the departure of the male from the female, it is the act of withdrawal."[82] In *Twilight in Italy*, Lawrence describes Milan—the headquarters for Futurist activity—as a city where the "process of disintegration was vigorous. . . . But always there was the same purpose stinking in it all, the mechanising, the perfect mechanising of human life."[83]

The most famous embodiment of Futurism in Lawrence's fiction is the sculptor Loerke, in *Women in Love*. Loerke's full symbolic weight can hardly be suggested by merely noting his connections with Futurism; he is in many ways beyond Futurism. Loerke is described as being "not satisfied with the Futurists," having taken its implications to the most extreme stages. He is, as Birkin says of him, "the wizard rat that swims ahead."[84] But Loerke's Futurist credentials are nevertheless clearly in order, as is Lawrence's own version of the implications embedded in Futurist theory. In a discussion of his latest project, a "great granite frieze for a great granite factory,"[85] Loerke tells Gudrun and Ursula:

> "Sculpture and architecture must go together. The day for irrelevant statues, as for wall pictures, is over. As a matter of fact sculpture is always part of an architectural conception. And since churches are all museum stuff, since industry is our business, now, then let us make our places of industry our art—our factory-area our Parthenon, *ecco*! . . ."
>
> ". . . There is not only *no need* for our places of work to be ugly, but their ugliness ruins the work, in the end. Men will not go on submitting to such intolerable ugliness. In the end it will hurt too much, and they

will wither because of it. And this will wither the *work* as well. They will think the work itself is ugly: the machines, the very act of labour. Whereas the machinery and the acts of labour are extremely, maddeningly beautiful. But this will be the end of our civilisation, when people will not work because work has become so intolerable to their senses, it nauseates them too much, they would rather starve. *Then* we shall see the hammer used only for smashing, then we shall see it. Yet here we are—we have the opportunity to make beautiful factories, beautiful machine-houses—we have the opportunity—."[86]

Even the most important insight that Lawrence felt Futurism had to offer—the nonhuman element in humanity—was one which probably would have surprised Marinetti. Not only was it comparatively little emphasized in Futurist declarations, but it clearly meant something quite different to Lawrence than it did to the Futurists. The difference is indicated in a letter which Lawrence wrote to Lady Ottoline Morrell in January 1915. Lawrence had just seen the latest work of the Bloomsburian painter Duncan Grant and had (mistakenly) determined that Grant was working from Futurist principles. He harangued the despairing and silent Grant about the "foolish waste"[87] of his efforts, a harangue so unpleasant to one witness, David Garnett—who had known and liked Lawrence since 1912—that Garnett felt he had to make a final break with him. Soon after, however, Lawrence wrote to Ottoline:

> We liked Duncan Grant very much. I *really* liked him. Tell him not to make silly experiments in the futuristic line, with bits of colour on a moving paper. Other Johnnies can do that. Neither to bother making marionettes—even titanic ones. But to seek out the terms in which he shall state his whole. He is after stating the Absolute—like Fra Angelico in the "Last Judgment"—a whole conception of the existence of man—creation, good, evil, life, death, resurrection, the separating of the stream of good and evil, and its return to the eternal source. It is an Absolute we are all after, a statement of the whole scheme—the issue, the progress through time—and the return—making unchangeable eternity.[88]

This rather unfortunate episode in Lawrence's life must have reverberated with some importance for Lawrence, because it is used as a model for an important episode in *Lady Chatterley's Lover*, published thirteen years after the event. Duncan Forbes, in that novel, is a very thinly disguised Duncan Grant; Mellors takes the place of Lawrence. If the scene in *Lady Chatterley's Lover* is rather different from the accounts that we have of Lawrence's and Grant's actual behavior,[89] perhaps it suggests Lawrence's version of the emotional reality of that afternoon in 1915. Certainly, it is evidence of Lawrence's continued resistance to the "futurist line" in modern art, as well as the addition of another dimension to the nature of that resistance.

> Duncan was a rather short, broad, dark-skinned, taciturn Hamlet of a fellow with straight black hair and a weird Celtic conceit of himself. His art was all tubes and valves and spirals and strange colors, ultra modern, yet with a certain power, even a certain purity of form and tone: only Mellors thought it cruel and repellent. He did not venture to say so, for Duncan was almost insane on the point of his art; it was a personal cult, a personal religion with him.
>
> They were looking at the pictures in the studio, and Duncan kept his smallish brown eyes on the other man. He wanted to hear what the gamekeeper would say. He knew already Connie's and Hilda's opinions.
>
> "It is like a pure bit of murder," said Mellors at last; a speech Duncan by no means expected from a gamekeeper.
>
> "And who is murdered?" asked Hilda, rather coldly and sneeringly.
>
> "Me! It murders all the bowels of compassion in a man."
>
> A wave of pure hate came out of the artist. He heard the note of dislike in the other man's voice, and the note of contempt. And he himself loathed the mention of bowels of compassion. Sickly sentiment!
>
> Mellors stood rather tall and thin, worn-looking gazing with flickering detachment that was something like the dancing of a moth on the wing, at the pictures.
>
> "Perhaps stupidity is murdered; sentimental stupidity," sneered the artist.
>
> "Do you think so? I think all these tubes and corrugated vibrations are stupid enough for anything, and pretty sentimental. They show a lot of self-pity and an awful lot of nervous self-opinion, seems to me."
>
> In another wave of hate, the artist's face looked yellow. But with a sort of silent hauteur he turned the pictures to the wall.[90]

Finally, then, Lawrence had to reject Futurism, even though it had been helpful in defining and exploring a new conceptual language, and had aided him in going beyond the limitations of the Georgian sensibility. From the beginning, when he found Futurist declarations to be "the most self-conscious, intentional, pseudo-scientific stuff on the face of the earth," until the end, when Mellors declares that Futurist art "murders all the bowels of compassion in a man," Lawrence was able to perceive that, despite its surface vitality, Futurism was at bottom following the wrong curve, the curve of pure intellectual, "scientific," dissolution.

It should be kept in mind, however, that although Lawrence's debts to Futurism are usually obscured by his more pungent (and better-known) criticism of it, the Futurist sensibility remained a significant point of focus for him, around which the continuing process of attraction and recoil could take place. Loerke may well embody the logical extension of Futurism, but other characters in *Women in Love* reveal the impact of Futurism in ways which are not so immediately apparent. Each of the major characters in *Women in Love* is rendered in symbolic and imagistic terms suggested by one radical element: for Ursula, earth; for Rupert, air; for Gudrun, fire; for Gerald, water. The impulse which led Lawrence to define his characters symbolically this way was the impulse to find the "unchangeable"—the "carbon"—which is the elemental force prior to character. It was an impulse which derived, in great part, from his assimilation of Futurism.

Lawrence, Imagism, and "Amygism"

I suggested earlier that every modern movement had at some time to wrestle with the implications of Futurism. The Imagists, though not particularly sympathetic to Futuristic principles, shared with that movement a pugnacity in aesthetic matters which, during the early years of the second decade, put them at the forefront of modernism. It even seems fair to say that the Futurists, particularly Marinetti, were as valuable to Pound and his group as were the much-celebrated dinner conversations and the *Complete Poetical Works* of T. E. Hulme. It was Hulme who perhaps first developed what was to become the essential conceptual floor plan of Imagism. But it was the Futurist onslaught, as much as anything, which broke down or preoccupied the traditional defenses, making it easier for the Imagists to break through.

Much of what Pound liked about the Futurists—their feeling that "the artist had to 'break up the surface of convention' and . . . to speak with the voice of the present"[91]—was a feeling shared by Lawrence. Pound's desire to eliminate cliché and to break away from the formal poetic models of the existing tradition was also shared by Lawrence during these years, as his argumentative letters to Edward Marsh clearly indicate. It is little wonder, then, that Lawrence would, sooner or later, enter the Imagists' orbit.

Lawrence knew most of the significant Imagists during what was perhaps their most fruitful period as a group, and was aware of the group's existence almost as soon as they were. He met Ezra Pound as early as November 1909, when Ford Madox Ford was guiding Lawrence through the perils of literary London. Both Lawrence and Pound were men noted for the speed with which they seized upon the essential, and on first acquaintance, Lawrence was able to seize upon the central difference between himself and Pound.

> I went on Tuesday to Violet Hunt's "at home" at the Reform Club in Adelphi Terrace, on the Embankment. It was very jolly. Elizabeth Martindale & Ellaline Terriss and Mary Cholmondeley were there— and Ezra Pound. He is a well-known American poet—a good one. He is 24, like me—but his god is beauty, mine, life. He is jolly nice: took me to supper at Pagnani's, and afterwards we went down to his room at Kensington. He lives in an attic, like a traditional poet—but the attic is a comfortable and well furnished one. He is an American Master of Arts & a professor of the Provençal group of languages, & he lectures once a week on the minstrels at the London polytechnic. He is rather remarkable—a good bit of a genius, & with not the least self-consciousness.
>
> This afternoon I am going up to tea with him & we are going out after to some friends who will not demand evening dress of us. He knows W. B. Yeats & all the Swells. Aren't the folks kind to me: it is really wonderful.[92]

They apparently saw a good deal of each other in late 1909 and early 1910; Lawrence once stayed the night in Pound's "attic" at 10 Church Walk after missing the train to Croydon.[93] In her memoir of Lawrence, Jessie Chambers recalled a luncheon with Lawrence, Violet Hunt, Ford Madox Ford, and Pound.

> A young American poet . . . startled me by springing to his feet and bowing from the waist with the stiff precision of a mechanical toy. . . .
>
> The young American poet was the life of the party. He flung out observations in an abrupt way that reminded me of his poetry. . . .
>
> I regarded him as an amiable buffoon.[94]

In another famous incident, which probably took place in December 1909, Lawrence, again shepherded by the ubiquitous Ford, went to the home of Ernest Rhys to meet the "Swells" and read some of his most recent work. Some twenty-two years later, Rhys remembered the evening in telling detail:

> When the two entered the room together, they made a curious contrast, for Ford always had the air of a man-about-town, well used to town

occasions, while Lawrence looked shy and countrified; perhaps a little overwhelmed by the fanfaron of fellow poets heard in the room, with W. B. Yeats and Ezra Pound dominating the scene. . . .

During the supper, Willie Yeats, always a good monologuer, held forth at length on this new art of bringing music and poetry together, and possibly Ezra Pound, who could also be vocal on occasion, may have felt he was not getting a fair share of the festivity. So, in order to pass the time perhaps, and seeing the supper table dressed with red tulips in glasses, he presently took one of the flowers and proceeded to munch it up. As Yeats, absorbed in his monologue, did not observe this strange behavior, and the rest of us were too well-bred to take any notice, Ezra, having found the tulip to his taste, did likewise with a second flower. Now, memory I admit is an artist, but not always to be trusted, and may have deceived me into recalling that by the end of supper all the tulips had been consumed. . . .

In his turn, Ford Madox Ford read us a witty burlesque, after which we persuaded D. H. Lawrence, who had been sitting silent in a corner, to read us some of his verse. He rose nervously but very deliberately, walked across to a writing desk whose lid was closed, opened it, produced a mysterious book out of his pocket, and sat down, his back to the company, and began to read in an expressive, not very audible voice. One could not hear every word or every line clearly, but what was heard left an impression of a set of love-poems, written with sincerity and not a little passion, interspersed with others written in dialect not easy to follow. . . .

Lawrence's reading went on and on, seemed as if it might go on the whole evening, and the other poets became restive, and chattered *sotto voce*. At the end of half an hour, these murmurings had increased, and one murmurer, with nod and gesture, seemed to ask his hostess to intervene. She appealed to me, and I whispered: "What am I to do?"

"Tell him he must want a little rest."

This I did, adding that if so inclined he might resume at midnight! He took it in good part, and getting up with an awkward little bow shut up book and desk, and retired to his corner. And now Ezra Pound, fortified, if anything, by the tulips, started up, asking if we minded "having the roof taken off the house." He went on to declaim in a resonant, histrionic voice, a little like Henry Irving with an American accent, his imaginative "Ballad of the Goodly Fere."[95] [See Appendix A]

The scene at Ernest Rhys's has been quoted at length not only because of its inherent interest, but also because it is suggestive of the yawning abyss of style and intention which separated Pound and Lawrence, two writers who, if they didn't much like each other, were certainly to learn something from each other. Here, in

Rhys's dining room, one is able to see the early Pound, bohemian poseur already at home in literary circles, interested in "having the roof taken off the house" of post-Victorian poetry, "often brilliant but an ass"[96]—and Lawrence, "shy and countrified," his back to his public, reading on until it, not he, was exhausted.

The night before a similar gathering in 1910, Lawrence wrote to Louie Burrows about the prospect of another evening at the Rhys's: "I am not very keen, and not much interested. I am no society man—it bores me. I like private people who will not talk current clippings."[97] One must wonder, then, what Lawrence thought of Pound, by that time fast becoming the demon salesman of modern poetry, with all of the charm and subtlety of a publicity agent. Pound was assuredly not one of those "private people who will not talk current clippings." One must wonder, too, what Lawrence had thought of literary London's chattering *sotto voce* while he read it his love poems. All too often, it seems, this was to be literary London's response to his work. Only six months later he would call the literary world "a disagreeable substratum under a fair country."[98]

During a conversation in 1929, Lawrence told Glenn Hughes, the first biographer of the Imagist school, that

> there never had been such a thing as imagism. It was all an illusion of Ezra Pound's, he said, and was nonsense. "In the old London days Pound wasn't so literary as he is now. He was more of a mountebank then. He practiced more than he preached, for he had no audience. He was always amusing."[99]

Lawrence, Hughes tells us, "joked a good deal about it."[100] Perhaps he was recalling the image of Ezra Pound with Ernest Rhys's red tulips tucked artistically down his gullet.

Still, it is unfortunate that no record remains of what Lawrence and Pound talked about during those early years, the gestation period of what would come to be called Imagism. But it would have been unlike Lawrence, and certainly unlike Pound, not to have known what the other was doing or thinking. There is some slight evidence which suggests that Lawrence, at least, did follow the development of Pound's poetry. During the summer of 1912, before the impact of the Imagists had really made itself felt, Lawrence and Frieda were in the Isartal, talking, says Frieda, about "style in writing, about the new style Americans had evolved—cinematographic, he called it."[101]

It had been in April of that year that Pound, Aldington, and H. D. had decided upon the three principles of good writing:

1. Direct treatment of the "thing" whether subjective or objective.
2. To use absolutely no word that does not contribute to the presentation.
3. As regarding rhythm: to compose in the sequence of the musical phrase, not in sequence of a metronome.[102]

About a month later, Pound christened the group "imagistes."

Pound's attitude toward Lawrence suggests that of a father who is constrained to love his son, but who nevertheless likes very little about him. In March 1913, Pound wrote to Harriet Monroe:

> Lawrence has brought out a vol. He is clever; I don't know whether to send in a review or not. We seem pretty well stuffed up with matter at the moment. (D. H. Lawrence, whom I mentioned in my note on the *Georgian Anthology*.) Detestable person but needs watching. I think he learned the proper treatment of modern subjects before I did. That was in some poems in *The Eng. Rev.*; can't tell whether he has progressed or retrograded as I haven't seen the book yet. He may have published merely on his prose rep.[103]

For Pound to have complimented Lawrence on the latter's modernity is intriguing—especially because of what is known of Pound's general attitude toward Lawrence's work (it "ultimately bores me"[104]) and also because it is practically impossible to determine what Pound might actually have meant. By March 1913, Pound had almost completely developed the early version of Imagist poetics, and it would seem at first that what he must have admired in Lawrence's early verse was some visible tendency toward Imagism. Yet this is unlikely, since Lawrence was not asked to contribute to *Des Imagistes*, the first and most strictly principled Imagist anthology, which was being assembled for publication at the very time of Pound's letter to Monroe.

To suggest that there was nothing like Imagism in Lawrence's work is, of course, not altogether accurate. Lawrence's early verse, like that of most of the poets functioning during the period, contains elements which could be called Imagist. Sandra Gilbert, for instance, notes some early poems of Lawrence's which, "though they may not have been consciously Imagist in intention, are certainly Imagist in mood."[105] Among those that she notes is "Baby Movements," the first lines of which she calls a "perfect little Imagist poem."[106]

> I wait for the baby to wander hither to me,
> Like a wind-shadow wandering over the water,
> So she may stand on my knee
> With her two bare feet on my hands
> Cool as syringa buds
> Cool and firm and silken as pink young peony flowers.[107]

Whether or not Pound was thinking of this poem is, and will probably remain, unknown; it was, however, published in the *English Review* before March 1913. Another poem which might have interested Pound was "Night Songs," which was published in the *English Review* in April 1910. Three stanzas from part two, "Tomorrow Night," run:

> When into the night the yellow light is roused like dust above the
> towns,
> Or like a mist the moon has kissed from off a pool in the midst of the
> downs:
>
> Our faces flower for a little hour pale and uncertain along the street,
> Daisies that waken all mistaken white-spread in expectancy to meet
>
> The luminous mist which the poor things wist was dawn arriving
> across the sky,
> When the dawn is far behind the star that the lamp-lit town has
> driven so high.[108]

These three stanzas, and the poem as a whole, read a bit like the Eliot of "Preludes" suffering a severe attack of Swinburne. Pound, however, may well have read such a poem while armed with a subconscious blue pencil, remembering only those elements which struck him as being "modern." For Pound in 1913, it did not actually take much to put a poet on the side of the angels; sustained performance, though desirable, was not necessary. One recalls Pound's praise for Henry Newbolt, who periodically made some sound declarations about poetry, or his praise for Wilfred Scawen Blunt, who forever stood above the general run of his contemporaries on the strength of one double sonnet which he had written in 1892.[109]

A more probable cause for Pound's declaration, however, was Lawrence's use of lower-class life, the experience of lower-class town and country folk, as his poetic subject; he did so without straining to moralize and without using bloated rhetoric. When

Pound came to review Lawrence's *Love Poems and Others* in July 1913, he condemned most of the poems in the volume, even those which now seem inclined toward some form of Imagism, as "a sort of pre-raphaelitish slush,"[110] but he nevertheless declared that when Lawrence "writes low-life narrative . . . there is no English poet under forty who can get within a shot of him."[111] Pound goes on to say:

> His prose training stands him in good stead in these poems. The characters are real. They are not stock figures of "the poor," done from the outside and provided with *cliché* emotions. . . .
> Mr. Lawrence has attempted realism and attained it. He has brought contemporary verse up to the level of contemporary prose, and that is no mean achievement.[112]

It is worth noting that Ford Madox Ford, to whom Pound was much indebted during this period, was most impressed by this same characteristic.

> There had been before him [Lawrence] novelists the sons of working men or of lower middle class origin. Their characters, at any rate in their earlier works, were always portrayed as of those classes and concerned, even to paroxysms of confusion, over social minutiae. They wilted under the eyes of butlers and waiters, were horribly confused over the use of fish-knives and aspirates. About Lawrence there was no sign of that either in his characters or in his personal life. His characters are perfectly self-sufficient and unembarrassed by the sense of class. They move with freedom in a world that seems to belong to them alone; they are beings of complete ignorance of class fetters and of confidence that they and their likes are the only persons that matter in the world. It was the same with Lawrence himself.[113]

It seems to be a reasonable speculation, then, to say that even those of Lawrence's early poems which now seem overwrought and lusciously post-Romantic, must have seemed, to Pound in 1913, unembarrassed evocations of lower-class life, casually if energetically written, and, when compared with the poetry being written all around him (for instance, by Masefield, Gibson, etc.) relievedly unpolished.

If unpolished poetry seems to be a little out of Pound's line, it should be remembered that during these years Pound was searching out any clear manifestation of energy and emotion in poetry, especially when it was manifested in what T. S. Eliot would later call "the accents of direct speech."[114] Form and technique would, perhaps, follow. Pound, after all, was given to justifying the limitations of his Imagist colleagues by declaring that they were very young, the implication being that a significant technique might yet come from further study of their craft and from an intensification of their efforts to make their work more precise. Perhaps Pound felt that Lawrence, in time, would become a worthwhile modern voice.

Even so, Lawrence was not asked to contribute to *Des Imagistes*, which, though finally published in February 1914, had been in the works since 1912, when Pound was first gathering likely prospects for his new movement. Pound's review of *Love Poems and Others*, which praises Lawrence for his "low-life" narratives, also suggests that Pound found very little which would justify Lawrence's inclusion in an anthology strictly for Imagists. His distaste for Lawrence's "middling-sensual erotic verses" made up of "his own disagreeable sensations"[115] in that early volume is reason enough for us to understand why Lawrence was not among the contributors. Evidently, Lawrence, though he had "learned the proper treatment of modern subjects" even before Pound, did "not show any signs of agreeing with the second specification"[116] (and perhaps even the first and third) of the original Imagist group's three principles of good writing. In any case, Pound could not have been overjoyed at the prospect of printing a poet who had already published in the first Georgian anthology. Pound was by now excoriating the Georgians, whom he considered ineffectual remnants of the ineffectual Romantic-Victorian tradition.

Lawrence, as Pound would say later, "was never an Imagist. He was an *Amy*gist" who never "accepted the Imagist program."[117] "Amygism" will be discussed later, in its historical context and in its relation to Lawrence, but Pound's claim that Lawrence was an "Amygist" confirms the probability that Lawrence's work, though modern in significant ways, was too much like that of Amy Lowell, who was also rejected for inclusion in *Des Imagistes* because her poetry was "the fluid, fruity, facile stuff we most wanted to avoid."[118]

Throughout these years, however, despite their evident disregard for each other, Lawrence and Pound maintained a connection. In 1913, for instance, Pound continually attempted to place Lawrence's poems with publishers, especially Harriet Monroe at *Poetry*. And as a prose writer, Lawrence was granted the "first place among the younger men"[119] by Pound, an opinion that would alter only slightly during subsequent years.

Lawrence apparently felt that he was being conscripted by the Imagists. In December 1913, Lawrence, predictably wary of the buzz saw of coterie warfare but nevertheless interested in a larger audience for his work, wrote a rather backhanded and nasty letter about Pound to Edward Garnett:

> The Hueffer-Pound faction seems inclined to lead me round a little as one of their show-dogs. They seem to have a certain ear in their possession. If they are inclined to speak my name into the ear, I don't care.[120]

But things moved quickly in those days, especially in poetic circles, and by early 1914, Pound had soured on Imagism, at least as it was originally conceived. Imagism simply was not comprehensive enough to satisfy him. By this time, he had become involved with Wyndham Lewis and Henri Gaudier-Brzeska, two men whose genius momentarily complemented Pound's own, and who were equally able and willing to proselytize for an aesthetic cause. At the same time, the remainder of the original group of Imagists—especially Richard Aldington and H. D.—had welcomed the giant American poetess Amy Lowell into their company.

Lowell was hardly one to be intimidated by Pound's heretofore dictatorial powers over the group. With the combined gifts of family money, energy, tact, and sheer presence, Lowell was able to orchestrate the remaining Imagists who were "fed up with Ezra."[121] Pound, who was at first indifferent but not hostile to Lowell's verse, apparently felt that she was an interloper into what before had been his territory. When Lowell organized a dinner to celebrate the publication of *Des Imagistes*, which was attended by all of its contributors, Pound

> rebuffed her attempts at seriousness with ill-bred, impertinent levity. In answer to her question about a precise formula for *Imagisme*, he left the table and came back in a few minutes wearing an old-fashioned tin tub on his head in caricature of a helmet of some knight-errant. He produced hilarous laughter, in which Amy joined, but hers was a hard and hurt laugh.[122]

Not only was Lowell shaken by Pound's "impudence and high-handed use of power," but she could also hardly abide his new friends—especially Gaudier-Brzeska—who were, claims Jean Gould, "revolting to her."[123]

The split between Pound and the original members of the Imagist group was, however, the result of more than a personality con-

flict between Pound and Amy Lowell. Pound's term for what Imagism became after Lowell's entrance into the group—
"Amygism"—is an appropriate one. What Pound meant by the
term can be perceived by juxtaposing his own work with Lowell's.
The hard, sharp edges of Pound's verse become blurred in Lowell's
verse, and the nondiscursive Image becomes discursive. The ter-
ritorial boundaries of the Image are no longer so carefully observed.

In "A Retrospect," which Pound wrote in 1918, he recalled the
origins and basic principles of the original school of Imagists, then
complains that those first principles were later blurred by "numerous people," no doubt including Lawrence as well as Lowell, who
"whatever their merits, do not show any signs of agreeing [to use
absolutely no word that does not contribute to the presentation of
the poem]."

> Indeed *vers libre* has become as prolix and as verbose as any of the
> flaccid varieties that preceded it. It has brought faults of its own. The
> actual language and phrasing is often as bad as that of our elders with-
> out even the excuse that the words are shovelled in to fill a metric
> pattern or to complete the noise of a rhyme-sound.[124]

Pound's memory is confirmed by his letters written during the
time of transition from Imagism to "Amygism." On 1 August 1914
Pound wrote to Lowell:

> . . . I should like the name "Imagisme" to retain some sort of a meaning.
> It stands, or I should like it to stand for hard light, clear edges. I can not
> trust any democratized committee to maintain that standard. Some will
> be splay-footed and some sentimental. . . .
> If anyone wants a faction, or if anyone wants to form a separate
> group, I think it can be done amicably, but I should think it wiser to
> split over an aesthetic principle. In which case the new group would
> find its name automatically, almost. The aesthetic issue would of itself
> give names to the two parties.[125]

There were no doubt a number of "aesthetic issues" involved in
Pound's dispute with Lowell, but of particular significance was his
insistence upon the poet's commitment to conceiving of the poem as
primarily an object in space, and his rejection of anything that
smacked of the continuity of events in time. For Pound, Lowell and
the remainder of the Imagist school had lapsed back into the sentimentality of the archaizing sensibility, of using art as an "opportunity for time travel."[126] Thus, when Pound wrote that Vorticism,

in contrast, "was an attempt to revive the sense of form,"[127] he was clarifying his sense that "Amygism" was a dilution of the spatial metaphor that he had originally developed to define Imagism.

It now appears, in fact, that the famous "doctrine of the Image," that elusive basis for Imagism which was promised (but never delivered) by the early Imagist school, was simply an earlier, less comprehensive version of the Vortex. John Gould Fletcher has written, with an interesting twist of emphasis, that Vorticist principles were only "an extension of the old principle of Imagism, developed to embrace all the arts."[128] Pound himself once declared: "Imagism was a point on the curve of my development. Some people remained at that point. I moved on."[129] What Pound moved on to, of course, was Vorticism.

Nevertheless, the "doctrine of the Image" was perhaps most adequately stated by Pound himself: "An 'Image' is that which presents an intellectual and emotional complex in an instant of time."[130] It is important to note that Pound's definition is a "description of spatial form, whose impact is instantaneous and non-discursive."[131] The Image, then, is a radiant truth situated out of time, without reference to anything but itself; it is unsentimental because it represents rather than expresses emotion. Like Lawrence's notion of symbolism, its impersonality "avoids the I and puts aside the egotist; and, in the whole, [allows us] to take our decent place." But the Image alone was found to be adequate only to poetry; for Pound, Imagism became simply a "distracting turbulence"[132] on the steady line which led to Vorticism. The Image was not enough; it could not incorporate the energies of movement and change; it "gave concreteness but not vitality and action."[133] The Image was static, not stable.

Pound's original commitment to space and stability, as against time and flux, hardened during his subsequent Vorticist phase, and it became a central and notable feature of difference between the original concept of the Imagists and of the Vorticists, as opposed to the Futurists, the "Amygists," and the Georgians.

It was, then, at the very moment that these issues were "in the air," and creating a considerable turbulence there, that Lawrence—at the invitation of Amy Lowell—entered the Imagist sphere. It was just at this time, too, that Lawrence's differences with the Georgians (his dispute with Edward Marsh had ended in December 1913) needed the confirmation of a supporting milieu which stood in opposition to the Georgian sensibility.

The Imagists stood firmly against the Georgians in most aesthetic particulars, although Pound, of course, felt that the original
group was lapsing back toward a kind of Georgian prolixity under
Amy Lowell's direction. The remaining members of the group,
however, maintained their earlier opinions of the Georgians.
Richard Aldington, for instance, felt that the Georgians were too
insular and provincial. They were, he would later write, "regional
in their outlook and in love with littleness. They took a little trip for
a little week-end to a little cottage where they wrote a little poem on
a little theme."[134] He complained, too, of their developing coterie
spirit:

> If one ventured a mild disapproval of the poetry of one of their innum-
> erable friends, the answer invariably was:
> "Oh, but he's *such* a nice fellow."
> So what?[135]

It can, and should, be said, however, that the Imagists (and later
the Vorticists) were in some ways simply an extreme fulfillment of
certain Georgian innovations and preoccupations: mainly, the desire to find and express a reality anterior to the flux of passing time.
Gordon Bottomley's declaration that his poetic "business has
seemed to be to look for the essentials of life, the part that does not
change,"[136] seems simply a slack formulation of significant Imagist-
Vorticist notions. In fact, the entire Georgian program, such as it
was, is similar in many ways to the major concerns expressed by
the Vorticists and the Imagists. But the Georgians' insistence on
finding an unchanging reality in major cosmic rhythms—night and
day, death and life, the procession of the seasons—as well as their
clear debt to the Romantic, projecting ego of Wordsworth, and
their subordination of the Image to narrative, all served to implicate
them in a sentimental and imprecise observance of "every form that
poetry of a former condition of life, no longer existing, has foisted
upon us."[137] Their values remained temporal, not spatial, and committed them to what T. E. Hulme called "the messiness and confusion of nature and natural things."[138]

Lawrence would continue to write from a world view that was
"highly Wordsworthian in its emphasis on organic relatedness to
nature."[139] But, like Keats, he objected to the "egotistical sublime,"
the continual projection of the ego onto the landscape, and he
recognized that it was no longer possible for him. For Wordsworth,

the fundamental themes of his culture, and therefore part of his own sense of self, were related to nature and to the landscape. When he described nature, claims David Perkins,

> the orchestrated culture of the age was summoned to mind. . . . When Wordsworth wrote about daffodils, he was invoking a hundred years of religious thought and feeling that had increasingly nourished intuitions of God in nature. . . . But when a Georgian poet wrote about daffodils, he was invoking only Romantic poetry.[140]

In any case, such was the context when Lawrence first appeared at Imagist—by this time "Amygist"—proceedings on 30 July 1914. Richard Aldington remembers the

> moment the door opened, and a tall slim young man, with bright red hair and the most brilliant blue eyes, came in with a lithe, springing step. . . .
> As guest of honour Lawrence sat next to Amy, and they made a curious contrast, if only because one was so lean and the other so plump. Probably Fletcher and H. D. appreciated more than I did the spectacle of the coal miner's son sitting at the right hand of a Lowell. . . .
> Amy came out well that evening. There was not a trace of condescension in her and she did a difficult thing well—she expressed her warm admiration for Lawrence's work without flattery or insincerity and without embarrassing him.[141]

This meeting of Imagists was "as notable for its success as the earlier one for its failure."[142] Lawrence wrote to Harriet Monroe—ironically, a contact from the days of Pound's influence—the next day:

> I was at dinner with Miss Lowell and the Aldingtons last night, and we had some poetry. But, my dear God, when I see all the understanding and suffering and the pure intelligence necessary for the simple perceiving of poetry, then I know it is an almost hopeless business to publish the stuff at all, and particularly in magazines. It must stand by, and wait and wait. So I don't urge anybody to publish me.[143]

Despite Lawrence's (slightly sarcastic) doubts, the upshot of the whole affair was that Lawrence was, indeed, published. In *Some Imagist Poets* (1915), edited by Lowell, there are seven of Lawrence's poems, as well as contributions from Aldington, H. D., John Gould Fletcher, F. S. Flint, and Lowell herself. Of Lawrence's poems that were included in the volume, only two—"Green" and "Ballad of Another Ophelia"—now seem to have been written in the Imagist, or even "Amygist," mode. His "Wedding Morn" was not included, although it was the opening lines of that poem,

> The morning breaks like a pomegranate
> In a shining crack of red . . .[144]

that Lowell used to counter Lawrence's objection that he was not really an Imagist. Still, for Lowell, unlike Pound, it was not so important for Lawrence to manifest Imagist leanings in order to be included in *Some Imagist Poets*.[145] Lawrence, claims Stanley Coffman, was "an Imagist only by courtesy of others."[146] Lowell, after all, had been able to replace Pound with Lawrence, and at the same time gather in a writer whom she considered more promising than Pound, one whose later work might shed glory and publicity on the movement which she now directed.[147] This did not happen, at least immediately; in fact, Lowell found herself in the position of having to defend Lawrence against hostile criticism quite soon after his entrance into the Imagist milieu.

The relationship between Lawrence and various members of the group—particularly Lowell, Aldington, and H. D.—continued and heightened in intensity during subsequent years. Lowell's biographer, Jean Gould, reports that "some of Lawrence's most perceptive, diverting, and delightful prose is to be found in his letters to Amy Lowell. In the correspondence files of the Lowell collection at the Houghton Library of Harvard University are fifty-five letters testifying to his art, his understanding of Amy's psyche, and the felicitous, enduring literary friendship which began with the dinner at the Berkeley Hotel."[148] Their relationship, curiously free of tension, was based on "loyalty and sympathetic understanding."[149] Lawrence himself, in a letter written in 1920, mentions the "odd congenital understanding"[150] between them.

For her part, Lowell continued to publish Lawrence's work—in the Imagist anthologies for 1916 and 1917, for instance—and to discuss it in various places in which he was otherwise unlikely to get a hearing. In one lecture, "Imagism Past and Present," which she delivered at the Brooklyn Institute in 1918, Lowell declared that Lawrence

> has no prototype that I can find. He is a poet of sensation, but of sensation as the bodily efflorescence of a spiritual growth. Other poets

have given us sensuous images; other poets have spoken of love as chiefly desire; but in no other poet does desire seem so surely "the outward and visible form of an inward and spiritual grace." . . . I do not hesitate to declare Mr. Lawrence to be a man of genius. He does not quite get his genius into harness; the cart of his work frequently overturns or goes awry; but it is no less Pegasus who draws it.[151]

Lawrence nevertheless maintained a certain objectivity toward her work. In November 1914, one of Lowell's poems in the War Number of *Poetry* enraged him. He wrote to Harriet Monroe:

It put me into such a rage—how dare Amy talk about bohemian glass and stalks of flame?—that in a real fury I had to write my war poem, because it breaks my heart, this war.
    I hate, and hate, and hate the glib irreverence of some of your contributors.[152]

And in 1916, he wrote in a letter to A. W. McLeod what must probably stand as his final word on Lowell:

I send you my copy of the Imagists' anthology from America. . . . I think H. D. is good: none of the others worth anything. Amy Lowell is James Russell Lowell's daughter [*sic*]. She is not a good poetess, I think. But she is a very good friend.[153]

Lawrence's relationship with H. D. was more interesting; he admired both her and her poetry. Richard Aldington, who was married to H. D. in 1917, has even declared that "Lawrence was for a time influenced by H. D."[154] The evidence of such an influence is, at best, slim, and Aldington does not elaborate his claim. Still, of all the Imagists, including Pound, H. D. was manifestly Lawrence's favorite.

It is their personal relationship, however, which is particularly intriguing. H. D.'s autobiographical novel, *Bid Me to Live*, makes a number of interesting suggestions, including, as Harry T. Moore has noted, "that Frieda tried to encourage Lawrence to make love to H. D. so that Frieda herself could have an affair with [Cecil] Gray, with whom, in actuality, H. D. ran away."[155] More interesting perhaps is that Lawrence (Rico in the novel) quite literally dominates *Bid Me to Live*. Much of the book is a passionate paean to Lawrence; even though the main issue of the volume is H. D.'s separation from Aldington, the last chapter is clearly directed to Lawrence. There she makes her separate peace with him, while always recognizing his genius. "Even if I don't agree with you, or don't like what you're saying," she says to Lawrence, "I know that the genius is there."[156] For H. D., Lawrence was "part of the cerebral burning, part of the inspiration";[157] if it cannot be said with certainty that Lawrence was influenced by H. D., it can be said that H. D. was influenced, perhaps even obsessed, by Lawrence.

The Imagist aesthetic discipline, although it does not seem to have radically altered Lawrence's art, buttressed certain notions that were in the process of formation during those years. Imagism also, it appears, provided Lawrence with a new way of talking about poetry—a way that he had been struggling to discover during his long epistolary debate with Edward Marsh.

In "Poetry of the Present" (1918), for instance, Lawrence sounds the Imagist bell while maintaining his characteristic independence. The voice of "Poetry of the Present" is certainly Lawrence's voice, but it nevertheless echoes a number of Imagist tenets and obsessions. The "rare new poetry,"[158] *vers libre*, must insist on its "own *nature*, . . . neither star nor pearl, but instantaneous like plasm."[159]

> It is the instant; the quick; the very jetting source of all will-be and has-been. The utterance is like a spasm, naked contact with all influences at once. It does not want to get anywhere. It just takes place.
>
> For such utterance any externally-applied law would be mere shackles and death. The law must come new each time from within.[160]

Poetry should look neither to the past nor the future, it should be the "sheer appreciation of the instant moment, life surging itself into utterance at its very well-head."[161]

> Give me nothing fixed, set, static. Don't give me the infinite or the eternal: nothing of infinity, nothing of eternity. Give me the still, white seething, the incandescence and the coldness of the incarnate moment: the moment, the quick of all change and haste and opposition: the moment, the immediate present, the Now.[162]

One hears in this text the reverberations of earlier battles, fought mainly by the Imagists on behalf of *vers libre*; one also recalls the Imagists' insistence on the instantaneous illumination of the present, and their suspicion of those ideas and emotions which, as Hulme said, "are grouped round the word infinite."[163] This was a particularly significant notion, and one with which all of the Imagists agreed. Richard Aldington, for instance, felt that this was the central idea behind the title of the movement itself:

> I think it [Des Imagistes] a very good and descriptive title, and it serves to enunciate some of the principles we most firmly believe in. It cuts us away from the "cosmic" crowd and it equally bars us off from the "abstract art" gang, and it annoys quite a lot of fools.[164]

Pound once cautioned Harriet Monroe to "damn the infinities, and the unendings, and the eternals! . . . Mistrust any poet using the word *cosmic.*"[165]

When "Poetry of the Present" is seen in the context of Lawrence's controversy with Edward Marsh and the Georgians, his fleeting connections but conceptual affinity with the Imagists (and Vorticists), and the implications of his own work during the period in question, it begins to take its decent place as a significant document in the swirling poetic controversies of the era.

Lawrence's letters also give evidence of his Imagist connections. In 1916, he wrote to Catherine Carswell:

> The essence of poetry with us in this age of stark and unlovely actualities is a stark directness, without a shadow of a lie, or a shadow of deflection anywhere. Everything can go, but this stark, bare, rocky directness of statement, this alone makes poetry, today.[166]

Such a statement would have been perfectly acceptable to Pound, as well as a confirmation of T. E. Hulme's early claim in "Romanticism and Classicism," one of the most important proto-Imagist documents: "I prophesy," said Hulme, "that a period of dry, hard, classical verse is coming."[167]

Lawrence's contact with Imagism and the Imagists was more direct and frequent than with any other literary milieu except, perhaps, the Georgians. Nevertheless, if Imagism is understood to be a manifestation of ideas and obsessions which were "in the air" during 1912 through 1914, it cannot be said to have had the impact on Lawrence that, say, Georgianism and Futurism had on him. It was far too limited in its scope to satisfy Lawrence. Futurism and Vorticism, much more than Imagism, revealed the essential features of the prewar *Zeitgeist*; they were the nodes in which innumerable ideas and feelings came together and surfaced. Unlike Imagism, Futurism and Vorticism were not so much expressions of a new aesthetic as they were spiritual and social manifestations.

Their roots are to be sought apart from art alone. Both were expressions, albeit extravagant ones, of genuinely fresh and creative energies that aimed to transform men as well as art. Lawrence never thought of anything else for long. One remembers, again, Lawrence's statement of intention of 1913: "I do write because I want folk—English folk—to alter, and have more sense."[168]

Wallace Stevens once observed that "not all objects are equal. The vice of imagism was that it did not recognize this."[169] Lawrence, who excoriated Joyce and Proust on similar grounds, no doubt observed this about his Imagist colleagues. It was always an important aspect of his art to differentiate meaningful experiences from others which were not so meaningful; the Imagist aesthetic, which continually referred only to itself for meaning, stopped far short of the scope necessary to alter English folk. Despite its reasonably successful attempt to create a voice for modern life, Imagism, like so much of the modern literature that it provoked, seems often "to exist in a vacuum, to spring from no particular society and to address no particular audience."[170]

In summary, then, Lawrence does not seem to have learned anything from Imagism that he had not been able to learn from his own development during these years—from his life with Frieda, his own work, his exercise in self-examination with Edward Marsh, his encounters with Futurism and with Thomas Hardy. There was, finally, nothing unique to Imagism that he needed to discover which could not have been assimilated, and probably was, from other sources.

Imagism did, however, give needed conceptual support to the direction in which he was already moving—as his later statements on the nature of poetry clearly suggest—and the Imagist milieu did provide him with an intellectually tough alternative to his still active Georgian fantasies. At the end of Lawrence's "transition stage" was, finally, something much more like Vorticism than Imagism, even though his contact with specific Imagists was infinitely more frequent and direct than it was with the Vorticists. Still, Lawrence, like Pound, must be seen as having passed through Imagism as a necessary phase of development, before moving on to a more comprehensive understanding of his art and his purpose.

7 Good-bye to All That: The Georgians, the War, and "England, My England"

Georgians and War: The Example of Rupert Brooke

"England, My England" is Lawrence's Parthian shot at both the Georgians and the England for which the Georgians stood. It is the fable of a failed Georgian; more precisely, perhaps, it is a fable about why Georgianism failed. It is, like so many of Lawrence's novels and tales, generated out of opposition, a final rejection notice to those with whom he had happily traveled only a short time before. In "England, My England," Lawrence glimpses the inner pattern, the hidden agenda, of Georgianism and says, in effect, "This is where your principles will lead. I will not be trapped there with you."

The story presents in fictive terms the pattern that Lawrence felt was manifesting itself in the war. The Georgian spirit had become flaccid and sentimental on the surface, nihilistic underneath. Like England itself, the Georgians entered the war with infinite cheerfulness or stoic acceptance, some—such as Rupert Brooke—because of their desire to throw off what they felt was a stifling and moribund culture, and others—such as Edward Marsh, who worked as Winston Churchill's secretary in the War Office—because of a misdirected sense of responsibility.

The same spirit that had embraced the primitive and the elemental now embraced the coming of the war. Rupert Brooke's diffident response upon hearing the declaration—"Well, if Armageddon's *on*, I suppose one should be there"[1]—soon developed into the delirious enthusiasm displayed by most of his friends and countrymen. The poems that Brooke wrote in 1914 (to be sure, long before the full horror of the war was known to anyone) express his feeling that the

war was somehow a solution to the malaise into which Britain had
fallen:

> Now, God be thanked Who has matched us with His hour,
>   And caught our youth, and wakened us from sleeping,
> With hand made sure, clear eye, and sharpened power,
>   To turn, as swimmers into cleanness leaping,
> Glad from a world grown old and cold and weary,
>   Leave the sick hearts that honour could not move,
> And half-men, and their dirty songs and dreary,
>   And all the little emptiness of love!²

Brooke hoped that the war would somehow revitalize life, even
more, that it would reinvest it with those very modes of being
which had come to seem more possible in the South Seas than in
England. The elemental vitality which stirred in more primitive
cultures, as well as the purifying literary and artistic violence of the
Futurists and Vorticists, was now to be found on every street
corner. Allegiance to some notion of England—and Brooke no
doubt hoped that it would be a notion similar to his own—again
took on that compulsive force which, if not looked at too closely,
resembles the intimacy of the community.

> Blow, bugles, blow! They brought us, for our dearth,
>   Holiness, lacked so long, and Love, and Pain.
> Honour has come back, as a king, to earth,
>   And paid his subjects with a royal wage;
> And Nobleness walks in our ways again;
>   And we have come into our heritage.³

"Holiness," "Honour," "Nobleness": Brooke's diction suggests
what Paul Fussell has described as the "collision . . . between
events and the public language used for over a century to celebrate
the idea of progress."⁴ Brooke's use of the word *holiness* to describe
what the war had brought, and what he felt had been "lacked so
long," is suggestive not only of his own feelings, but also of the
feelings of the Georgians as a whole. In *Letters from America*, Brooke
uses *holiness* to generate an entire pattern of associative images,
mostly rural, gentle and—for lack of a better word—Forsterian,
which describe what he, along with the other Georgians, had insisted upon as the only alternative for a culture gone rotten with
commercialism and industry.

He [Brooke is writing of "a friend," who is astonishingly similar to Brooke himself] was immensely surprised to perceive that the actual earth of England held for him a quality which he found in A——, and in a friend's honour, and scarcely anywhere else, a quality which, if he'd ever been sentimental enough to use the word, he'd have called "holiness." His astonishment grew as the full flood of "England" swept him on from thought to thought. He felt the triumphant helplessness of a lover. Grey, uneven little fields, and small, ancient hedges rushed before him, wild flowers, elms and beeches, gentleness, sedate houses of red brick, proudly unassuming, a countryside of rambling hills and friendly copses. He seemed to be raised high, looking down on a landscape compounded of the western view from the Cotswolds, and the Weald, and the high land in Wiltshire, and the Midlands seen from the hills above Prince's Risborough. . . . And continually he seemed to see the set of a mouth which he knew for his mother's, and A——'s face, and, inexplicably, the face of an old man he had once passed in a Warwickshire village. To his great disgust, the most commonplace sentiments found utterance in him. At the same time he was extraordinarily happy.[5]

The world for which the Georgians had written was smashed in 1914, as was the world for which they had wished. The fine, gently heroic figures who populate the poems of Brooke and Davies, as well as the yeoman heroes of Forster's *Howards End*, had become worse than valueless; they had, for Lawrence, become dangerous. By 1915, Lawrence had come to believe not only that the Georgian sensibility allowed participation in the war, but that it was also deeply implicated in the war's cause. "They are fools, and vulgar fools, and cowards who will always make a noise because they are afraid of silence," Lawrence wrote to Gordon Campbell.

I don't even mind if they're killed. But I do mind those who, being sensitive, will receive such a blow from the ghastliness and mechanical, obsolete, hideous stupidity of war, that they will be crippled beings further burdening our sick society. Those that die, let them die. But those that live afterwards—the thought of them makes me sick.[6]

When Brooke himself died in 1915, Lawrence, playing off the myth that had already grown up around the "soldier-poet," wrote of him:

The death of Rupert Brooke fills me more and more with the sense of the fatuity of it all. He was slain by bright Phoebus' shaft—it was in keeping with his general sunniness—*it was the real climax of his pose*. I first heard of him as a Greek god under a Japanese sunshade, reading poetry in his pyjamas, at Grantchester,—at Grantchester upon the lawns where the river goes. Bright Phoebus smote him down. It is all in the saga.

O God, O God, it is all too much of a piece: it is like madness.[7] [Italics mine]

And Brooke's pose, Lawrence felt, was part of a larger loss of integrity. After some time spent with some soldiers at Bodmin, he wrote:

> . . . I liked the men. They all seemed so *decent*. And yet they all seemed as if they had *chosen wrong*. It was the underlying sense of disaster that overwhelmed me. They are all so brave, to suffer, but none of them brave enough, to reject suffering. They are all so noble, to accept sorrow and hurt, but they can none of them demand happiness. Their manliness all lies in accepting calmly this death, this loss of their integrity. They must stand by their fellow man: that is the motto. . . .
>
> This is the most terrible madness. And the worst of it all, is, that it is a madness of righteousness. . . . Yet they accepted it all: they accepted it, as one of them said to me, with wonderful purity of spirit—I could howl my eyes out over him—because "they believed first of all in their duty to their fellow man." . . . So we toil in a circle of pure egoism.[8]

To the war poet, Robert Nichols,* he wrote, "The courage of death is *no courage* any more: *the courage to die has become a vice.*"[9]

By the time Lawrence wrote "England, My England," he clearly felt that sentimentality, the thoughtless indulgence of emotional energy, the denial of spiritual responsibility, and the inability to "fulfil that which is *really* in us"[10]—all Georgian weaknesses, according to Lawrence—had become the source of most human evil.

---

*It is no accident that most of the best-known war poets—Owen, Sassoon, Graves, Blunden, and Edward Thomas—were to become, in one way or another, closely associated with the Georgian group. This came about partially because of the war poets' use of the English countryside as a symbolic (and actual) contrast to the horror of the trenches, as well as the central image of the England for which they thought they were fighting. Sassoon, for instance, recalls that in the midst of a German barrage, he was "meditating about England, visualizing a grey day down in Sussex; dark green woodlands with pigeons circling above the tree-tops; dogs barking, cocks crowing, and all the casual tappings and twinklings of the countryside. . . . It was for all that, I supposed, that I was in the front-line with soaked feet, trench mouth, and feeling short of sleep" (Siegfried Sassoon, *Memoirs of an Infantry Officer*, p. 69). Wilfred Owen, who never lived to see his association with the Georgians made explicit, wrote on New Year's Eve, 1917: "I go out of this year a Poet, my dear Mother, as which I did not enter it. I am held peer by the Georgians; I am a poet's poet" (Harold Owen and John Bell, eds., *The Collected Letters of Wilfred Owen*, p. 521).

> One should stick by one's own soul, and by nothing else. In one's soul, one knows the truth from the untruth, and life from death. And if one betrays one's own soul-knowledge one is the worst of traitors.[11]

As an artist, Lawrence felt that it was his business to seek out and expose the traitorous soul, to follow the war

> home to the heart of the individual fighters—not to talk in armies and nations and numbers—but to track it home—home—their war—and it's at the bottom of almost every Englishman's heart—the war—the desire of war—the *will* to war—and at the bottom of every German's.[12]

"England, My England"

"England, My England" has for its hero a prototypical Georgian who refuses the responsibility for his own life, and it is made, as one critic has noted, of "materials which could be viewed historically as Georgian melancholy pastoral."[13] Perhaps more thoroughly than anything else he wrote, "England, My England" combines Lawrence's desire to "get to the bottom of almost every Englishman's heart" with his opposition to the specific cultural direction that he felt was being taken by the Georgians.

"England, My England" (see Appendix B) begins with a landscape: the "shaggy wildness"[14] that surrounds Egbert and Winifred's cottage in Hampshire. Essentially, it is the kind of primitive landscape that had haunted writers such as Hardy and Conrad (and would later haunt Wells in *The Croquet Player*), and that would become progressively more important to Lawrence.

> Strange how the savage England lingers in patches: as here, amid these shaggy gorse commons, and marshy, snake-infested places near the foot of the South Downs. The spirit of place lingering on primeval, as when the Saxons came, so long ago.[15]

> That was Crockham. The spear of modern invention had not passed through it, and it lay there secret, primitive, savage as when the Saxons first came. And Egbert and she were caught there, caught out of the world.[16]

As in *The White Peacock* and *The Rainbow*, much of what we are to make of the characters in the story depends upon their relationship with the landscape they inhabit. In "England, My England" we first discover Egbert working at the edge of the common, attempting to cut a garden path.

> He had cut the rough turf and bracken, leaving the grey, dryish soil bare. But he was worried because he could not get the path straight, there was a pleat between his brows. He had set up his sticks, and taken the sights between the big pine trees, but for some reason everything seemed wrong.[17]

Everything seems wrong because Egbert refuses to confront the reality of the landscape that surrounds him; he tries instead to make the landscape conform to his notion of what it should be. Egbert wants to make the essentially savage, snake-infested reality of Crockham part of his "living romance."[18]

> Ah, how he loved it! The green garden path, the tufts of flowers, purple and white columbines, and great Oriental red poppies with their black chaps and mulleins tall and yellow: this flamy garden which had been a garden for a thousand years, scooped out in the little hollow among the snake-infested commons. He had made it flame with flowers, in a sun-cup under its hedges and trees. So old, so old a place! And yet he had re-created it.
>
> The timbered cottage with its sloping, cloak-like roof was old and forgotten. It belonged to the old England of hamlets and yeomen. Lost all alone on the edge of the common, at the end of a wide, grassy briar-entangled lane shaded with oak, it had never known the world of to-day. Not till Egbert came with his bride. And he had come to fill it with flowers.[19]

The attempt to fill wildness with flowers may well be commendable for one of E. M. Forster's characters, but Lawrence clearly wants us to understand that to attempt to sweeten the truth is tantamount to a failure to recognize it. And such a failure is dangerous. One recalls the charges which he had leveled at Abercrombie in 1914: "There's something wrong with his soul."[20]

Later, when Egbert's various failures trap him between the combined effects of Godfrey's power, Winifred's duty, and the "marsh-venomous atmosphere"[21] of the landscape, he is thrown back onto his own resources and finds that he has none. The landscape, the "savage old spirit of the place,"[22] then has its way with him. It becomes both a cause and a reflection of Egbert's ultimate dissolution, and at the same time it suggests the elemental savagery which always lies just under the surface—ready to re-establish primacy whenever men refuse to take the responsibility for their own lives.

Egbert's nostalgic dream of a purer past, the old England recreated with flowers, is shown to be the surface to a "deeper nihilism and a longing for death."[23]

Egbert himself is a dilettante, "an amateur—a born amateur."[24] He loves "the past, the old music and dances and customs of old England"[25] and, like his "ineffectual"[26] friends in London (one thinks here of The Poetry Bookshop), he tampers with "the arts, literature, painting, sculpture, music."[27] He is not absolutely contemptible, nor is he weak. But, as F. R. Leavis has remarked, the theme of his tale is, in part, "the impossibility of making a *life* with no more than this."[28]

> No, it was not that he didn't earn money. It was not that he was idle. He was *not* idle. He was always doing something, always working away, down at Crockham, doing little jobs. But, oh dear, the little jobs—the garden paths—the gorgeous flowers—the chairs to mend, old chairs to mend!
> It was that he stood for nothing. . . .
> He, the higher, the finer, in his way the stronger, played with his garden, and his old folk-songs and Morris dances, just played.[29]

The central incident in the story, his daughter's crippling fall on a sickle that Egbert had "left lying about after cutting the grass,"[30] comes as a direct result of Egbert's dilettantism. It is precisely the kind of thing that would come from the "living romance" of his life, from "playing" at things instead of working at them. Egbert did not, indeed could not, recognize "the difference between work and romance."[31]

> He worked so hard, and did so little, and nothing he ever did would hold together for long. . . . He had not been brought up to come to grips with anything, and he thought it would do. Nay, he did not think there was anything else except little temporary contrivances possible, he who had such a passion for his old enduring cottage, and for the old enduring things of the bygone England. Curious that the sense of permanency in the past had such a hold over him, whilst in the present he was all amateurish and sketchy.[32]

As *Women in Love* makes clear, there are no accidents for Lawrence. So, the amateurish sketchiness that has been shown to be the dominant pattern of Egbert's life also determines his response to his daughter's fall.

He had taken his handkerchief and tied it round the knee. Then he lifted the still sobbing child in his arms, and carried her into the house and upstairs to her bed. In his arms she became quiet. But his heart was burning with pain and with guilt. He had left the sickle there lying on the edge of the grass, and so his first-born child whom he had loved so dearly had come to hurt. But then it was an accident—it was an accident. Why should he feel guilty? It would probably be nothing, better in two or three days. Why take it to heart, why worry? He put it aside.[33]

Here, made explicit for the first time, Egbert refuses responsibility. The guilt is there, but the force of responsibility is absent.

He could not help feeling that Winifred was laying it on rather. Surely the knee itself wasn't hurt! Surely not. It was only a surface cut.[34]

Egbert's inability to assume responsibility for the seriousness of his daughter's injury soon leads, as irresponsibility usually does in Lawrence, to crisis.

Egbert's relationship with Winifred is, from the beginning, marked by the same absence of direction. They were "a beautiful couple";[35] she "loved him, this southerner, as a higher being"[36] and he "loved her in a passion with every fibre of him"[37]—but their relationship is purely sensual, the stuff of romance. Crockham itself, "caught out of the world" and paid for by her father, feeds their illusion.

He worked away, in his shirt-sleeves, worked all day intermittently doing this thing and the other. And she, quiet and rich in herself, seeing him stooping and labouring away by himself, would come to help him, to be near him. . . .

Town-bred, everything seemed to her splendid, and the very digging and shovelling itself seemed romantic.[38]

Throughout the early part of the story, Lawrence even suggests that Egbert and Winifred "collected" each other like curios, much as both are interested in collecting the curios and customs of the past. Winifred, for instance, is described as part of the landscape— "a red-flowered bush in motion,"[39] with "hawthorn robustness,"[40] etc.—and it is appropriate that her marriage portion is, in fact, the old English land that Egbert hopes to recreate and fill up with flowers. Even Joyce, the daughter, is described as being a "wild little daisy-spirit,"[41] a "light little cowslip child. She was like a little poem in herself."[42]

But the life of romance, no matter how superficially pleasant, exacts its price. When Joyce is born, romance recedes, and Egbert can generate nothing to take its place.

> After the child was born, it was never quite the same between him and Winifred. The difference was at first hardly perceptible. But it was there. In the first place Winifred had a new centre of interest. . . . The responsibility of motherhood was the prime responsibility in Winifred's heart: the responsibility of wifehood came a long way second. . . .
>
> Her husband—? Yes, she loved him still. But that was like play.[43]

And after Joyce is injured, Winifred stops playing altogether. "She had what the modern mother so often has in the place of spontaneous love: a profound sense of duty towards her child,"[44] and her sense of duty throws her back into the sturdy, protective arms of her father. Just as Egbert represents the spirit of Georgian England in decay, Godfrey Marshall represents the older, "robust and Christmassy,"[45] Victorian England. In the Georgian milieu, the Victorian father figure may no longer dominate the foreground, but he is still powerful and responsible—"the pillar, the source of life, the everlasting support."[46]

> In his own small circle he would emanate power, the single power of his own blind self. With all his spoiling of his children, he was still the father of the old English type. He was too wise to make laws and to domineer in the abstract. But he had kept, and all honour to him, a certain primitive dominion over the souls of his children, the old, almost magic prestige of paternity. There it was, still burning in him, the old smoky torch of paternal godhead.[47]

By making the Marshalls Catholic, Lawrence suggests the power of tradition and certainty at Godfrey Marshall's back, which gives sanction to his actions. Lawrence does not exactly commend Godfrey and his "will-to-power"[48] to us, but he does suggest that there is at least *something there*, and that it is solid where Egbert's tradition is mere paste.

That "something" expresses itself in immediate action and firm direction. When Godfrey, "implacable in his responsibility,"[49] directs Joyce and Winifred to London, Egbert is left behind, "bareheaded and a little ignominious."[50] Alone and "out of it,"[51]

Egbert begins to submit to the blank actuality of his life, to the principle which he had heretofore denied:

> Then with the empty house around him at night, all the empty rooms, he felt his heart go wicked. The sense of frustration and futility, like some slow, torpid snake, slowly bit right through his heart. Futility, futility, futility: the horrible marsh-poison went through his veins and killed him. . . .
>
> His heart went back to the savage old spirit of the place: the desire for old gods, old, lost passions, the passion of the cold-blooded, darting snakes that hissed and shot away from him, the mystery of blood-sacrifices, all the lost, intense sensations of the primeval people of the place, whose passions seethed in the air still, from those long days before the Romans came. The seethe of a lost, dark passion in the air. The presence of unseen snakes.[52]

But for Egbert, as for Rupert Brooke and Georgian England itself, the war arrives in time to give purpose—however savage—to his sense of "frustration and futility." Brooke himself provides an instructive comparison. In his letters of 1914, Brooke repeatedly declares that before the war he had been unsure of the aim and purpose of his life. But in November 1914, he writes: "The central purpose of my life, the aim and end of it, now, the thing God wants of me, is to get good at beating Germans. That's sure."[53] To G. Lowes Dickinson, a man surely unsympathetic to Brooke's wartime avidity, he says, "I hope you don't think me very reactionary and callous for taking up this function of England. There shouldn't be war—but what's to be done, but fight Prussia? . . . I wish everyone I know were fighting."[54]

It is precisely this kind of claim—soldiering as a "function of England," the invocation of God as justification, the desire for what Lawrence himself calls "this terrible glamour of camaraderie"[55]—that finally reveals the moral cowardice which Lawrence perceives at "the bottom of almost every Englishman's heart."

Still, Egbert does not feel, at first, like one of Brooke's "swimmers into cleanness leaping"; he is, in fact, indifferent.

> Egbert was well-bred, and this was part of his natural understanding. It was merely unnatural to him to hate a nation *en bloc.* Certain individuals he disliked, and others he liked, and the mass he knew nothing about. Certain deeds he disliked, certain deeds seemed natural to him, and about most deeds he had no particular feeling. . . .[56]

And yet, war! War! Just war! Not right or wrong, but just war itself. Should he join? Should he give himself over to war? The question was in his mind for some weeks. Not because he thought England was right and Germany wrong. Probably Germany was wrong, but he refused to make a choice. Not because he felt inspired. No. But just—war.[57]

Egbert's "natural understanding" disallows even the *possibility* of responsible choice, but his situation demands that he must break from the pattern established during his leisurely days of romance; he can no longer refuse "to reckon with the world."[58] There is in him nothing like the crude, yet positive, power that drives Godfrey; there is only the baffling, wicked savagery that emanates from the landscape at Crockham. Godfrey, of course, "whose soul was quick with the instinct of power,"[59] can reckon with the world—and does. To join the army, he tells Egbert, "is the best thing you could do."[60]

Egbert joins immediately, subjecting himself to another power—equally ignominious—"the power of the mob-spirit of a democratic army."[61]

In the ugly intimacy of the camp his thoroughbred sensibilities were just degraded. But he had chosen, so he accepted. An ugly little look came on to his face, of a man who has accepted his own degradation.[62]

Lawrence's intense feelings about the "mob-spirit" are well known. The army generated in Lawrence an entirely new set of images, images which are perhaps raised to their highest pitch in the famous "Nightmare" chapter of *Kangaroo*. The point of the chapter, as Neil Myers has correctly observed, "is not that Lawrence's expression of outrage is vulgarly direct, but that it is appropriate to what evokes it."[63] The same nightmare visions appear again and again in his stories, in *Women in Love,* and in his letters of the period.

Yesterday, at Worthing, there were many soldiers. Can I ever tell you how ugly they were. "To insects—sensual lust." I like sensual lust—but insectwise, no—it is obscene. I like men to be beasts—but insects—one insect mounted on another—oh God! The soldiers at Worthing are like that—they remind me of lice or bugs: "to insects—sensual lust." They will murder their officers one day. They are teeming insects. What massive creeping hell is let loose nowadays.

It isn't my disordered imagination. There is a wagtail sitting on the gate-post. I see how sweet and swift heaven is. But hell is slow and creeping and viscous and insect-teeming: as is this Europe now, this England.[64]

And again:

> But it was a great shock, that barracks experience—that being escorted by train, lined up on station platforms, marched like a criminal through the streets to a barracks. The ignominy is horrible, the humiliation. And even this terrible glamour of camaraderie, which is the glamour of Homer and of all militarism, is a decadence, a degradation, a losing of individual form and distinction, a merging in a sticky male mass.[65]

What is essential here, though, at least as it relates to "England, My England," is Lawrence's insistence that joining the "mob-spirit" reveals a "deeper sense of catastrophe."[66] The process which inexorably leads Egbert to the "mob-spirit" and to war derives from his individual inadequacy and futility; Egbert must inevitably reveal himself to be, in Kingsley Widmer's phrase, a "Georgian hero of ineffectual sensitivity demanding universal destruction."[67]

Egbert's death in the trenches explicitly reveals his underlying destructive impulse:

> Were they stars in the dark sky? Was it possible it was stars in the dark sky? Stars? The world? Ah, no, he could not know it! Stars and the world were gone for him, he closed his eyes. No stars, no sky, no world. No, no! The thick darkness of blood alone. It should be one great lapse into the thick darkness of blood in agony.
>
> Death, oh, death! The world all blood, and the blood all writhing with death. The soul like the tiniest little light out on a dark sea, the sea of blood. And the light guttering, beating, pulsing in a windless storm, wishing it could go out, yet unable.
>
> There had been life. There had been Winifred and his children. But the frail death-agony effort to catch at straws of memory, straws of life from the past, brought on too great a nausea. No, no! No Winifred, no children. No world, no people. Better the agony of dissolution ahead than the nausea of the effort backwards. Better the terrible work should go forward, the dissolving into the black sea of death, in the extremity of dissolution, than that there should be any reaching back towards life. To forget! To forget! Utterly, utterly to forget, in the great forgetting of death. To break the core and the unit of life, and to lapse out on the great darkness. Only that. To break the clue, and mingle and commingle with the one darkness, without afterwards or forwards. . . . Let the will of man break and give up.[68]

Once again, Rupert Brooke's letters provide an instructive example of the kind of sensibility which Lawrence condemns in Egbert. In a letter to his Georgian friend, John Drinkwater, Brooke writes:

> On service one has a great feeling of fellowship, and a fine thrill, like nothing else in the world. And I'd not be able to exist, for torment, if I weren't doing it. Not a bad place and time to die, Belgium, 1915? I want to kill my Prussian first. Better than coughing out a civilian soul amid bedclothes and disinfectant and gulping medicines in 1950. The world'll be tame enough after the war, for those that see it. I had hopes that England'ld get on her legs again, achieve youth and merriment, and slough the things I loathe—capitalism and feminism and hermaphroditism and the rest. But on maturer consideration, pursued over muddy miles of Dorset, I think there'll not be much change. What there is for the better, though. Certain sleepers have awoken in the heart.
> Come and die. It'll be great fun.[69]

With Egbert, as with Brooke himself, died much of that for which he stood. It was, perhaps, altogether too appropriate that Winston Churchill used Brooke's name as a rallying cry to send so many other Englishmen to their death in the trenches. Brooke and the Georgians, Lawrence felt, had betrayed that which they had earlier seemed to herald: "a new order, a new earth,"[70] where men could be "happy *together*, in unanimity, not hostility, creating, not destroying."[71]

Lawrence never completely relinquished his belief in the possibility of a "new world," the world he had envisioned at the end of *The Rainbow*. But the Georgian spirit, the very spirit which had helped to give partial shape and vitality to that book, had ultimately revealed itself to be, at best, a "falling back"[72] to the "testimony of the past";[73] at worst, it was a futile gesture leading inevitably to a final dissolution in war and death. "We must have the courage," Lawrence wrote in 1916,

> to cast off the old symbols, the old traditions: at least, put them aside, like a plant in growing surpasses its crowning leaves with higher leaves and buds. There is something beyond the past. The past is no justification. Unless from us the future takes place, we are death only.[74]

And again, in 1917:

> What I did through individuals, the world has done through the war.

But alas, in the world of Europe I see no Rainbow. I believe the deluge of iron rain will destroy the world here, utterly: no Ararat will rise above the subsiding iron waters. There is a great *consummation* in death, or sensual ecstasy, as in the Rainbow. But there is also death which is the rushing of the Gadarine swine down the slope of extinction. And this is the war in Europe. We have chosen our extinction in death, rather than our Consummation. So be it: it is not my fault.[75]

Lawrence apparently hoped that "England, My England" would achieve something worthwhile, even if only in the distant future. In a letter to Catherine Carswell he wrote:

It upsets me very much to hear of [the death in battle of] P[ercy] L[ucas]. I did not know he was dead. I wish that story ["England, My England"] at the bottom of the sea, before ever it had been printed. Yet, it seems to me, man must find a new expression, give a new value to life, or his women will reject him, and he must die. I liked M[adeleine] L[ucas], the best of the M[eynall]s really. She was the one who was capable of honest love: she and M[?]. L[ucas] was, somehow, a spiritual coward. But who isn't? I ought never, never to have gone to live at [Greatham]. Perhaps M[adeleine] L[ucas] won't be hurt by that wretched story—that is all that matters. If it was a true story, it shouldn't really damage.

P. S. . . .

No, I *don't* wish I had never written that story. It should do good, at the long run.[76]

Still, it seems unlikely that Lawrence would have held out too much hope for this. His major intention in writing the story was, after all, something quite different. As he once wrote to S. S. Koteliansky:

My dear Kot, I feel anti-social. I want to blow the wings off these fallen angels. I want to bust 'em up. I feel that everything I do is a shot at these fallen angels of mankind. Wing the brutes.[77]

"England, My England" is one of Lawrence's more pointed attempts to "wing" a functioning center of the British cultural milieu—the Georgians—and it stands as one of his most powerful explosives for satisfying his intention to "lay a mine under their foundations."[78]

8   Extensions and Conclusions

Extensions: Cambridge and Bloomsbury

Many of the elements in the Georgian sensibility that Lawrence had found dangerous and had violently rejected in "England, My England"—the sense of extended adolescence, the underlying lust for war, the failure to confront the reality of a decaying England with the necessary toughness—were crystallized in a more influential form in the Cambridge-Bloomsbury milieu. In some ways, Lawrence's succession of involvements with the Edwardians, the Georgians, the Futurists, and the Imagists inevitably led to his brief, tenuous, but painful connection with Cambridge and Bloomsbury. And, like the associations which have been detailed in the previous chapters, his connection with the Cambridge-Bloomsbury milieu had important consequences for his subsequent work.

Lawrence's entrance into this milieu, so "obviously a civilisation,"[1] as John Maynard Keynes has remarked, was made possible by a new acquaintance—Bertrand Russell. Their relationship was bitter and brief, but it does seem to describe more or less accurately the contours of Lawrence's response to Cambridge-Bloomsbury as a whole.

Lawrence and Russell first met under the aegis of Lady Ottoline Morrell, and they decided to collaborate on a series of speeches against the war and on the direction that England would have to take subsequent to it. Naturally, they differed—"more," said Russell later, "than either differed from the Kaiser."[2] Before their differences became inflamed, however, Russell invited Lawrence to Cambridge to discuss their plans and meet some of his friends, notably Keynes and G. E. Moore. Even before he went, Lawrence realized that his entrance into Russell's world would not be easy.

"You must put off your further knowledge and experience," Lawrence wrote to Russell, and talk to me my way, and be with me, or I feel a babbling idiot and an intruder. My world is real, it is a true world, and it is a world I have in my measure understood. But no doubt you also have a true world, which I can't understand. It makes me sad to conclude that. But you must live in my world, while I am there. Because it is also a real world. And it is a world you can inhabit with me, if I can't inhabit yours with you. . . .[3]

Also I feel frightfully important coming to Cambridge—quite momentous the occasion is to me. I don't want to be horribly impressed and intimidated, but am afraid I may be. I only care about the revolution we shall have. . . . I am afraid of concourses and clans and societies and cliques—not so much of individuals. Truly I am rather afraid.[4]

More potent than his fears, however, was Lawrence's insatiable desire to find a group which could help him establish a new foundation for English life. Paul Delany has noted that "Lawrence's Messianic phase—the time when he imagined himself a prophet called to save England, and to build a new Jerusalem on the ruins of the old"[5]—coincided with the time of Lawrence's intimacy with Russell. Delany probably overstates the case for Lawrence's "Messianic" posture. He bases it far too heavily on a rather literal reading of Lawrence's utopian fantasies, especially Rananim.* Still, what needs to be pointed out here is the extent to which Lawrence persistently desired a connection with the larger world, a connection which had, at least to his eye, access to the traditional centers of power in England. It is no accident that he would attempt to establish such a connection by making contact with another small, relatively isolated intellectual enclave which, at the time, he thought had the potential to join with him in a full-throated onslaught on contemporary English failings. So, five days after he had completed *The Rainbow,* a time during which his vision of a regenerated England had reached its highest pitch, he was breakfasting at Cambridge with Russell and Keynes.

---

*As a political program, Rananim can be taken seriously only at the cost of denying Lawrence a lick of sense. Delany does seem to take it seriously, and consequently finds it, at best, "an agreeable pipedream," and at worst the pitiable thrummings of a politically inept, would-be messiah.

Like the schemes in so many of his novels, Rananim was less important as an actual program for action than as a vortex of significant, if often contradictory, aims and desires which Lawrence—as he always did—built into a concrete image. Rananim, like Birkin's cat "Mino" in *Women in Love*, ultimately fails as an image because it is never more than partially comprehended, a sign inadequate to what it signifies. Rananim is finally crucial to Lawrence only as a symbol, a key fantasy based on his driving impulse toward some notion of community.

That meeting, Lawrence said afterward, "was one of the crises of my life."[6] All that Keynes remembered of it was that Lawrence was "morose from the outset and said very little, apart from indefinite expressions of irritable dissent, all the morning. . . . His reactions were incomplete and unfair, but they were not usually baseless. . . . Lawrence was oblivious of anything valuable [Cambridge] may have offered—it was a *lack* that he was violently apprehending."[7]

Lawrence expressed his feelings about that "lack" when he returned home to Frieda. The men he had met at Cambridge, he told her, "walked up and down the room and talked about the Balkan situation and things like that, and they know nothing about it."[8] In his next letter to Russell, Lawrence declared:

> It is true Cambridge made me very black and down. I cannot bear its smell of rottenness, marsh-stagnancy. I get a melancholic malaria. How can so sick people rise up? They must die first.[9]

Lawrence's subsequent letters to Russell became increasingly peevish and contentious until finally, in September 1915, he writes:

> The enemy of all mankind, you are, full of the lust of enmity. It is *not* the hatred of falsehood which inspires you. It is the hatred of people, of flesh and blood. It is a perverted, mental blood-lust. Why don't you own it.
> Let us become strangers again. I think it is better.[10]

Lawrence had come to feel that Russell was the very image of the rigid, enclosed Englishman whose desire to *know* made it impossible for him to experience new realities. And Russell, who had originally been attracted to Lawrence because of the "energy and passion of his feelings"[11] and who once told Ottoline Morrell that Lawrence was "infallible,"[12] finally came to believe that Lawrence was a "positive force for evil" whose ideas "led straight to Auschwitz."[13]

Lawrence's relationship with Russell now seems to have been destined for failure; it was as inevitable a failure as a relationship between, for instance, William Blake and Jeremy Bentham. As early as February 1915, Lawrence had declared to Russell that "one must fulfil one's vision as much as possible. And the drama shall be between individual men and women, not between nations and classes."[14] Already, then, Lawrence had announced the central difference which would in time shatter their relationship.

Lawrence's response to Russell and, more importantly, to what he thought Russell stood for, hardly seems curious after following Lawrence's progress among the various cultural milieus that constituted England's cultural matrix throughout the years between 1908 and 1915. It becomes even less curious when it is noted that the Georgians had very strong connections with Cambridge. It was at Cambridge that Edward Marsh, whose undergraduate career overlapped with those of Russell and G. E. Moore, first developed and solidified his characteristic habits of mind. Christopher Hassall has observed that "the climate of thought which centred in Moore and Russell in the middle 'nineties found no more characteristic product than Eddie Marsh."[15] Myron Simon has extended the connection to include the entire Georgian circle.

> Like the chief members of the Bloomsbury group, the founders of Georgian poetry were Cambridge men whose religious views were agnostic, whose political views were liberal, whose literary views were anti-Victorian, and whose basic intellectual orientation derived from Russell and Moore. Although scarcely noted heretofore, the contribution of Cambridge to the character of the Georgian movement was decisive.[16]

It needs to be remembered here that at the time Lawrence visited Russell and Keynes at Cambridge, he had just broken free from the Georgian sensibility. He had finally moved beyond the "shadowy and funny" Georgians and poems such as Abercrombie's "The End of the World," where "everything is mean and rather sordid," and which made Lawrence feel that there was "something going bad in [Abercrombie's] soul."[17] He had gone beyond them to let his "demon" see for itself. Lawrence brought this new, hard-won, astringent, Vorticist-like vision, this new belief in the impersonal, to Cambridge, and found it crawling with egos. And what he found at Cambridge was more dangerous than the acquiescent Georgian sensibility because it had its source in the most finely tuned traditions of English intellectual life.

Paul Delany and Quentin Bell have both suggested that Lawrence's intense dislike for the Bloomsbury-Cambridge milieu was elicited as much as anything else by his horror of what came to be called "Bloomsbuggery"—especially as it was represented by John Maynard Keynes. The root of Lawrence's "misery and hostility and rage" at the Cambridge breakfast, says Delany, "was Keynes's homosexuality."[18] It was Cambridge's prevailing homoeroticism, as well as its rationalism and cynicism, Delany notes, that made Lawrence feel "that his hope of enlisting [its] political support was bound to be disappointed."[19] Quentin Bell goes a bit farther, suggesting that Lawrence "felt himself menaced, not so much by an external as by an internal force. Could it not be that by discovering, or rather suspecting, homosexual passion, not only in others but within himself, he brought forth swarming creatures from the recesses of his mind that could be scotched but not killed . . . ?"[20]

Delany and Bell are both hovering around the center of Lawrence's "crisis." It would be absurd to suggest that Lawrence and Cambridge-Bloomsbury parted ways on purely ideological grounds. It would be absurd because Lawrence never responded to anything on purely ideological grounds. Ideologies, Lawrence insisted on noticing, have people behind them.

Still, the major reason that the meeting at Cambridge was one of the crises of Lawrence's life was precisely that Cambridge, through its Bloomsbury extension, was beginning to dominate a large part of England's cultural life. It can, of course, be said, as Quentin Bell has noted, that in 1915 Bloomsbury was "almost a non-entity."[21] To the larger world this may well have been so; its greatest weight in British cultural affairs would not be felt until the 1920s. But the "literary" people Lawrence knew and with whom he maintained contact during the early war years—Murry and Mansfield, Ottoline Morrell, David Garnett, E. M. Forster, Mark Gertler, S. S. Koteliansky, Russell—all had more or less direct ties with Bloomsbury and more or less circled in and around Bloomsbury's widening orbit. Lawrence was kept well abreast of the group's movements and activities during this time, and he could not have failed to notice that something of importance had coalesced in those regions. Lawrence clearly perceived this, and the perception heightened his frenzy over finding it simply another false trail in his search for a force that could lead the way toward the regeneration of England. Cambridge was "our disease, not our hope,"[22] because it represented a serious and articulate opposition to his own ideas for a regenerated England, an opposition which was infinitely more persuasive than the rapidly fading Georgian sensibility. The Cambridge-Bloomsbury milieu was more dangerous than the Georgian milieu because it was more potent. In Cambridge and in Bloomsbury, Lawrence felt he had located the evil genius behind the continuing decomposition of English character and English culture.

It is not, of course, completely fair to Bloomsbury to use Bertrand Russell and Cambridge as its measure. Russell, at best, was a peripheral member of the Bloomsbury circle. To Lawrence, however, Russell was part of the same fabric that clothed Bloomsbury. He shared many of the same friends, the same attitudes, and the same cultural position as the Bloomsburians. As far as Lawrence was concerned, Russell, David Garnett, Lady Ottoline, John Maynard Keynes, and all of the Bloomsburians were part of the "embodiment of an assumption"[23] which was, perhaps unintentionally, "responsible for spreading the new ideas of 'modern' morality."[24]

The "modern morality" and the assumptions upon which it was based were things that Lawrence passionately despised. The basic assumptions of "modern morality," he felt, were poisonous: the primacy of reason; the available truths of science; the superiority of exquisite states of mind developed through the contemplation of beauty, art, and cultured conversation, all of which were served up in tureens of irony, irreverence, and condescension. Lawrence felt that the primary value of Bloomsbury—the cultivation of personal relationships—had become artificial, intellectualized, and debased as a spawning ground for titillating sensations, meaningless talk, and the "horror of little swarming selves."[25]

In a famous letter written during the time of those skirmishes with the Cambridge-Bloomsbury set, Lawrence declares that hearing

> these young people talking really fills me with black fury: they talk endlessly, but endlessly—and never, never a good or real thing said. Their attitude is so irreverent and blatant. They are cased each in a hard little shell of his own, and out of this they talk words. . . . I cannot stand it. I *will not* have people like this—I had rather be alone. They made me dream in the night of a beetle that bites like a scorpion.[26]

Although these words were directed at two rather minor Bloomsburians (he never formally met Virginia Woolf or Lytton Strachey), they stand in tone and imagery as a culmination of Lawrence's disgust with Bloomsbury and as the beginning of a crucial new kind of thrust to his imagination. Not everyone in Bloomsbury or Cambridge made Lawrence dream of beetles, but it was a dream that soon made inroads into his vision of reality as well as the vision of his fiction. One side—the underside—of what was to become a series of related polarities in Lawrence's fiction, was defined and clarified by his response to the Cambridge-Bloomsbury milieu.

When one thinks of many of the major and minor characters in the novels and stories after 1915, one thinks of characters who had their models in Bloomsbury and in Cambridge: Hermione and Malleson in *Women in Love*, Owen and Villiers in *The Plumed Serpent*, Clifford Chatterley, Michaelis and Duncan Forbes in *Lady Chatterley's Lover*, Bertie Reid (Lawrence's most powerful indictment of Bertrand Russell) in "The Blind Man," Rico Carrington in *St. Mawr*. One is put in touch with Lawrence's disgust with the Cambridge-Bloomsbury milieu almost every time one thinks of Lawrence's cultured, upper-middle-class, sexless, backboneless, effete English people, against whom Lawrence continually places himself in vital opposition. Lawrence's rejection of sterility was a direct corollary of his quest for the cultural accommodation of vitality, and though his images of vitality changed from book to book, the targets of his rejection continued to be modeled upon those figures and movements that he had come to know, and despise, by 1915.

What about the Bloomsbury Group's response to Lawrence? There is little that can be said with assurance. Bloomsbury may have been privately fascinated by Lawrence, but it noted him publicly with a studied indifference. Nevertheless, what we know about the Bloomsbury Group, through the work of Quentin Bell, Nigel Nicolson, Michael Holroyd, Leon Edel, S. P. Rosenbaum, and others, suggests that the group would never have given access to Lawrence in 1915, then in the most aggressively prophetic and angry phase of his development. But at least one of them, Virginia Woolf, wrote in 1931: "Now I realise with regret that a man of genius wrote in my time and I never read him."[27] Woolf had, in fact, read some of Lawrence's work before 1931 and was staggeringly cool toward it. But Woolf insists that she had never before been in a position to take him seriously because the "obscene objurgations" of John Middleton Murry, "that bald necked blood dripping vulture,"[28] had kept her attention removed from Lawrence until after Lawrence's death. Murry was, however, surely not the whole reason. There was nothing in the Bloomsbury ethos which would suggest that Lawrence and Woolf could ever have admired each other, and there was no one essential to the Bloomsbury Group—except, perhaps, Forster, and he was always on the periphery—who was in any important way sympathetic to Lawrence's work, his person, or his aims.

From Lawrence's perspective, Cambridge and Bloomsbury offered an anti-Victorian rebellion that was less committed to maturity and responsibility than even the Georgians had been. The

Georgians, at least, had offered an alternative identity for England. The Cambridge-Bloomsbury milieu, Lawrence felt, offered nothing more than meaningless talk and ironic detachment. And although Lawrence, too, felt it necessary to reject the Victorian sense of England, he nevertheless insisted upon a new kind of maturity and responsibility, a continuing commitment to the total texture of English life, which could in time replace the values that had been lost.

Conclusions

Much of what Lawrence felt, or had come to feel, about the cultural centers of prewar English life was confirmed and extended by his brief encounter with the Cambridge-Bloomsbury milieu. Put simply, Lawrence felt that he was living in an age of decadence. "I think there is no future for England: only a decline and fall," Lawrence wrote in 1915. "That is the dreadful and unbearable part of it: to have been born into a decadent era, a decline of life, a collapsing civilisation."[29]

The signs of decadence were everywhere: in the acquiescence of man to machine; in the increasing intrusion of mental processes into the structure of events; in the horror of England's trying to save itself from rot by the awful remedy of war; in the pervasive lack of reverence for *anything;* in the failure to acknowledge both the human and nonhuman elements of value; in the inability to replace human beings into a significant relationship with what Lawrence sometimes calls Nature, or Woman, or "the other," or the "Great Will":

> Every living soul believes that all things real are within the scope of a Great Will which is working itself out in all things, but also and most vitally in the soul itself. This I call a belief in God, or belief in Love— what you like. Now if a soul believes that the Great Will is working in all things, even though itself be thwarted and deformed and frustrated, that is what I call a *dead* belief: not a living belief. Because every *living* soul believes that, whatever the conditions, there will be that conjunction between the conditions and the soul itself which shall fulfill the Great Will.[30]

This "dead belief" is *"much more insidious* than atheism"[31] because it trivializes experience; it is "doing dirt" on life. Without intense experience, the "adventure" of living,

one tries by an act of volition to invest the mere process of living with
the zest that circumstance fails to provide. Experience itself is an adventure, one says; every moment of it, if life be rightly lived, can be made
significant, every act has importance, has even, some have averred, an
equal importance.[32]

Lawrence develops this point in "Surgery for the Novel—or a
Bomb," an essay in which he "feels the pulses" of Joyce, Dorothy
Richardson, and Marcel Proust and hears instead the "death-rattle
in their throats."[33]

So there you have the "serious" novel, dying in a very long-drawn-
out fourteen-volume death-agony, and absorbedly, childishly interested in the phenomenon. "Did I feel a twinge in my little toe, or didn't
I?" asks every character of Mr. Joyce or of Miss Richardson or
M. Proust. Is my aura a blend of frankincense and orange pekoe and
boot-blacking, or is it myrrh and bacon-fat and Shetland tweed? The
audience round the death-bed gapes for the answer. And when, in a
sepulchral tone, the answer comes at length, after hundreds of pages:
"It is none of these, it is abysmal chloro-coryambasis," the audience
quivers all over, and murmurs: "That's just how I feel myself."
Which is the dismal, long-drawn-out comedy of the death-bed of the
serious novel. It is self-consciousness picked into such fine bits that the
bits are most of them invisible, and you have to go by smell. Through
thousands and thousands of pages Mr. Joyce and Miss Richardson tear
themselves to pieces, strip their smallest emotions to the finest threads,
till you feel you are sewed inside a wool mattress that is being slowly
shaken up, and you are turning to wool along with the rest of the
woolliness.[34]

In a culture in which experience had been defused and neutralized, Lawrence felt that the need to re-evaluate experience was
more important than it had ever been. Consequently, his most
potent novels—*Women in Love* and *The Rainbow*—are structured as a
series of paradigmatic experiences which are juxtaposed against
each other in order to illuminate the possibility for both triumph
and failure in human life.
After the war, Lawrence was compelled to search for lost sources
of vitality in a style his generation had rejected and in places where
his generation had refused to go. He becomes increasingly adamant
about the necessity of rejecting the old, decayed world in order to
begin again, and his subsequent books are verbal explosives for use
in carrying out the demolition. As he says himself, "when the war

is over, then, in the debacle, one can hope to shove a stiletto into the stout heart of Britannia."[35] It is fair to say that, after 1915, almost everything Lawrence writes is an act of clearing away the debris of the old England in order to establish a bedrock on which a new, vital England can be built. For Lawrence, as for Blake and Nietzsche before him, the "way down is the way up."

His search had to extend to Mexico, New Mexico, Australia, and Etruscan places because no answers could be found among the acknowledged sources of British culture. For him, these sources were "dead as nails—nothing there."[36] As long as England remained under their sway it would continue to be "artificially held *together* by the social mechanism."[37] In such a world, experience would be, as Virginia Woolf describes it, "a luminous halo, a semi-transparent envelope surrounding us from the beginning of consciousness to the end,"[38] and the business of the novelist would therefore be to

> record the atoms as they fall upon the mind in the order in which they fell . . . [to] trace the pattern, however disconnected and incoherent in appearance, which each sight or incident scores upon the consciousness.[39]

In contrast, for Lawrence the novel must help one to "be alive, to be man alive, to be whole man alive: that is the point."[40] The novel

> can inform and lead into new places the flow of our sympathetic consciousness, and it can lead our sympathy away in recoil from things gone dead. Therefore, the novel, properly handled, can reveal the most secret places of life: for it is in the *passional* secret places of life, above all, that the tide of sensitive awareness needs to ebb and flow, cleansing and freshening.[41]

It was this, and little more, that Lawrence insisted was the great "want of the English people."[42]

Lawrence's belief in the decadence of England was not simply the result of a temperamental inclination to see the failure of everyone around him, as some of his "destructive hagiographers" have implied; it was at least partially the result of Lawrence's continually frustrating journey through the shifting centers of England's cultural life. There, where Lawrence hoped to find the nucleus of a new life for English folk, he found nothing. From those centers, however, Lawrence assimilated new ways of thought and new ways of expression. Much of what we find characteristically Lawrentian is the result of those assimilations, and we can "place" Lawrence nearer the center of his era by recognizing them. He "roamed in the belly of his era" to find a way out of what it had become; he loathed the modern era in order that, someday, he could love it.

Appendix A: The Night Pound Ate the Tulips

This incident was first reported by Ernest Rhys in his *Everyman Remembers* (1931), and has been accepted without qualification by the biographers of Lawrence, Pound, and Ford. (See Harry T. Moore, *The Priest of Love*; Charles Norman, *Ezra Pound*; Arthur Mizener, *The Saddest Story*; Edward Nehls, *D. H. Lawrence: A Composite Biography*.) The incident is well enough known by now that it has become a commonplace example of literary life in London during the period, as well as an example of Pound's and Lawrence's differing styles of dealing with that milieu. In using the Rhys soirée as an exemplary incident, this study has been no exception to the rule.

There are, however, certain inconsistencies in Rhys's account which should be noted. Rhys did not date the incident at all, but Violet Hunt—with whom Ford Madox Ford was quite intimate at the time—does date it; in her unpublished Diary, Hunt dates the occasion 18 December 1909 (Arthur Mizener, *The Saddest Story*, p. 552). If this is so, it should have surprised the biographers of John Davidson, who, Rhys tells us, "came very late" and, "after some persuasion," read his poem "In Romney Marsh" to the assembled guests (Ernest Rhys, *Everyman Remembers*, pp. 247–48). Davidson, unfortunately for him and for our attempts to date this incident, had disappeared from his home in Penzance on 23 March 1909, and was not seen again until some fishermen found his body on 18 September 1909 (J. Benjamin Townsend, *John Davidson: Poet of Armageddon*, pp. 1–15). Literary London was well aware of Davidson's disappearance; Arthur Conan Doyle even intervened and was the first to suggest the possibility of what was eventually found to be the truth—Davidson had committed suicide. Curiously, Davidson's biographer, J. Benjamin Townsend, uses the Rhys party as an example of Davidson's uneasiness in literary circles, but says only "that this *soirée* must have taken place in the last few months of Davidson's life." (Townsend, pp. 168–69).

Someone is wrong, and other evidence suggests that it is Rhys himself. Rhys tells us, at the beginning of his chapter on this literary gathering, that Lawrence was a "completely unknown poet," but that Ford had "discovered" him and had written to ask Rhys if he could bring Lawrence along. Ford's discovery of Lawrence (recounted in his *Portraits from Life*) took place in July or August, months after Davidson's disappearance, and Lawrence did not actually meet Ford until September. If, then, Lawrence had been "discovered" and knew Ford by the time of the Rhys party, John Davidson could not have been there.

Other evidence from Lawrence's letters, especially two that he wrote to Louie Burrows, tend to confirm Violet Hunt's claim that the party took place in December. The first, written on 20 November 1909, suggests that Lawrence had never met Rhys until mid-November.

> Last Sunday I went up to lunch with Ford Madox Hueffer, & with Violet Hunt, who is rich, & a fairly well-known novelist. They were both delightful. Hueffer took me to tea at Ernest Rhy's [*sic*]: he edits heaps of classics—Dent's Everyman's, for instance. He is very nice indeed, and so is his wife, Grace Rhys, who writes stories. [James T. Boulton, ed., *Lawrence in Love: Letters to Louie Burrows*, p. 46]

If, as this letter suggests, Lawrence had not met Rhys before mid-November, the soirée in question could hardly have taken place before Davidson's death, in March.

The second letter, written to Louie Burrows on 11 December 1909, describes his intention to go' to the Rhyses' "next week" (Boulton, p.47), making Violet Hunt's date of 18 December appear more definitive.

> Next week I am going up to Grace Rhys [*sic*] to meet various poetry people. I am to take some of my unpublished verses to read. I do not look forward to these things much. I shall feel such a fool. [Boulton, p. 47]

We cannot be certain, of course, that this was not a different, if similar, occasion than the one described by Rhys in *Everyman Remembers*. The Rhyses were in the habit of giving such parties quite often. Still, we can be certain that of the "poetry people" who did appear, John Davidson was not among them.

The inconsistencies in Rhys's anecdote are by now obvious. If Davidson was there, the party must have taken place before 23 March, before Lawrence's poems were in Ford's hands, and before Lawrence had met either Ford or Rhys. If Lawrence came with Ford, who had recently "discovered" him, Davidson could not have been there. The combined evidence of Violet Hunt's Diary and Lawrence's own letter to Louie Burrows (11 December 1909) would tend to confirm the probability that Rhys, writing some twenty-two years later, must have conflated one memorable evening with another.

All of this is not intended to suggest that we dismiss Rhys's anecdote as being untrue, as, say, we have had to dismiss some of Ford Madox Ford's anecdotal tales. The Rhyses' party is too instructive and too engaging to dismiss; it is already too much a part of what we think we know about Lawrence and about Pound. Still, memories such as Rhys's should be taken with a degree of caution; ghosts may give the lie to them.

Appendix B: The *English Review* "England, My England"

The text used for this discussion is the revised text of December 1921. The original 1915 text (published in the *English Review* for October) contains all of the essential elements, with the exception of the explicit descriptions of the Crockham landscape, that appear in the later version. The larger implications of the landscape in the later version do exist in the 1915 text, but they are much more vaguely apprehended. In the early version, Crockham is surrounded by a "shaggy, ancient heath"; it

> has no relation with the world; it held its cup under heaven alone, and was filled forever with peace and sunshine and loveliness. . . . It was held up only to heaven; the world entered not at all. [Lawrence, "England, My England," *English Review* 21 (October 1915):239]

The essentials of Egbert's character (Evelyn in the 1915 text)— his dilettantism, his indifference, and his underlying current of nihilism— exist in summary form in the earlier version. Evelyn, for instance, derives a "basic satisfaction" from "being part of the great warrior motion" (Lawrence, "England, My England," p. 244). Such satisfactions apparently extend to the killing of Germans, too; even after Evelyn is critically wounded, he manages to exhibit his destructive tendencies by shooting three Germans at close range.

In the 1915 text, the relationship between Evelyn and Winifred is more explicitly tense and hostile. She is, for instance, the first to direct Evelyn toward joining the army, and quite clearly she does so out of hostility, rather than out of a sense of duty. Still, the "living romance" quality is the dominant factor in their relationship.

Perhaps the most glaring difference between the original and the final versions is the amount of emphasis that Lawrence places on the war scenes. The 1921 text spends little time with them; the original version, as perhaps could be expected from a story written during wartime (and especially for the *English Review*, which devoted most of its pages to features like "War and Creative Art" and "A Way to End the War"), gives fully half of its pages over to descriptions of Evelyn's life in the trenches. That Lawrence deleted them from the final version suggests that they were not among those aspects of the story which had any real significance for him.

What Lawrence had felt on his pulses in 1915 was much more consciously apprehended in late 1921. "England, My England," as it now stands, is not only much superior, but is also a more articulate and more comprehensive statement of what Lawrence felt about the failures of Georgian England.

Notes

Chapter 1: Introduction

1. John Lehmann, *A Nest of Tigers: The Sitwells in Their Times* (Boston: Little, Brown, 1968), pp. 62–63.

2. D. H. Lawrence, "Note" in *CP* (New York: Viking, 1973), p. 28.

3. Aldous Huxley, *Collected Essays* (New York: Harper, 1958), p. 116.

4. Frank Kermode, *D. H. Lawrence* (New York: Viking, 1973) p. 26.

5. Edmund Gosse, *Some Diversions of a Man of Letters* (London: Heinemann, 1920), p. 303.

6. Richard Aldington, quoted by C. K. Stead, *The New Poetic: Yeats to Eliot* (New York: Harper Torchbooks, 1966), p. 98.

7. Harold Monro, *Some Contemporary Poets (1920)* (London: Leonard Parsons, 1920), p. 16.

8. Malcolm Bradbury, *The Social Context of Modern English Literature* (New York: Schocken, 1971), p. 54.

9. Paul Fussell, *The Great War and Modern Memory* (New York: Oxford University Press, 1975), p. 76.

10. Samuel Hynes, *The Edwardian Turn of Mind* (Princeton, N.J.: Princeton University Press, 1968), p. 5.

11. Vivian de Sola Pinto, *Crisis in English Poetry 1880–1940* (New York: Harper Torchbooks, 1958), p. 118.

12. Ibid., p. 152.

13. D. D. Paige, ed., *The Letters of Ezra Pound 1907–1941* (New York: Harvest, 1950), p. 13.

14. Michael Holroyd, *Lytton Strachey: A Critical Biography*, vol. 1 (New York: Holt, Rinehart and Winston, 1967), p. 416.

15. Stephen Spender, *Love-Hate Relations: English and American Sensibilities* (New York: Vintage, 1975), p. 228.

16. Ibid.

17. E. M. Forster, *The Longest Journey* (Norfolk, Conn.: New Directions, n. d.), p. 77.

18. Ibid., p. 26.

19. Ibid., p. 206.

20. Ibid., p. 88.

21. Ezra Pound, quoted in T. S. Matthews, *Great Tom: Notes toward the Definition of T. S. Eliot* (New York: Harper and Row, 1974), p. 57.

22. Harry T. Moore, ed., *CL*, 1: 204.

23. Brewster Ghiselin, "D. H. Lawrence and a New World," *The Western Review* 11 (1947): 154.

24. See G. K. Chesterton, *Lunacy and Letters*, ed. Dorothy Collins (New York: Sheed and Ward, 1958), p. 94.

25. D. H. Lawrence, *Studies in Classic American Literature* (New York: Viking, 1968), p. 6.

26. Moore, *CL*, 1: 482.

27. D. H. Lawrence, "Democracy," in *Phoenix*, p. 718.

28. Raymond Williams, *Culture and Society 1780/1950* (New York: Harper and Row, 1958), p. 205.

29. Raymond Williams, *The English Novel from Dickens to Lawrence* (New York: Oxford University Press, 1970), p. 183.

Chapter 2: Lawrence and the Edwardians, 1908–1912

1. Harry T. Moore, ed., *CL*, 1: 31.

2. W. H. Mallock, quoted by Kenneth Hopkins, *The Poets Laureate* (New York: Library Publishers, 1955), p. 177.

3. Jerome Buckley, *The Victorian Temper: A Study in Literary Culture* (New York: Vintage, 1964), p. 126.

4. John Davidson, "The Crystal Palace," in M. Lindsay, ed., *John Davidson: A Selection of His Poems* (London: Hutchinson, 1961), pp. 183, 191.

5. Samuel Hynes, *The Edwardian Turn of Mind* (Princeton, N.J.: Princeton University Press, 1968), p. 5.

6. H. G. Wells, quoted by Hynes, ibid., p. 7.

7. Ford Madox Ford, quoted by Stephen Spender, *Love-Hate Relations: English and American Sensibilities* (New York: Vintage, 1975), p. 190.

8. W. B. Yeats, ed., *The Oxford Book of Modern Verse, 1892–1935* (New York: Oxford University Press, 1936), pp. xi–xii.

9. C. F. G. Masterman, *In Peril of Change* (London: T. Fisher Unwin, 1905), pp. xii–xiii.

10. Rebecca West, "Uncle Bennett," in *The Strange Necessity: Essays by Rebecca West* (Garden City, N.Y.: Doubleday, Doran, 1928), p. 215.

11. Samuel Hynes, "Introduction: A Note on 'Edwardian,'" in *Edwardian Occasions: Essays on English Writing in the Early Twentieth Century* (New York: Oxford University Press, 1972), p. 5.

12. Vivian de Sola Pinto, *Crisis in English Poetry: 1880–1940* (New York: Harper Torchbooks, 1958), p. 118.

13. Wylie Sypher, *Loss of Self in Modern Literature and Art* (New York: Vintage, 1962), p. 35.

14. Henry James, "The Younger Generation," in Leon Edel and Gordon Ray, eds., *Henry James and H. G. Wells* (London: Rupert Hart-Davis, 1958), p. 184.

15. Virginia Woolf, "Mr. Bennett and Mrs. Brown," in *The Captain's Death Bed and Other Essays* (New York: Harcourt, Brace, 1950), p. 105.

16. Leonard Woolf and James Strachey, eds., *Virginia Woolf and Lytton Strachey: Letters* (London: Hogarth Press, 1956), p. 35.

17. William Bellamy, *The Novels of Wells, Bennett and Galsworthy: 1890–1910* (New York: Barnes and Noble, 1971), p. 22.

18. H. G. Wells, *Tono-Bungay* (Boston: Houghton Mifflin, 1966), p. 268.

19. Moore, *CL*, 1: 88.

20. H. G. Wells, *Experiment in Autobiography: Discoveries and Conclusions of a Very Ordinary Brain (since 1866)* (New York: Macmillan, 1934), pp. 390, 396–97.

21. Kenneth Rexroth, "Henry James and H. G. Wells," in *Assays* (New York: New Directions, 1961), p. 115.

22. H. V. Marrot, ed., *Life and Letters of John Galsworthy* (New York: Scribner's, 1936), p. 724.

23. John Galsworthy, quoted by Keith Sagar, *The Art of D. H. Lawrence* (London: Cambridge University Press, 1966), p. 69.

24. D. H. Lawrence, "John Galsworthy," in *Phoenix*, pp. 542–43.

25. Allan Wade, ed., *The Letters of W. B. Yeats* (New York: Macmillan, 1955), p. 803.

26. Malcolm Brown, "The Craftsman as Critic," in Douglas A. Hughes, ed., *The Man of Wax: Critical Essays on George Moore* (New York: New York University Press, 1971), p. 336.

27. George Moore, quoted by Malcolm Brown, "The Craftsman as Critic," p. 336.

28. Edward Garnett, ed., *Letters from W. H. Hudson* (London: Nonesuch, 1923), p. 116.

29. Ibid., p. 141.

30. Henry James, "The Younger Generation," p. 180.

31. Compton Mackenzie, *Literature in My Time* (Freeport, New York: Books for Libraries Press, 1967), pp. 190–91.

32. Christopher Gillie, *Movements in English Literature 1900–1940* (London: Cambridge University Press, 1975), p. 10.

33. Moore, *CL*, 1: 388.

34. Violet Hunt, quoted by Harry T. Moore, *The Priest of Love: A Life of D. H. Lawrence* (New York: Farrar, Straus and Giroux, 1974), p. 128.

35. Helen Corke, "D. H. Lawrence as I Saw Him," *Renaissance and Modern Studies* IV (1960): 11.

36. Carolyn Heilbrun, *The Garnett Family* (New York: Macmillan, 1961), p. 95.

37. Edward Garnett, "Mr. D. H. Lawrence and the Moralists," in *Friday Nights* (London: Jonathan Cape, 1929), p. 118.

38. Ibid., pp. 124–25.

39. Ibid., p. 120.

40. W. L. George, *A Novelist on Novels* (London: W. Collins, 1918), pp. 99–100.

41. Viola Meynell, ed., *Letters of J. M. Barrie* (New York: Scribner's, 1947), p. 200.

42. Arnold Bennett, *The Evening Standard Years: "Books and Persons" 1926–1931*, ed. Andrew Mylett (London: Chatto and Windus, 1974), p. 212.

43. James Hepburn, ed., *Letters of Arnold Bennett*, vol. 3 (London: Oxford University Press, 1966), pp. 345–46.

44. Arnold Bennett, *The Evening Standard Years*, p. 164.

45. Moore, *CL*, 1: 234.

46. See Rose Marie Burwell, "A Catalogue of Lawrence's Reading from Early Childhood," *D. H. Lawrence Review* 3 (1970): 193–296.

47. Moore, *CL*, 1: 51.

48. H. G. Wells, *Tono-Bungay*, p. 11.

49. C. F. G. Masterman, *The Condition of England* (London: Methuen, 1960), p. 181.

50. Ibid., p. 178.

51. H. G. Wells, *Tono-Bungay*, p. 14.

52. Ibid.

53. Ibid., p. 316.

54. Ibid.

55. Moore, *CL*, 1: 519

56. Ibid., pp. 378–79.

57. D. H. Lawrence, *Women in Love* (New York: Modern Library, 1950), p. 109. The English country house, so long the symbol of "an Utopian compromise between community and country isolation" (Angus Wilson, *The Wild Garden*, p. 30), had, by the early twentieth century, become the symbolic focus—a microcosm—of the disintegration of traditional English society. Houses, in fact, are quite often the central source of plot, characterization, and theme in Edwardian novels and plays. One thinks not only of *Tono-Bungay*, but also of *The Man of Property*, *Howards End*, and the later, but still Edwardian, *Heartbreak House*. By the 1920s, the stock of the traditional English country house had dropped so sharply that its major literary use was as a scene for murder.

58. C. F. G. Masterman, *England after War* (New York: Harcourt, Brace, 1923), p. 260.

59. Ford Madox Ford, *Portraits from Life* (Boston: Houghton Mifflin, 1937), p. 86.

60. C. F. G. Masterman, *The Condition of England*, p. 161.

61. Ibid.

62. D. H. Lawrence, *The White Peacock* (Carbondale, Ill.: Southern Illinois University Press, 1966), p. 212.

Chapter 3: Lawrence and the Georgians: Significant Affinities

1. Harry T. Moore, ed., *CL*, 1: 150.

2. Ibid., p. 152.

3. Ibid., p. 62.

4. Ibid., p. 172.

5. D. H. Lawrence, *"Georgian Poetry 1911–1912,"* in *Phoenix*, p. 304.

6. Edmund Gosse, quoted by James Reeves, ed., *Georgian Poetry* (Harmondsworth, Middlesex: Penguin, 1962), p. xiv.

7. Allen Upward, quoted by Wallace Martin, *The New Age under Orage* (Manchester: Manchester University Press, 1967), p. 128.

8. Lascelles Abercrombie, quoted by Robert H. Ross, *The Georgian Revolt: Rise and Fall of a Poetic Ideal 1910–1922* (London: Faber and Faber, 1967), p. 39.

9. D. D. Paige, ed., *The Letters of Ezra Pound 1907–1941* (New York: Harvest, 1950), p. 10.

10. Leonard Woolf, *Beginning Again: An Autobiography of the Years 1911 to 1918* (New York: Harcourt Brace Jovanovich, 1964), p. 36.

11. Gregory Bantock, "The Social and Intellectual Background," in Boris Ford, ed., *The Modern Age*, The Pelican Guide to English Literature #7 (Harmondsworth, Middlesex: Penguin, 1964), p. 14.

12. Samuel Hynes, *The Edwardian Turn of Mind* (Princeton, N.J.: Princeton University Press, 1968), p. 350.

13. Quoted by Hynes, *The Edwardian Turn of Mind*, p. 350.

14. J. A. V. Chapple, *Documentary and Imaginative Literature 1880–1920* (London: Blandford Press, 1970), p. 221.

15. John Gross, *The Rise and Fall of the Man of Letters* (New York: Collier, 1969), p. 229.

16. Arnold Bennett, *Books and Persons: Being Comments on a Past Epoch* (London: Chatto and Windus, 1917), p. 297.

17. A. R. Orage, quoted by Wallace Martin, *The New Age under Orage*, pp. 108–109.

18. Virginia Woolf, "Mr. Bennett and Mrs. Brown," in *The Captain's Death Bed and Other Essays* (New York: Harcourt, Brace, 1950), p. 96.

19. Ibid., p. 110.

20. Ibid., p. 103.

21. Ibid., p. 105.

22. Ibid., p. 104.

23. Ibid., p. 110.

24. George Dangerfield, *The Strange Death of Liberal England 1910–1914* (New York: Capricorn, 1961), p. viii.

25. Hynes, *The Edwardian Turn of Mind*, p. 326.

26. Virginia Woolf, *Roger Fry: A Biography* (New York: Harcourt, Brace, 1940), p. 153.

27. Wilfred Scawen Blunt, *My Diaries: Being a Personal Narrative of Events 1888–1914*, vol. 2, (New York: Knopf, 1921), p. 330. It is worth noting that a similar phrase was used about Turner in the 1840s, which led Ruskin to write *Modern Painters*. Ruskin himself then used it in the 1870s when attacking Whistler.

28. Quoted by Hynes, *The Edwardian Turn of Mind*, p. 329.

29. Arnold Bennett, quoted by Hynes, *The Edwardian Turn of Mind*, p. 332.

30. Quoted by Hynes, *The Edwardian Turn of Mind*, p. 342.

31. Geoffrey Keynes, ed., *The Letters of Rupert Brooke* (New York: Harcourt, Brace and World, 1968), p. 327.

32. Edward Marsh, quoted by Christopher Hassall, *A Biography of Edward Marsh* (New York: Harcourt, Brace, 1959), pp. 231–32.

33. Hynes, *The Edwardian Turn of Mind*, p. 343.

34. Gilbert Phelps, *The Russian Novel in English Fiction* (London: Hutchinson's University Library, 1956), p. 171.

35. Virginia Woolf, "The Russian Point of View," in *Collected Essays*, vol. 1 (London: Hogarth, 1966), p. 242. In *Dickens and His Readers*, George H. Ford has pointed out the inability of the early modern reader to see the broad connections between Dostoevsky and Dickens. Such connections are indisputably there, but one suspects that readers like Virginia Woolf were more attuned to Dostoevsky's fiercely satirical indictments of basic Victorian assumptions (the attack on the Crystal Palace in *Notes from Underground*, for instance) than to Dickens's comic vision.

36. Patrick Bridgewater, *Nietzsche in Anglosaxony* (n. p.: Leicester University Press, 1972), p. 13.

37. Michael Hamburger, *Contraries: Studies in German Literature* (New York: Dutton, 1970), p. 203.

38. Hynes, *The Edwardian Turn of Mind*, p. 311.

39. Samuel Hynes, "Harold Monro," in *Edwardian Occasions* (New York: Oxford University Press, 1972), p. 98.

40. Dangerfield, p. 433.

41. Ibid.

42. John Wain, "Poetry," in C. B. Cox and A. E. Dyson, eds., *The Twentieth Century Mind 1: 1900–1918* (London: Oxford University Press, 1972), p. 397.

43. Stephen Spender, *Love-Hate Relations: English and American Sensibilities* (New York: Vintage, 1975), p. 221.

44. Edward Marsh, *A Number of People* (New York: Harper, 1939), p. 321.

45. Ross, pp. 27–28.

46. Marsh, p. 320.

47. Ibid.

48. Hassall, p. 190.

49. Rupert Brooke, quoted by Dangerfield, p. 430.

50. W. H. Davies, "A Greeting," in *The Complete Poems of W. H. Davies* (Middletown, Conn.: Wesleyan University Press, 1965), p. 167.

51. John Drinkwater, "The Fires of God," in *Georgian Poetry 1911–1912* (London: The Poetry Bookshop, 1912), pp. 81–82.

52. Ezra Pound, *Literary Essays of Ezra Pound*, ed. with intro. by T. S. Eliot (New York: New Directions, 1968), p. 41.

53. Edmund Gosse, quoted by Ross, p. 146.

54. Quoted by Ross, p. 146.

55. Quoted by Richard J. Stonesifer, *W. H. Davies: A Critical Biography* (London: Jonathan Cape, 1963), p. 100.

56. Evelyn Waugh, *A Little Learning: An Autobiography* (Boston: Little, Brown, 1964), p. 76.

57. Arthur Waugh, *Tradition and Change: Studies in Contemporary Literature* (London: Chapman and Hall, 1919), p. 16.

58. Ibid., pp. 16, 17.

59. Ibid., p. 27.

60. Ibid., p. 32.

61. H. G. Wells, *Tono-Bungay* (Boston: Houghton Mifflin, 1966), p. 18.

62. Ross, p. 146.

63. See Myron Simon, "The Georgian Poetic," in Robert Scholes, ed. *Papers of the Midwest Modern Language Association #1* (Iowa City, Ia.: Midwest Modern Language Association, 1969).

64. Arthur Waugh, pp. 14–15.

65. Ibid., p. 15.

66. Keynes, p. 328.

67. Lawrence, *"Georgian Poetry 1911–1912,"* p. 305.

68. C. K. Stead, *The New Poetic: Yeats to Eliot* (New York: Harper Torchbooks, 1964), pp. 87–88.

69. Kenneth Rexroth, *D. H. Lawrence: Selected Poetry*, ed. with intro. by Kenneth Rexroth (New York: Viking, 1961), p. 1.

70. Lawrence, *"Georgian Poetry 1911–1912,"* p. 304.

71. Ibid.

72. Ibid., p. 305.

73. Ibid., p. 304.

74. Ibid.

75. Ibid.

76. Ibid., p. 306.

77. Ibid., p. 304.

78. Ibid.

79. Ibid.

80. Ibid.

81. Ibid.

82. Ibid., p. 305.

83. Ibid., pp. 305–6.

84. Ibid., p. 306.

85. Ibid., p. 305.

86. Ibid., p. 306.

87. Ibid.

88. Ibid.

89. David Daiches, *Poetry in the Modern World* (Chicago: University of Chicago Press, 1940), p. 53.

90. Edward Marsh, quoted by Hassall, p. 194.

91. Herbert Palmer, *Post-Victorian Poetry* (London: Dent, 1938), p. 94.

92. Marsh, p. 322.

93. Ibid., p. 323.

94. Lascelles Abercrombie, "The Sale of Saint Thomas," in *Georgian Poetry 1911–1912*, p. 20.

95. Sandra Gilbert, *Acts of Attention* (Ithaca, N.Y.: Cornell University Press, 1972), p. 56.

96. Lawrence, "Snap-dragon," in *Georgian Poetry 1911–1912*, pp. 113, 115–16.

97. Gilbert, p. 57.

98. Lawrence, "Snap-dragon," p. 116.

99. Rupert Brooke, "Town and Country," in *Georgian Poetry 1911–1912*, p. 43.

100. Ibid.

101. Ibid.

102. Ibid.

103. Ibid., p. 44.

104. Edwin Muir, *One Foot in Eden* (London: Faber and Faber, 1956), title.

105. R. G. N. Selgãdo, "Review of *Complete Poems*," *The Critical Quarterly* 7 (Winter 1965): 391.

106. Robert Langbaum, "Lord of Life, Kings in Exile: Identity and Sexuality in D. H. Lawrence," *The American Scholar* 45 (Winter 1975/1976): p. 809.

107. Selgãdo, p. 391.

108. Robert Coombes, "Hardy, de la Mare, and Edward Thomas," in Boris Ford, ed., *The Modern Age*, p. 149.

109. Tom Marshall, *The Psychic Mariner* (New York: Viking, 1970), p. 42.

110. A. Alvarez, "D. H. Lawrence: The Single State of Man," in Harry T. Moore, ed., *A D. H. Lawrence Miscellany* (Carbondale, Ill.: Southern Illinois University Press, 1959), p. 344.

111. Jessie Chambers (E. T.), *D. H. Lawrence: A Personal Record* (London: Jonathan Cape, 1935), p. 52.

112. Marshall, p. 65.

113. Ibid., p. 66.

114. D. H. Lawrence, "The North Country," *CP*, p. 148.

115. Ibid., p. 149.

116. Gordon Bottomley, "The Viaduct," in *Chambers of Imagery* (First series) (no place: E. Mathews, 1907), p. 20.

117. Gordon Bottomley, "Iron-founders and others," in *Chambers of Imagery* (Second series) (no place: E. Mathews, 1912), p. 19.

118. Lawrence, "*Georgian Poetry 1911–1912*," p. 305.

119. Ibid., p. 306.

120. Quoted by R. P. Draper, ed., *D. H. Lawrence: The Critical Heritage* (New York: Barnes and Noble, 1970), p. 56.

121. Michael Reck, *Ezra Pound: A Close-Up* (New York: McGraw-Hill, 1967), p. 14.

122. Stephen Spender, *The Struggle of the Modern* (Berkeley and Los Angeles: University of California Press, 1965). p. 160.

123. F. R. Leavis, *New Bearings in English Poetry: A Study of the Contemporary Situation* (London: Chatto and Windus, 1932), p. 64.

124. Marsh, p. 321.

125. Harold Monro, *Some Contemporary Poets (1920)* (London: Leonard Parsons, 1920), p. 25.

126. Ezra Pound, quoted by Hassall, p. 193.

127. Alun R. Jones, *The Life and Opinions of T. E. Hulme* (London: Gollancz, 1960), p. 30.

128. Jones, p. 35.

129. Wain, "Poetry," p. 394.

130. Graham Hough, *Image and Experience* (London: Duckworth, 1960), p. 70.

131. D. D. Paige, ed., p. 4.

132. Ibid., p. 12.

133. Ibid., p. 13.

134. Hough, p. 69.

135. Stead, p. 49.

136. Marsh, pp. 322–23.

137. Stead, p. 57.

138. W. W. Gibson, quoted by Ross, p. 125.

139. John Drinkwater, *Discovery* (Boston: Houghton Mifflin, 1933), p. 229.

140. Palmer, p. 94.

141. W. H. Davies, quoted by Ross, p. 129.

142. Walter de la Mare, quoted by Marsh, p. 327.

143. Moore, *CL*, l: 261.

144. Ibid., pp. 153–54.

145. Ibid., p. 182.

146. Ibid., p. 200.

147. Ibid.

148. Ibid., p. 183.

149. Ibid., p. 82.

150. Ibid., p. 74.

151. Ibid., p. 164.

152. Ibid., p. 134.

153. Ibid., p. 204.

154. Ibid., p. 183.

Chapter 4: Landscape and Community: *The White Peacock* and *The Rainbow*

1. Myron Simon, "The Georgian Poetic," in Robert Scholes, ed., *Papers of the Midwest Modern Language Association* #1 (Iowa City, Ia.: Midwest Modern Language Association, 1969), p. 132.

2. Geoffrey Keynes, ed., *The Letters of Rupert Brooke* (New York: Harcourt, Brace and World, 1968), pp. 258–59.

3. Ibid., p. 270.

4. James T. Boulton, ed., *Lawrence in Love: Letters to Louie Burrows* (Nottingham: University of Nottingham Press, 1968), p. 2.

5. Harry T. Moore, ed., *CL* l: 203.

6. Ibid.

7. E. M. Forster, "Pessimism in Literature," in *Albergo Empedocle and Other Writings*, ed. with an intro. by George H. Thomson (New York: Liveright, 1971), p. 144.

8. Ibid.

9. Ibid., pp. 132, 133.

10. Ibid., p. 136.

11. Ibid., p. 145.

12. Forster, "The Beauty of Life," in *Albergo Empedocle and Other Writings*, p. 175.

13. Ibid., p. 172.

14. Ibid., p. 171, 175.

15. E. M. Forster, *Howards End*, ed. Oliver Stallybrass (London: Camelot Press, 1978), p. 229.

16. Malcolm Bradbury, *The Social Context of Modern English Literature* (New York: Schocken Books, 1971), p. 46.

17. Forster, *Howards End*, p. 23.

18. Ibid., p. 212.

19. Ibid., p. 337.

20. Ibid., p. 195.

21. Ibid., p. 172.

22. Ibid., p. 129.

23. Ibid., p. 320.

24. Ibid.

25. Ibid.

26. Ibid., p. 337.

27. Ibid., p. 179.

28. Bradbury, p. 52.

29. Forster, *Howards End*, p. 215.

30. Ibid., p. 264.

31. Harold Monro, quoted by F. R. Leavis, *New Bearings in English Poetry: A Study of the Contemporary Situation* (London: Chatto and Windus, 1932), p. 6.

32. Ibid.

33. Forster, *Howards End*, p. 27.

34. E. M. Forster, *England's Pleasant Land: A Pageant Play* (London: Hogarth Press, 1940), p. 8.

35. L. A. G. Strong, quoted by Richard J. Stonesifer, *W. H. Davies: A Critical Biography* (London: Jonathan Cape, 1963), p. 99.

36. Harold Monro, quoted by Joy Grant, *Harold Monro and the Poetry Bookshop* (Berkeley and Los Angeles: University of California Press, 1967), p. 54. Monro had called these principles "the first principles of *our* [meaning English] Futurism." Monro was, in 1913, attracted to Italian Futurism until Marinetti's appearance in London cooled his enthusiasm. Again, however, attention should be paid to the lack of demarcation between apparently different schools and to the surprising extent to which any new movement—even Futurism—was likely to be adopted as a part of a new program for British literature.

37. Simon, "The Georgian Poetic," p. 132.

38. Gordon Bottomley, quoted by Simon, p. 132.

39. Simon, p. 131.

40. Raymond Williams, *The Country and the City* (New York: Oxford University Press, 1973), p. 258.

41. Stephen Spender, *Love-Hate Relations: English and American Sensibilities* (New York: Vintage, 1975), p. 137.

42. Ford Madox Ford, *Portraits from Life* (Boston: Houghton Mifflin, 1937), p. 209.

43. Nathan Scott, Jr., "The Broken Center," in Rollo May, ed., *Symbolism in Religion and Literature* (New York: George Braziller, 1960), p. 196.

44. D. H. Lawrence, *The Trespasser* (London: Heinemann, 1955), p. 75.

45. Ibid., p. 60.

46. Ibid., p. 17.

47. Ibid., p. 66.

48. Ibid., p. 67.

49. Moore, *CL*, l: 66–67.

50. Ibid., p. 77.

51. Ibid., p. 151.

52. Williams, *The Country and the City*, p. 252.

53. Forster, *Howards End*, p. 209.

54. E. M. Forster, *A Room with a View* (New York: Alfred Knopf, 1925), p. 111.

55. Aldous Huxley, "Wordsworth in the Tropics," in *Collected Essays* (New York: Harper, 1958), p. 3.

56. D. H. Lawrence, "England, My England," in *CSS*, 2: 304.

57. D. H. Lawrence, *St. Mawr together with "The Princess"* (London: Martin Secker, 1925), p. 180.

58. Moore, *CL*, l: 263.

59. Claude M. Sinzelle, quoted by Michael Squires, *The Pastoral Novel: Studies in George Eliot, Thomas Hardy, and D. H. Lawrence* (Charlottesville, Va.: University Press of Virginia, 1974), pp. 177–78.

60. Squires, p. 178.

61. George H. Ford, *Double Measure: A Study of the Novels and Stories of D. H. Lawrence* (New York: Norton, 1965), p. 47.

62. D. H. Lawrence, *The White Peacock*, ed. Matthew J. Bruccoli (Carbondale, Ill.: Southern Illinois University Press, 1966), p. 67.

63. Baruch Hochman, *Another Ego* (Columbia, S.C.: University of South Carolina Press, 1970), pp. 25–26. Michael Squires's study of the pastoral novel notes three features which are "especially salient and stable in both the pastoral tradition and the pastoral novel": "Pastoral contrasts, the development of a circumscribed pastoral world, and the correspondence between landscape and character" (Michael Squires, *The Pastoral Novel*, p. 18). All of these, he finds, are present in *The White Peacock*.

64. Robert Gajdusek, "A Reading of *The White Peacock*," in Harry T. Moore, ed., *A D. H. Lawrence Miscellany* (Carbondale, Ill.: Southern Illinois University Press, 1959), p. 192.

65. Lawrence, *The White Peacock*, pp. 171–72.

66. Ibid., p. 68.

67. Ibid., p. 210.

68. Ibid., p. 50.

69. Ibid.

70. Ibid., p. 115.

71. Ibid., p. 139.

72. Ibid., p. 8.

73. Ibid., p. 27.

74. Ibid., p. 75.

75. Kenneth Inniss, *D. H. Lawrence's Bestiary* (The Hague: Mouton, 1971), p. 109.

76. Lawrence, *The White Peacock*, p. 161.

77. Ibid.

78. Ibid., p. 145. George H. Ford, in his discussion of *The White Peacock* in *Double Measure*, has devised a similar spectrum "of darkness and light." Arranging the characters along a nature-civilization spectrum changes the order only slightly—Cyril moves closer to the center and Leslie far to one end. Ford's warning that such a spectrum is "a horizontal bar,

not a scale of values arranged vertically," and that "tilting the bar so that the dark side appears to be on top is the commonest mistake in interpretations of *The White Peacock*" still holds true (George H. Ford, *Double Measure*, p. 49).

79. Lawrence, *The White Peacock*, p. 145.

80. Ibid., p. 168.

81. Ibid., p. 309.

82. Ibid., p. 311.

83. Ibid., p. 312.

84. Ibid., p. 310.

85. Ibid., p. 280.

86. Ibid., p. 278.

87. Ibid., p. 280.

88. Ibid., p. 166.

89. Ibid., p. 163.

90. Ibid., p. 165.

91. Ibid.

92. Ibid.

93. Ibid.

94. Ibid., p. 260.

95. Ibid., p. 329.

96. Ibid., p. 320.

97. Ibid., p. 315.

98. Ibid., p. 340.

99. Ibid., p. 354.

100. Ibid., p. 283.

101. Ibid., p. 307.

102. Ibid., pp. 288–89.

103. Ibid., p. 335.

104. Ibid., p. 291.

105. Ibid., p. 334.

106. Ibid., p. 259.

107. Ibid., p. 334.

108. Ibid., pp. 334–35.

109. Ibid., pp. 291–92.

110. Ibid., p. 233.

111. Ibid., p. 234.

112. Graham Hough, *The Dark Sun: A Study of D. H. Lawrence* (London: Duckworth, 1970), p. 53.

113. Bradbury, p. 50.

114. D. H. Lawrence, *Sons and Lovers* (New York: Viking, 1964), p. 420.

115. Eugene Goodheart, *The Utopian Vision of D. H. Lawrence* (Chicago: University of Chicago Press, 1963), p. 8.

116. Harold E. Toliver, *Marvell's Ironic Vision* (New Haven, Conn.: Yale University Press, 1965), p. 89.

117. Peter Laslett, *The World We Have Lost: England before the Industrial Age* (New York: Scribner's, 1973), p. 5.

118. Ibid.

119. Lawrence, *Sons and Lovers*, p. 420.

120. Raymond Williams, *Culture and Society 1780/1950* (New York: Harper Torchbooks, 1958), pp. 205–6.

121. D. H. Lawrence, "Nottingham and the Mining Country," in *Phoenix*, p. 133.

122. Ibid., pp. 135–36.

123. Moore, *CL*, 1: 318.

124. Ibid., 2: 989–90.

125. D. H. Lawrence, *Studies in Classic American Literature* (New York: Viking, 1968), p. 54.

126. D. H. Lawrence, "Love," in *Phoenix*, pp. 155–56.

127. Goodheart, p. 30.

128. D. H. Lawrence, *The Rainbow* (New York: Viking, 1969), p. 344–45.

129. Lawrence, *St. Mawr*, p. 114.

130. Terry Eagleton, *Exiles and Emigrés* (New York: Schocken Books, 1970), p. 208.

131. Mark Schorer, "D. H. Lawrence and the Spirit of Place," in Moore, ed., *A D. H. Lawrence Miscellany*, p. 286.

132. D. H. Lawrence, "Study of Thomas Hardy," in *Phoenix*, p. 419.

133. Scott Sanders, *D. H. Lawrence: The World of the Five Major Novels* (New York: Viking, 1974), p. 77.

134. Ibid., p. 80.

135. Ibid.

136. Lawrence, "Study of Thomas Hardy," p. 407.

137. Lawrence, *The Rainbow*, p. 2.

138. Ibid.

139. Ibid., p. 3.

140. Ibid.

141. Ibid., p. 6.

142. Ibid.

143. Ibid.

144. Ibid., p. 7.

145. Ibid., p. 2.

146. Ibid.

147. David Cavitch, *D. H. Lawrence and the New World* (N.Y.: Oxford University Press, 1969), p. 39.

148. Lawrence, *The Rainbow*, p. 437.

149. Ibid., p. 438.

150. Ibid.

151. Ibid., p. 487.

152. Ibid., p. 488.

153. Ibid.

154. Ibid.

155. Ibid., p. 486.

156. Ibid., p. 489.

157. Ibid., pp. 491–92.

158. Ibid., p. 490.

159. Ibid., p. 492.

160. Ibid., p. 495.

161. F. R. Leavis, *D. H. Lawrence: Novelist* (New York: Clarion, 1969), pp. 142–43.

162. Ibid., p. 143.

163. George H. Ford, *Double Measure*, p. 162.

164. Ibid., pp. 161–62.

Chapter 5: Lawrence's Break with the Georgians

1. Horace Gregory, *D. H. Lawrence: Pilgrim of the Apocalypse* (New York: Grove, 1957), p. 1.

2. Ibid., p. 4.

3. Ibid., p. 10.

4. Lascelles Abercrombie, "The Sale of St. Thomas," *Georgian Poetry 1911–1912* (London: The Poetry Bookshop, 1917), p. 20.

5. Harry T. Moore, ed., *CL*, 1: 47.

6. D. H. Lawrence, *Georgian Poetry 1911–1912*," in *Phoenix*, pp. 305–6.

7. Lawrence, "Surgery for the Novel—or a Bomb," in *Phoenix*, p. 518.

8. Lawrence, "*Georgian Poetry 1911–1912*," p. 305. As early as 1907, W. W. Gibson showed signs that, at least for him, the world was not always "fairly bubbling and glittering." His introductory poem to *Daily Bread* (1910) suggests his movement of mind during these years:

All life moving to one measure—
Daily bread, daily bread—
Bread of life, and bread of labour,
Bread of bitterness and sorrow,
Hand-to-mouth, and no to-morrow,
Dearth for housemate, death for neighbour . . .

"Yet when all the babes are fed,
Love, are there not crumbs to treasure?"
                    [W. W. Gibson, *Daily Bread*, epigraph]

But Gibson's sallies into social verse were always mild-mannered. His work, for the most part, was a watery reflection of the Edwardian stock-in-trade: the literature of social therapy. Though his subjects were often drawn from the lives of the laboring classes, his emphasis was always on the "life-song of humanity." In some ways, Gibson's career was a pale recapitulation of the cultural movement from the 1890s to the Edwardian period.

9. Christopher Hassall, *Rupert Brooke: A Biography* (London: Faber and Faber, 1972), p. 354.

10. Geoffrey Keynes, ed., *The Letters of Rupert Brooke* (New York: Harcourt, Brace and World, 1968), p. 440.

11. Ibid., p. 380.

12. Rupert Brooke, *Letters from America* (London: Sidgwick and Jackson, 1916), p. 161.

13. Ibid., p. 167.

14. W. Somerset Maugham, *The Summing Up* (Garden City, N.Y.: Doubleday, Doran, 1939), p. 192.

15. Ibid., p. 196.

16. Ibid., pp. 197–98.

17. Ibid., p. 198.

18. W. H. Hudson, quoted by John Lester, *Journey through Despair, 1880–1914: Transformations in British Literary Culture* (Princeton, N.J.: Princeton University Press, 1968), p. 121.

19. John Gould Fletcher, *Life Is My Song* (New York: Farrar and Rinehart, 1937), p. 68.

20. Octavio Paz, *Children of the Mire: Modern Poetry from Romanticism to the Avant-Garde*, translated by Rachel Phillips (Cambridge, Mass.: Harvard University Press, 1974), p. 35.

21. Ibid., p. 9.

22. E. M. Cioran, *The Fall into Time,* translated by Richard Howard (Chicago: Quadrangle, 1970), p. 92.

23. D. H. Lawrence, *The Lost Girl* (New York: Viking, 1968), p. 350.

24. D. H. Lawrence, *Twilight in Italy*, in *D. H. Lawrence and Italy* (New York: Viking, 1972), p. 135.

25. Ibid., p. 151.

26. Moore, *CL*, 1: 208.

27. Lawrence, *The Lost Girl*, p. 328.

28. Ibid.

29. D. H. Lawrence, *The Rainbow* (New York: Viking, 1969), p. 495.

30. Ibid.

31. Moore, *CL*, 1: 519.

32. Ibid., p. 366.

33. Ibid., p. 519.

34. Ibid., p. 336.

35. Percy Lubbock, ed., *Letters of Henry James*, vol. 2 (New York: Scribner's, 1920), p. 384.

36. Lionel Trilling, "On the Modern Element in Modern Literature," in Irving Howe, ed., *Literary Modernism* (Greenwich, Conn.: Fawcett Premier, 1971), p. 60.

37. Moore, *CL*, 1: 131.

38. Ibid., p. 191.

39. Ibid., p. 250.

40. Ibid.

41. Christopher Hassall, *A Biography of Edward Marsh* (New York: Harcourt, Brace and World, 1959), p. 270.

42. Lawrence, *"Georgian Poetry 1911–1912,"* p. 305.

43. Moore, *CL*, 1: 278.

44. Ibid.

45. Ibid., p. 236.

46. Lawrence, *"In the American Grain*, by William Carlos Williams," in *Phoenix*, p. 336.

47. Moore, *CL*, 1: 279.

48. Eugene Goodheart, *The Utopian Vision of D. H. Lawrence* (Chicago: University of Chicago Press, 1963), p. 41.

49. James T. Boulton, ed. *Lawrence in Love: Letters to Louie Burrows* (Nottingham: University of Nottingham Press, 1968), p. 84.

50. Lawrence, "German Books: Thomas Mann," in *Phoenix*, p. 308.

51. Ibid.

52. Ibid., p. 308–9.

53. Ibid., p. 309.

54. Ibid.

55. Ibid., p. 312.

56. Ibid.

57. Ibid., p. 313.

58. Moore, *CL*, 1: 47–48.

59. D. H. Lawrence, *Sons and Lovers* (New York: Viking, 1964), p. 152.

60. Edward Marsh, quoted by Hassall, *A Biography of Edward Marsh*, p. 282.

61. Edward Marsh, *A Number of People* (New York: Harper, 1939), p. 322.

62. Robert Nichols, quoted by Hassall, *A Biography of Edward Marsh*, p. 506.

63. Marsh, quoted ibid., p. 507.

64. Moore, *CL*, 1: 219–20.

65. Ibid., p. 221.

66. Ibid., p. 224.

67. Ibid., p. 225.

68. D. H. Lawrence, "Foreword to *Collected Poems*," in *CP*, p. 851.

69. Moore, *CL*, 1: 230.

70. Marsh, quoted by Hassall, *A Biography of Edward Marsh*, p. 251.

71. Moore, *CL*, 1: 233–34.

72. Ibid., pp. 231–32.

73. Ibid., p. 236. It is worth noting that Marsh himself consciously practiced what he called critical "Diabolization," defined by Christopher Hassall as "the act of a critic whose declared aim is 'to find fault and be as carping as possible for the eventual benefit of the work in hand'" (Hassall, *A Biography of Edward Marsh*, p. 691). Lawrence, when discussing Davies—and later, Abercrombie—seems to be functioning much in this capacity.

74. Ibid., pp. 236–37.

75. Ibid., p. 244.

76. Ibid., pp. 242–44.

77. Ibid., pp. 244–46.

78. Marsh, quoted by Hassall, *A Biography of Edward Marsh*, p. 255.

79. Ibid., p. 260.

80. Ibid., p. 235.

81. Marsh, p. 228.

82. Moore, *CL*, 1: 249.

83. Ibid.

84. Ibid., p. 252.

85. Ibid.

86. Ibid., p. 253.

87. Aldous Huxley, ed., *The Letters of D. H. Lawrence* (London: Heinemann, 1932), p. 167.

88. Moore, *CL*, 1: 218.

89. Ibid., p. 269.

90. Ibid., p. 425.

91. Hassall, *A Biography of Edward Marsh*, p. 382.

92. Marsh, p. 228.

93. Ibid., p. 234.

94. J. B. Harmer, *Victory in Limbo: Imagism in 1908–1917* (London: Secker and Warburg, 1975), p. 26.

95. Ibid., p. 27.

96. Edward Storer, quoted in ibid., p. 28.

97. Ezra Pound, "A Retrospect," in *Literary Essays of Ezra Pound* (New York: New Directions, 1968), p. 9.

98. Edgar Wind, *Art and Anarchy* (New York: Vintage, 1969), p. 18.

99. Lawrence, "*Georgian Poetry 1911–1912*," p. 305.

100. Abercrombie, "The Sale of St. Thomas," pp. 20–21.

101. Robert H. Ross, *The Georgian Revolt: Rise and Fall of a Poetic Ideal, 1910–1922* (London: Faber and Faber, 1967), p. 158.

102. J. C. Squire, quoted ibid., p. 155.

103. John Drinkwater, quoted ibid., p. 151.

104. Lawrence, "Study of Thomas Hardy," in *Phoenix*, p. 431.

105. Squire, quoted by Ross, p. 155.

106. Ibid., p. 210.

107. Ezra Pound, "The Serious Artist," in *Literary Essays of Ezra Pound*, pp. 43–44.

108. Pound, quoted by Noel Stock, *The Life of Exra Pound* (New York: Pantheon, 1970), p. 159.

109. Stephen Spender, *Love-Hate Relations: English and American Sensibilities* (New York: Vintage, 1975), p. 142.

110. Lawrence, "Study of Thomas Hardy," p. 419.

111. Ibid.

112. Baruch Hochman, *Another Ego* (Columbia, S.C.: University of South Carolina Press, 1970), p. 41.

113. Raymond Williams, *The Country and the City* (New York: Oxford University Press, 1973), p. 255, 258.

114. D. H. Lawrence, *Studies in Classic American Literature* (New York: Viking, 1968), p. 24.

115. Ibid., p. 26.

116. Ibid., p. 23.

117. Moore, *CL*, 1: 278–79.

118. Marsh, quoted by Hassall, *A Biography of Edward Marsh*, p. 268.

119. Ibid., p. 273.

Chapter 6: "Another Language Almost": The Impact of Futurism, Imagism, and Vorticism

1. Angus Wilson, *Anglo-Saxon Attitudes* (New York: Viking, 1956), p. 6.

2. Max Wildi, "The Birth of Expressionism in the Work of D. H. Lawrence," *English Studies* 19 (December 1937): p. 241.

3. Ibid., pp. 241–42.

4. Harry T. Moore, ed., *CL*, 1: p. 282.

5. Wildi, p. 258.

6. Ford Madox Ford, "Impressionism and Poetry," in *Critical Writings of Ford Madox Ford*, ed. by Frank MacShane (Lincoln, Neb.: University of Nebraska Press, 1964), p. 141.

7. D. H. Lawrence, *The Rainbow* (New York: Viking, 1969), p. 2.

8. Moore, *CL*, 1: p. 264.

9. Ibid.

10. Ibid., p. 279.

11. Ibid., p. 263.

12. Ibid., p. 282.

13. Ibid.

14. Ibid., p. 273.

15. Ibid.

16. Ibid., p. 264.

17. Ibid., p. 242.

18. Ibid.

19. Ibid., p. 241.

20. Douglas Goldring, quoted by John Lester, *Journey through Despair, 1880–1914: Transformations in British Literary Culture* (Princeton, N. J.: Princeton University Press, 1968), p. 127.

21. Ezra Pound, "The Serious Artist," *Literary Essays of Ezra Pound*, ed. by T. S. Eliot (New York: New Directions, 1968), p. 49.

22. Wyndham Lewis, quoted by William C. Wees, *Vorticism and the English Avant-Garde* (Toronto: University of Toronto Press, 1972), pp. 57–58.

23. Ezra Pound, "I gather the limbs of Osiris," in William Cookson, ed., *Selected Prose 1909–1965* (New York: New Directions, 1975), p. 25.

24. Hugh Kenner, *The Pound Era* (Berkeley and Los Angeles: University of California Press, 1971), p. 173.

25. Ibid., p. 147.

26. Ezra Pound, *Gaudier-Brzeska: A Memoir* (New York: New Directions, 1970), p. 92.

27. Kenner, p. 146.

28. Wyndham Lewis, quoted by Wees, p. 161.

29. Kenner, p. 146.

30. Amédée Ozenfant, *Foundations of Modern Art*, New American Edition, augmented (New York: Dover, 1952), p. 266.

31. Lawrence, *The Rainbow*, p. 489.

32. Stephen Spender, *The Struggle of the Modern* (Berkeley and Los Angeles: University of California Press, 1965), p. 84.

33. Wyndham Lewis, quoted in Timothy Materer, "The English Vortex: Modern Literature and the 'Pattern of Hope,'" *Journal of Modern Literature* 3 (July 1974): 1129.

34. Spender, p. 84.

35. Lawrence, *The Rainbow*, p. 495.

36. Walter Pater, *Studies in the History of the Renaissance* (London: Macmillan, 1873), p. 209.

37. Ibid.

38. John Lester, p. 31.

39. Geoffrey Barraclough, *An Introduction to Contemporary History* (Baltimore: Penguin, 1968), p. 240.

40. Kenneth Burke, *Attitudes toward History* (Boston: Beacon, 1961), p. 30.

41. Marianne W. Martin, *Futurist Art and Theory, 1900–1915* (Oxford: Clarendon Press, 1968), p. 38.

42. Richard Aldington, quoted by Robert H. Ross, *The Georgian Revolt: Rise and Fall of a Poetic Ideal, 1910–1922* (London: Faber and Faber, 1967), p. 59.

43. Edward Marsh, *A Number of People* (New York: Harper, 1939), pp. 295–96.

44. James Gibbons Huneker, *Ivory, Apes and Peacocks* (New York: Scribner's, 1915), p. 266.

45. Filippo Tommaso Marinetti, "The Founding and Manifesto of Futurism," in R. W. Flint, ed., *Marinetti: Selected Writings* (New York: Farrar, Straus and Giroux, 1972), pp. 41–42.

46. Moore, *CL*, l: 279–80.

47. Mark Kinkead-Weekes, "The Marble and the Statue," in Maynard Mack and Ian Gregor, eds., *Imagined Worlds* (London: Methuen, 1968), p. 380.

48. Ibid.

49. Moore, *CL*, 1: 281–82.

50. Mark Schorer, "*Women in Love* and Death," in Mark Spilka, ed., *D. H. Lawrence: A Collection of Critical Essays* (Englewood Cliffs, N.J.: Prentice-Hall, 1963), p. 51.

51. R. E. Pritchard, *D. H. Lawrence: Body of Darkness* (London: Hutchinson University Library, 1971), pp. 20–21.

52. H. M. Daleski, *The Forked Flame* (London: Faber and Faber, 1965), pp. 76–77.

53. Frank Kermode, *D. H. Lawrence* (New York: Viking, 1973), p. 25.

54. Ibid., p. 28.

55. D. H. Lawrence, *Fantasia of the Unconscious*, in *Psychoanalysis and the Unconscious and Fantasia of the Unconscious* (New York: Viking, 1972), p. 57.

56. D. H. Lawrence, "Study of Thomas Hardy," in *Phoenix*, p. 479.

57. Ibid., p. 477.

58. Ibid.

59. Moore, *CL*, 1: 291.

60. Filippo Tommaso Marinetti, "Technical Manifesto of Futurist Literature," in R. W. Flint, ed., *Marinetti: Selected Writings*, p. 85.

61. Ibid.

62. Ibid., p. 84.

63. Ibid., p. 87.

64. Ibid.

65. Moore, *CL*, 1: 302.

66. C. E. M. Joad, *Decadence* (New York: Philosophical Library, 1949), p. 15.

67. Moore, *CL*, 1: 269.

68. Ibid.

69. Ibid., p. 241.

70. Ibid., p. 302.

71. Mary Freeman, *D. H. Lawrence: A Basic Study of His Ideas* (Gainsville, Fla: University of Florida Press, 1955), p. 73.

72. D. H. Lawrence, *Studies in Classic American Literature* (New York: Viking, 1968), p. 146.

73. Burke, p. 30.

74. Ibid., p. 32.

75. Ibid., p. 33.

76. Moore, *CL*, 1: 482.

77. Freeman, p. 74.

78. Burke, p. 30.

79. D. H. Lawrence, "The Crown," in *Phoenix II*, p. 366.

80. D. H. Lawrence, *Twilight in Italy*, in *D. H. Lawrence and Italy* (New York: Viking, 1968), p. 62.

81. Moore, *CL*, 1: 280.

82. Lawrence, "Study of Thomas Hardy," p. 464.

83. Lawrence, *Twilight in Italy*, p. 168.

84. D. H. Lawrence, *Women in Love* (New York: Modern Library, 1960), p. 488.

85. Ibid., p. 482.

86. Ibid., pp. 482–83.

87. Moore, *CL*, 1: 308.

88. Ibid.

89. See David Garnett, *The Flowers of the Forest* (New York: Harcourt Brace, 1956), pp. 34–36.

90. D. H. Lawrence, *Lady Chatterley's Lover* (New York: Grove Press, 1957), pp. 345–46.

91. Noel Stock, *The Life of Ezra Pound* (New York: Pantheon, 1970), p. 115.

92. James T. Boulton, ed., *Lawrence in Love: Letters to Louie Burrows* (Nottingham: Nottingham University Press, 1968), pp. 46–47.

93. See Noel Stock, p. 77, and Harry T. Moore, *The Priest of Love* (New York: Farrar, Straus and Giroux, 1974), p. 115.

94. Jessie Chambers (E. T.), *D. H. Lawrence: A Personal Record* (London: Jonathan Cape, 1935), pp. 171–72.

95. Ernest Rhys, *Everyman Remembers* (New York: Cosmopolitan Book Corporation, 1931), pp. 243–47.

96. William Carlos Williams, *Autobiography* (New York: Random House, 1951), p. 58.

97. Boulton, ed., p. 50.

98. Moore, *CL*, 1: 62.

99. Glenn Hughes, *Imagism and the Imagists* (New York: The Humanities Press, 1960), p. 170.

100. Hughes, p. 170.

101. Frieda Lawrence, *"Not I, But the Wind . . ."* (New York: Viking, 1934), p. 43.

102. Ezra Pound, "A Retrospect," in *Literary Essays of Ezra Pound*, p. 3.

103. D. D. Paige, ed., *The Letters of Ezra Pound 1907–1941* (New York: Harvest, 1950), p. 17.

104. Ibid., p. 301.

105. Sandra Gilbert, *Acts of Attention* (Ithaca, N.Y.: Cornell University Press, 1972), p. 35.

106. Ibid., p. 36.

107. D. H. Lawrence, "Baby-Movements," in *CP*, p. 916.

108. Lawrence, "Night Songs," in *CP*, p. 920.

109. See Noel Stock, p. 128.

110. Ezra Pound, "D. H. Lawrence," in *Literary Essays of Ezra Pound*, p. 387.

111. Ibid.

112. Ibid., p. 388.

113. Ford Madox Ford, *Return to Yesterday* (New York: Liveright, 1972), p. 375.

114. T. S. Eliot, quoted by Stanley Coffman, *Imagism: A Chapter for the History of Modern Poetry* (Norman, Okla.: University of Oklahoma Press, 1951), p. 217.

115. Pound, "D. H. Lawrence," p. 387.

116. Pound, "A Retrospect," p. 3. Not everyone has agreed with Pound that there were no Imagist elements to be found in *Love Poems and Others*. William Pratt, in his anthology of Imagist verse, includes thirteen of Lawrence's poems, three of which were published in *Love Poems and Others* (see William Pratt, *The Imagist Poem*).

117. Paige, ed., p. 212.

118. Richard Aldington, *Life for Life's Sake* (New York: Viking, 1941), p. 137.

119. Paige, ed., p. 22.

120. Moore, *CL*, 1: 259.

121. Aldington, p. 139.

122. Jean Gould, *Amy: The World of Amy Lowell and the Imagist Movement* (New York: Dodd, Mead, 1975), p. 128.

123. Ibid., p. 127.

124. Pound, "A Retrospect," p. 3.

125. Paige, ed., p. 38.

126. Kenner, p. 25.

127. Ezra Pound, quoted by J. B. Harmer, *Victory in Limbo: Imagism in 1908–1917* (London: Secker and Warburg, 1975), p. 179.

128. John Gould Fletcher, quoted by Wees, p. 61.

129. Ezra Pound, quoted by Hughes, p. 38.

130. Pound, "A Retrospect," p. 4.

131. Monroe K. Spears, *Space against Time in Modern Poetry* (Fort Worth, Tex.: Texas Christian University Press, 1972), p. 9.

132. Kenner, p. 173.

133. Frank Kermode, *Romantic Image* (New York: Vintage, 1964), p. 133.

134. Aldington, p. 110.

135. Ibid., p. 149.

136. Gordon Bottomley, quoted by Myron Simon, "The Georgian Poetic," in Robert Scholes, ed., *Papers of the Midwest Modern Language Association #1* (Iowa City, Ia.: Midwest Modern Language Assocation, 1969), p. 132. C. K. Stead, in comparing poems by the Georgian Edward Thomas and the Imagist H. D., finds that he can discern where "the most important motives of the two groups coincided, and where they differed" (C. K. Stead, *The New Poetic*, p. 101). He finds similarities in their attempts to "realize with precision one intensely experienced moment" which suggests "something beyond itself"; in their "intense reaction against generalization and abstraction"; in their verbal simplicity and unpretentiousness; in their "expression of precise emotions or states of mind." The differences involve form (especially rhyme), diction, and the use—in Thomas—of narrative (Stead, pp. 102–5).

137. Ezra Pound, quoted by C. K. Stead, *The New Poetic: Yeats to Eliot* (New York: Harper Torchbooks, 1964), p. 107.

138. T. E. Hulme, "Modern Art and Its Philosophy," in *Speculations*, ed. by Herbert Read (London: Routledge and Kegan Paul, 1965), p. 96.

139. Robert Langbaum, "Lords of Life, Kings in Exile: Identity and Sexuality in D. H. Lawrence," *The American Scholar* 45 (Winter 1975/1976): 807.

140. David Perkins, *A History of Modern Poetry: From the 1890's to the High Modernist Mode* (Cambridge, Mass.: Harvard University Press, 1976), p. 216.

141. Aldington, p. 141.

142. Gould, p. 129.

143. Moore, *CL*, 1: 288.

144. Lawrence, "Wedding Morn," in *CP*, p. 58.

145. See Coffman, *Imagism;* Moore, *The Priest of Love;* Gould, *Amy*.

146. Coffman, p. 30.

147. See Coffman, *Imagism;* Gould, *Amy*.

148. Gould, p. 132.

149. Ibid., p. 327.

150. Moore, *CL*, 1: 622.

151. Amy Lowell, quoted by Gould, p. 243.

152. Moore, *CL*, 1: 294.

153. Ibid., p. 495.

154. Aldington, p. 140.

155. Harry T. Moore, *The Priest of Love: A Life of D. H. Lawrence* (New York: Farrar, Straus and Giroux, 1974), p. 283.

156. H. D., *Bid Me to Live: (A Madrigal)* (New York: Grove, 1960), p. 183.

157. Ibid., p. 67.

158. Lawrence, "Poetry of the Present," in *CP*, p. 185.

159. Ibid.

160. Ibid.

161. Ibid., p. 183.

162. Ibid., pp. 182–83.

163. T. E. Hulme, "Romanticism and Classicism," in *Speculations*, p. 127.

164. Richard Aldington, quoted by Coffman, p. 166.

165. Ezra Pound, quoted by Harriet Monroe, *A Poet's Life: Seventy Years in a Changing World* (New York: Macmillan, 1938), p. 266.

166. Moore, *CL*, 1: 413.

167. Hulme, "Romanticism and Classicism," p. 133.

168. Moore, *CL*, 1: 204.

169. Wallace Stevens, "Adagia," in *Opus Posthumous*, ed. Samuel French Morse (New York: Knopf, 1957), p. 161.

170. Graham Hough, *Image and Experience* (London: Duckworth, 1960), p. 70.

Chapter 7: Good-bye to All That: The Georgians, the War, and "England, My England"

1. Rupert Brooke, *Letters from America* (London: Sidgwick and Jackson, 1916), p. 180. Graham Greene, in his autobiography, *A Sort of Life*, recalls that in August 1914 "a German master was denounced to my father as a spy because he had been seen under the railway bridge without a hat, [and] a dachshund was stoned in the High Street" (Graham Greene, *A Sort of Life*, p. 66). Incidents of the same temper were hardly unfamiliar to Lawrence and his "Hunnish" wife.

2. Rupert Brooke, "Peace," in *The Collected Poems of Rupert Brooke* (New York: John Lane, 1915), p. 107.

3. Brooke, "The Dead," in ibid., p. 109.

4. Paul Fussell, *The Great War and Modern Memory* (New York: Oxford University Press, 1975), p. 169.

5. Brooke, *Letters from America*, pp. 177–78.

6. Harry T. Moore, ed., *CL* 1: 290–91.

7. Ibid., p. 337. It can hardly be disputed that Lawrence used his neighbor at Greatham, Percy Lucas (brother of light-essayist E. V. Lucas), as the central model for his story. Lawrence himself wrote Lady Cynthia Asquith to tell her that she would find "in the *English Review* for next month a story about the Lucases" (Moore, *CL*, 1: 364). Nevertheless, Percy Lucas's daughter has argued that although Lawrence accurately described an incident which happened to Lucas—the sickle incident—Lawrence "did not know Percy, and nor did he need to for the creation of Egbert" (Barbara Lucas, "Apropos of 'England, My England,'" p. 292). This seems to be an accurate perception and holds true for most of Lawrence's models. In any case, though Percy Lucas was certainly not an "official" Georgian, the rather skimpy evidence (including his brother's work) suggests that he fitted the Georgian mold—at least as Lawrence saw it in 1915.

8. Ibid., p. 459.

9. Ibid., p. 384.

10. Ibid., p. 498.

11. Ibid., p. 509.

12. Ibid., p. 295.

13. Kinsley Widmer, *The Art of Perversity: D. H. Lawrence's Shorter Fictions* (Seattle: University of Washington Press, 1962), p. 17.

14. D. H. Lawrence, "England, My England," in *CSS*, 2: 303.

15. Ibid.

16. Ibid., p. 307.

17. Ibid., p. 303.

18. Ibid., p. 308.

19. Ibid., pp. 303–4.

20. Moore, *CL*, 1: 278.

21. Lawrence, "England, My England," p. 323.

22. Ibid.

23. Widmer, p. 21.

24. Lawrence, "England, My England," p. 307.

25. Ibid., p. 308.

26. Ibid.

27. Ibid.

28. F. R. Leavis, *D. H. Lawrence: Novelist* (New York: Clarion, 1969), p. 266.

29. Lawrence, "England, My England," pp. 311–12.

30. Ibid., p. 317.

31. Ibid., p. 307.

32. Ibid.

33. Ibid., p. 317.

34. Ibid., pp. 317–18.

35. Ibid., p. 304.

36. Ibid., p. 306.

37. Ibid.

38. Ibid., p. 307.

39. Ibid., p. 304.

40. Ibid.

41. Ibid., p. 309.

42. Ibid.

43. Ibid.

44. Ibid.

45. Ibid., p. 305.

46. Ibid., p. 309.

47. Ibid., p. 314.

48. Ibid.

49. Ibid., p. 321.

50. Ibid.

51. Ibid., p. 309.

52. Ibid., pp. 323–24.

53. Geoffrey Keynes, ed., *The Letters of Rupert Brooke* (New York: Harcourt, Brace and World, 1968), p. 631.

54. Ibid., p. 627.

55. Moore, *CL*, 1: 456.

56. Lawrence, "England, My England," p. 326.

57. Ibid., p. 327.

58. Ibid.

59. Ibid.

60. Ibid., p. 328.

61. Ibid., p. 327.

62. Ibid., p. 328.

63. Neil Myers, "Lawrence and the War," *Criticism* 4 (Winter 1962): 48.

64. Moore, *CL*, 1: 337–38.

65. Ibid., p. 456.

66. Ibid., p. 457. In one way, at least, Brooke's prediction was accurate—though not in the way he thought. The savagery that underlies postwar British civilization found its ablest chronicler in Evelyn Waugh, and its ablest chronicle in his *A Handful of Dust*.

67. Widmer, p. 21.

68. Lawrence, "England, My England," pp. 332–33.

69. Keynes, ed., pp. 654–55.

70. Moore, *CL*, 1: 476.

71. Ibid., p. 402.
72. Ibid., p. 466.
73. Ibid.
74. Ibid., pp. 466–67.
75. Ibid., p. 519.
76. Catherine Carswell, *The Savage Pilgrimage* (London: Chatto and Windus, 1932), p. 59. Curiously, the first paragraph of this letter does not appear in Moore or Huxley, although the postscript does appear. Carswell, however, quotes it in *The Savage Pilgrimage*, and indicates that both the missing paragraph and the postscript were part of the same letter.
77. Moore, *CL*, 1: 429.
78. Ibid., p. 336.

Chapter 8: Extensions and Conclusions

1. John Maynard Keynes, "My Early Beliefs," in *Two Memoirs* (London: Rupert Hart-Davis, 1949), p. 79.
2. Bertrand Russell, *Portraits from Memory and Other Essays* (New York: Clarion, 1969), p. 111.
3. Harry T. Moore, ed., *CL* 1: 324.
4. Ibid., pp. 327–28.
5. Paul Delany, *D. H. Lawrence's Nightmare* (New York: Basic Books, 1978), p. 64.
6. David Garnett, *The Flowers of the Forest* (New York: Harcourt, Brace and Co., 1956), p. 54.
7. Keynes, "My Early Beliefs," pp. 78, 80.
8. D. H. Lawrence, quoted by Frieda Lawrence, *"Not I, But the Wind . . ."* (New York: Viking, 1934), p. 82.
9. Moore, *CL*, 1: 330.
10. Ibid., p. 367.
11. Russell, p. 112.
12. Russell, quoted by Ottoline Morrell, *Ottoline: The Early Memoirs of Lady Ottoline Morrell*, ed. Robert Gathorne-Hardy (London: Faber and Faber, 1963), p. 276.
13. Russell, pp. 112, 114.
14. Moore, *CL*, 1: 324.
15. Christopher Hassall, *A Biography of Edward Marsh* (New York: Harcourt, Brace, 1959), p. 66.
16. Myron Simon, "The Georgian Poetic," in Robert Scholes, ed., *Papers of the Midwest Modern Language Association # 1* (Iowa City, Ia.: Midwest Modern Language Association, 1969), p. 125.
17. Moore, *CL*, 1: 278–79.
18. Delany, p. 79.
19. Ibid., p. 80.
20. Quentin Bell, *Bloomsbury*, Pageant of History Series (London: Weidenfeld and Nicolson, 1968), p. 76.
21. Quentin Bell, "Introduction," *The Diary of Virginia Woolf*, vol. 1, ed. Anne Olivier Bell (New York: Harcourt Brace Jovanovich, 1977), p. xxv.
22. Moore, *CL*, 1: 491.
23. Frank Swinnerton, *The Georgian Scene: A Literary Panorama* (New York: Farrar and Rinehart, 1934), p. 339.

24. Noel Annan, *Leslie Stephen: His Thought and Character in Relation to his Time* (Cambridge, Mass.: Harvard University Press, 1952), p. 124. In *A Mirror for Anglo-Saxons*, Martin Green has pointed out that Lawrence's Cambridge-Bloomsbury acquaintances "were not moving in any parallel direction to him," and that their "forms of gaiety and rebellion were not to his sense healthy" (p. 160). Lytton Strachey, for instance, "with his sickliness, his Pyrrhonism, his formality of manner and irony of tone," would come to be seen after the war as the "realist, clear-sighted moralist, and arbiter of manners" for the new direction that England would take (pp. 161–62). England, Green insists, had to make a major cultural choice by the end of the war, and its choice was for Strachey and Keynes and Russell—not for Lawrence.

25. Moore, *CL*, 1: 333.

26. Ibid., pp. 332–33.

27. Nigel Nicolson and Joanne Trautmann, eds., *The Letters of Virginia Woolf*, vol. 4 (New York: Harcourt Brace Jovanovich, 1979), p. 315.

28. Ibid.

29. Moore, *CL*, 1: 383.

30. Ibid., p. 341.

31. Ibid.

32. C. E. M. Joad, *Decadence: A Philosophical Inquiry* (New York: Philosophical Library, 1949), pp. 98–99.

33. D. H. Lawrence, "Surgery for the Novel—or a Bomb," in *Phoenix*, p. 517.

34. Ibid., pp. 517–18.

35. Moore, *CL*, 1: 475.

36. D. H. Lawrence, *Women in Love* (New York: Modern Library, 1950), p. 64.

37. Ibid.

38. Virginia Woolf, "Modern Fiction," in *Collected Essays*, vol. 2 (London: Hogarth, 1966), p. 106.

39. Ibid., p. 107.

40. Lawrence, "Why the Novel Matters," in *Phoenix*, p. 537.

41. D. H. Lawrence, *Lady Chatterley's Lover* (New York: Grove, 1957), pp. 117–18.

42. Moore, *CL*, 1: 183.

Selected Bibliography

Aldington, Richard. *Life for Life's Sake*. New York: Viking, 1941.

————. *Portrait of a Genius, But . . .* London: Heinemann, 1950.

Aldridge, John W., ed. *Critiques and Essays on Modern Fiction: 1920–1951*. New York: Ronald Press, 1952.

Annan, Noel. *The Disintegration of an Old Culture*. London: Oxford University Press, 1966.

————. *Leslie Stephen: His Thought and Character in Relation to His Time*. Cambridge, Mass.: Harvard University Press, 1952.

Asquith, Lady Cynthia. *Diaries 1915–1918*. Edited by E. M. Horsley. New York: Knopf, 1969.

————. *Remember and Be Glad*. London: James Barrie, 1952.

Asquith, Herbert. *Moments of Memory: Recollections and Impressions*. New York: Scribner's, 1938.

Auden, W. H. *The Dyer's Hand and Other Essays*. New York: Random House, 1962.

————. *Forewords and Afterwords*. New York: Random House, 1973.

Baird, James. *Ishmael: A Study of the Symbolic Mode in Primitivism*. Baltimore: Johns Hopkins University Press, 1956.

Barraclough, Geoffrey. *An Introduction to Contemporary History*. Baltimore: Penguin, 1968.

Bedient, Calvin. *Architects of the Self: George Eliot, D. H. Lawrence and E. M. Forster*. Berkeley and Los Angeles: University of California Press, 1972.

Bell, Anne Olivier, ed. *The Diary of Virginia Woolf*. 2 vols. New York and London: Harcourt Brace Jovanovich, 1977.

Bell, Clive. *Art*. London: Chatto and Windus, 1913.

————. *Civilization: An Essay*. New York: Harcourt, Brace, 1928.

————. *Old Friends*. London: Chatto and Windus, 1956.

Bell, Quentin. *Bloomsbury*. London: Weidenfeld and Nicolson, 1968.

————. *Virginia Woolf: A Biography*. New York: Harcourt Brace Jovanovich, 1972.

Bellamy, William. *The Novels of Wells, Bennett and Galsworthy: 1890–1910*. New York: Barnes and Noble, 1971.

Bennett, Arnold. *Books and Persons: Being Comments on a Past Epoch*. London: Chatto and Windus, 1917.

———. *The Evening Standard Years: "Books and Persons" 1926–1931*. Edited by Andrew Mylett. London: Chatto and Windus, 1974.

———. *The Journal of Arnold Bennett*. New York: Viking, 1933.

Bergonzi, Bernard. *Heroes' Twilight*. London: Constable, 1965.

———. *The Turn of a Century*. New York: Barnes and Noble, 1973.

———, ed. *The Twentieth Century*. London: Barrie and Jenkins, 1970.

Bersani, Leo. *A Future for Astyanax: Character and Desire in Literature*. Boston: Little, Brown, 1976.

Blackmur, R. P. *Form and Value in Modern Poetry*. Garden City, N.Y.: Doubleday Anchor, 1952.

Blunden, Edmund. *Undertones of War*. New York: Harvest, 1965.

Blunt, Wilfrid Scawen. *My Diaries: Being a Personal Narrative of Events 1888–1914*. 2 vols. New York: Knopf, 1921.

Bottomley, Gordon. *Chambers of Imagery*. First series. N.p.: E. Mathews, 1907.

———. *Chambers of Imagery*. Second series. N.p.: E. Mathews, 1912.

Boulton, James T., ed. *Lawrence in Love: Letters to Louie Burrows*. Nottingham: University of Nottingham Press, 1968.

Bradbury, Malcolm. *Possibilities: Essays on the State of the Novel*. London: Oxford University Press, 1973.

———. *The Social Context of Modern English Literature*. New York: Schocken Books, 1971.

Bridgewater, Patrick. *Nietzsche in Anglosaxony*. N.p.: Leicester University Press, 1972.

Brooke, Rupert. *The Collected Poems of Rupert Brooke*. New York: John Lane, 1915.

———. *Letters from America*. With a Preface by Henry James. London: Sidgwick and Jackson, 1916.

———. *The Prose of Rupert Brooke*. Edited with an Introduction by Christopher Hassall. London: Sidgwick and Jackson, 1956.

Brower, Reuben A., ed. *Twentieth-Century Literature in Retrospect*. Harvard English Studies #2. Cambridge, Mass.: Harvard University Press, 1971.

Brown, Norman O. *Closing Time*. New York: Random House, 1973.

———. *Life against Death: The Psychoanalytical Meaning of History*. New York: Vintage, 1959.

Buckle, Richard. *Diaghilev*. New York: Atheneum, 1979.

Buckley, Jerome. *The Victorian Temper: A Study in Literary Culture*. New York: Vintage, 1964.

Bullough, Geoffrey. *The Trend of Modern Poetry*. Edinburgh and London: Oliver and Boyd, 1934.

Burke, Kenneth. *Attitudes toward History*. Boston: Beacon, 1961.

Burwell, Rose Marie. "A Catalogue of Lawrence's Reading from Early Childhood." *D. H. Lawrence Review*, Fall 1970, pp. 193–296.

Calinescu, Matei. *Faces of Modernity: Avant-Garde, Decadence, Kitsch*. Bloomington and London: Indiana University Press, 1977.

Callow, Phillip. *Son and Lover: The Young Lawrence*. London: The Bodley Head, 1975.

Campbell, Roy. *Broken Record*. London: Boriswood, 1934.

Carpenter, Edward. *Civilisation: Its Cause and Cure*. Boston: Tao Books, 1971.

Carrington, Noel, editor. *Mark Gertler: Selected Letters*. London: Rupert Hart-Davis, 1965.

Carswell, Catherine. *The Savage Pilgrimage*. London: Chatto and Windus, 1932.

Carter, John. "*The Rainbow* Prosecution." *Times Literary Supplement* 496 (27 February 1969): 216.

Cavitch, David. *D. H. Lawrence and the New World*. New York: Oxford University Press, 1969.

Chambers, Jessie (E. T.). *D. H. Lawrence: A Personal Record*. London: Jonathan Cape, 1935.

Chapple, J. A. V. *Documentary and Imaginative Literature 1880–1920*. London: Blandford Press, 1970.

Chesterton, G. K. *Autobiography*. London: Hutchinson, 1937.

———. *The Common Man*. New York: Sheed and Ward, 1950.

———. *Lunacy and Letters*. Edited by Dorothy Collins. New York: Sheed and Ward, 1958.

Church, Richard. *The Voyage Home*. New York: The John Day Co., 1966.

Cioran, E. M. *The Fall into Time*. Translated by Richard Howard. Chicago: Quadrangle, 1970.

Clarke, Colin. *River of Dissolution: D. H. Lawrence and English Romanticism*. London: Routledge and Kegan Paul, 1969.

Clough, Rosa T. *Futurism*. New York: Wisdom Library, 1961.

Coffman, Stanley. *Imagism: A Chapter for the History of Modern Poetry*. Norman, Okla.: University of Oklahoma Press, 1951.

Connolly, Cyril. *Enemies of Promise and Other Essays: An Autobiography of Ideas.* Garden City, N.Y.: Doubleday Anchor, 1960.

Corke, Helen. "D. H. Lawrence as I Saw Him." *Renaissance and Modern Studies* 4 (1960): 5–13.

———. *D. H. Lawrence: The Croydon Years.* Austin, Tex.: University of Texas Press, 1965.

Cox, C. B., and Dyson, A. E., eds. *The Twentieth Century Mind 1: 1900–1918.* London: Oxford University Press, 1972.

Cox, C. B., and Dyson, A. E., eds. *Word in the Desert.* London: Oxford University Press, 1968.

D., H. (Doolittle, Hilda) *Bid Me to Live: (A Madrigal).* New York: Grove Press, 1960.

Daiches, David. *Poetry and the Modern World.* Chicago: University of Chicago Press, 1940.

Daleski, H. M. *The Forked Flame.* London: Faber and Faber, 1965.

Dangerfield, George. *The Strange Death of Liberal England 1910–1914.* New York: Capricorn, 1961.

Davidson, John. *John Davidson: A Selection of His Poems.* Edited by M. Lindsay. London: Hutchinson, 1961.

Davies, W. H. *The Complete Poems of W. H. Davies.* Middletown, Conn.: Wesleyan University Press, 1965.

Deakin, William. "D. H. Lawrence's Attacks on Proust and Joyce." *Essays in Criticism* 6 (October 1957): 383–403.

Delany, Paul. *D. H. Lawrence's Nightmare: The Writer and His Circle in the Years of the Great War.* New York: Basic Books, 1978.

Delavenay, Emile. *D. H. Lawrence and Edward Carpenter: A Study in Edwardian Transition.* New York: Taplinger, 1971.

———. *D. H. Lawrence: The Man and His Work.* London: Heinemann, 1972.

de Sola Pinto, Vivian. *Crisis in English Poetry 1880–1940.* New York: Harper Torchbooks, 1958.

Downie, R. Angus. *Frazer and the Golden Bough.* London: Gollancz, 1970.

Drabble, Margaret. *Arnold Bennett.* New York: Knopf, 1974.

Draper, R. P., ed. *D. H. Lawrence: The Critical Heritage.* New York: Barnes and Noble, 1970.

Drinkwater, John. *Discovery.* Boston and New York: Houghton Mifflin, 1933.

Eagleton, Terry. *Exiles and Emigrés.* New York: Schocken Books, 1970.

Edel, Leon, and Ray, Gordon, eds. *Henry James and H. G. Wells.* London: Rupert Hart-Davis, 1958.

Edwards, E. P. *Bad Fish*. London: Malign Fiesta Press, 1957.

Ellmann, Richard. *Golden Codgers: Biographical Speculations*. New York: Oxford University Press, 1973.

Fiedler, Leslie. *The Collected Essays of Leslie Fiedler*. 2 vols. New York: Stein and Day, 1971.

Fletcher, John Gould. *Life Is My Song*. New York: Farrar and Rinehart, 1937.

Ford, Boris, ed. *The Modern Age*. The Pelican Guide to English Literature #7. Harmondsworth, Middlesex: Penguin, 1964.

Ford, Ford Madox. *Critical Writings of Ford Madox Ford*. Edited by Frank MacShane. Lincoln, Neb.: University of Nebraska Press, 1964.

————. *Portraits from Life*. Boston: Houghton Mifflin, 1937.

————. *Return to Yesterday*. New York: Liveright, 1972.

Ford, George H. *Dickens and His Readers: Aspects of Novel-Criticism since 1836*. New York: Norton, 1965.

————. *Double Measure: A Study of the Novels and Stories of D. H. Lawrence*. New York: Norton, 1965.

Forster, E. M. *Abinger Harvest*. New York: Harcourt, Brace and World, 1964.

————. *Albergo Empedocle and other Writings*. Edited by George H. Thomson. New York: Liveright, 1971.

————. *England's Pleasant Land: A Pageant Play*. London: Hogarth Press, 1940.

————. *Howards End*. Edited by Oliver Stallybrass. London: Camelot Press, 1973.

————. *A Room with a View*. New York: Knopf, 1925.

Fraser, G. S. *The Modern Writer and His World*. Baltimore: Pelican, 1964.

Frazer, Sir James. *The Golden Bough*. 1 vol. Abridged edition. New York: Macmillan, 1972.

Freeman, Mary. *D. H. Lawrence: A Basic Study of His Ideas*. Gainesville, Fla.: University of Florida Press, 1955.

Freud, Sigmund. *Civilization and Its Discontents*. Translated by James Strachey. New York: Norton, 1962 (1930).

Friedman, Alan. *The Turn of the Novel*. New York: Oxford University Press, 1966.

Fussell, Paul. *The Great War and Modern Memory*. New York: Oxford University Press, 1975.

Garnett, David, ed. *Carrington: Letters and Extracts from Her Diaries*. London: Jonathan Cape, 1970.

————. *The Flowers of the Forest*. New York: Harcourt, Brace and Co., 1956.

Garnett, Edward. *Friday Nights*. London: Jonathan Cape, 1929.

———, ed. *Letters from John Galsworthy: 1900–1932*. London: Jonathan Cape, 1934.

———, ed. *Letters from W. H. Hudson*. London: Nonesuch, 1923.

Gauguin, Paul. *Noa Noa*. Translated by O. F. Theis. New York: Noonday, 1974.

Gay, Peter. *Weimar Culture: The Outsider as Insider*. New York: Harper and Row, 19687.

George, W. L. *A Novelist on Novels*. London: W. Collins, 1918.

George, W. L., and Forbes-Robertson, Phillip. *A London Mosaic*. New York: Stokes, 1921.

Gerhardi, William. *Memoirs of a Polyglot*. New York: Knopf, 1931.

Ghiselin, Brewster. "D. H. Lawrence and a New World." *The Western Review* 11 (1947):150–59.

Gibson, Wilfred Wilson. *Daily Bread*. In Three Books. New York: Macmillan, 1912.

Gilbert, Sandra. *Acts of Attention*. Ithaca, New York: Cornell University Press, 1972.

Gill, Richard. *Happy Rural Seat: The English Country House and the Literary Imagination*. New Haven, Conn.: Yale University Press, 1972.

Gillie, Christopher. *Movements in English Literature 1900–1940*. London: Cambridge University Press, 1975.

Goldring, Douglas. *Reputations: Essays in Criticism*. New York: Thomas Seltzer, 1920.

Goodheart, Eugene. *The Cult of the Ego*. Chicago: University of Chicago Press, 1968.

———. *The Utopian Vision of D. H. Lawrence*. Chicago: University of Chicago Press, 1963.

Goodwin, K. L. *The Influence of Ezra Pound*. London: Oxford University Press, 1966.

Gosse, Edmund. *Some Diversions of a Man of Letters*. London: Heinemann, 1920.

Gould, Jean. *Amy: The World of Amy Lowell and the Imagist Movement*. New York: Dodd, Mead and Co., 1975.

Grant, Joy. *Harold Monro and the Poetry Bookshop*. Berkeley and Los Angeles: University of California Press, 1967.

Graves, Robert. *The Common Asphodel: Collected Essays on Poetry 1922–1949*. London: Hamish Hamilton, 1971.

———. *Good-bye to All That*. New York: Doubleday Anchor, 1957.

Gray, Cecil. *Peter Warlock: A Memoir of Philip Heseltine*. London: Jonathan Cape, 1934.

Green, Martin. *Children of the Sun: A Narrative of "Decadence" in England after 1918*. New York: Basic Books, 1976.

————. *A Mirror for Anglo-Saxons: A Discovery of America, a Rediscovery of England*. New York: Harper and Brothers, 1960.

————. *The von Richthofen Sisters: The Triumphant and Tragic Modes of Love*. New York: Basic Books, 1974.

Greene, Graham. *A Sort of Life*. New York: Simon and Schuster, 1971.

Gregory, Horace. *Amy Lowell: Portrait of the Poet in Her Time*. New York: Thomas Nelson, 1958.

————. *D. H. Lawrence: Pilgrim of the Apocalypse*. N.Y.: Grove, 1957.

Gross, Harvey. *The Contrived Corridor: History and Fatality in Modern Literature*. Ann Arbor: University of Michigan Press, 1971.

Gross, John. *The Rise and Fall of the Man of Letters*. New York: Collier, 1969.

Hahn, Emily. *Lorenzo: D. H. Lawrence and the Women Who Loved Him*. Philadelphia and New York: Lippincott, 1975.

Hamburger, Michael. *Contraries: Studies in German Literature*. New York: Dutton, 1970.

————. *The Truth of Poetry: Tensions in Modern Poetry from Baudelaire to the Nineteen-Sixties*. New York: Harcourt, Brace and World, 1969.

Hardy, Barbara. *The Appropriate Form*. London: The Athlone Press, 1964.

Harmer, J. B. *Victory in Limbo: Imagism in 1908–1917*. London: Secker and Warburg, 1975.

Harrington, Michael. *The Accidental Century*. Baltimore: Penguin, 1966.

Harrod, R. F. *The Life of John Maynard Keynes*. London: Macmillan, 1951.

Hart-Davis, Rupert. *Hugh Walpole: A Biography*. New York: Harcourt, Brace and World, 1952.

Hassall, Christopher. *A Biography of Edward Marsh*. New York: Harcourt, Brace and Co., 1959.

————. *Rupert Brooke: A Biography*. London: Faber and Faber, 1972.

Heilbrun, Carolyn. *The Garnett Family*. New York: Macmillan, 1961.

Hepburn, James, ed. *Letters of Arnold Bennett*. 3 vols. London: Oxford University Press, 1966.

Hibbard, G. R., ed. *Renaissance and Modern Essays*. New York: Barnes and Noble, 1966.

Hochman, Baruch. *Another Ego*. Columbia, S.C.: University of South Carolina Press, 1970.

Hoffman, Frederick J. *Freudianism and the Literary Mind*. New York: Grove Press, 1959.

———. "From Surrealism to 'The Apocalypse.'" *Journal of English Literary History* 15 (1948): 147–65.

Holroyd, Michael. *Lytton Strachey: A Critical Biography*. 2 vols. New York: Holt, Rinehart and Winston, 1967.

Hopkins, Kenneth. *The Poets Laureate*. New York: Library Publishers, 1955.

Hough, Graham. *The Dark Sun: A Study of D. H. Lawrence*. London: Duckworth, 1970.

———. *Image and Experience*. London: Duckworth, 1960.

Howe, Irving, ed. *Literary Modernism*. Greenwich, Conn.: Fawcett Premier, 1971.

Howe, Marguerite Beede. *The Art of the Self in D. H. Lawrence*. Athens, Ohio: Ohio University Press, 1977.

Hughes, Douglas A., ed. *The Man of Wax: Critical Essays on George Moore*. New York: New York University Press, 1971.

Hughes, Glenn. *Imagism and the Imagists*. New York: The Humanities Press, 1960.

Hulme, T. E. *Further Speculations*. Edited by Sam Hynes. Lincoln, Neb.: University of Nebraska Press, 1962.

———. *Speculations*. Edited by Herbert Read. London: Routledge and Kegan Paul, 1965.

Huneker, James Gibbons. *Ivory, Apes and Peacocks*. New York: Scribner's, 1915.

Huxley, Aldous. *Collected Essays*. New York: Harper, 1958.

———. *Crome Yellow*. London: Chatto and Windus, 1921.

———, ed. *The Letters of D. H. Lawrence*. London: Heinemann, 1932.

Hynes, Samuel. *Edwardian Occasions: Essays on English Writing in the Early Twentieth Century*. New York: Oxford University Press, 1972.

———. *The Edwardian Turn of Mind*. Princeton, N.J.: Princeton University Press, 1968.

Inniss, Kenneth. *D. H. Lawrence's Bestiary*. The Hague: Mouton, 1971.

Joad, C. E. M. *Decadence: A Philosophical Inquiry*. New York: Philosophical Library, 1949.

John, Augustus. *Chiaroscuro: Fragments of Autobiography*. New York: Pellegrini and Cudahy, 1952.

Johnstone, J. K. *The Bloomsbury Group: A Study of E. M. Forster, Lytton Strachey, Virginia Woolf, and Their Circle*. New York: Farrar, Straus, 1954.

Jones, Alun R. *The Life and Opinions of T. E. Hulme*. London: Gollancz, 1960.

Kallich, Martin. *The Psychological Milieu of Lytton Strachey*. New York: Bookman Associates, 1961.

Kaplan, Harold. *The Passive Voice*. Athens, Ohio: Ohio University Press, 1966.

Kenner, Hugh. *Gnomon: Essays on Contemporary Literature*. New York: Aston-Honor, 1958.

———. *The Pound Era*. Berkeley and Los Angeles: University of California Press, 1971.

Kermode, Frank. *D. H. Lawrence*. New York: Viking, 1973.

———. *Romantic Image*. New York: Vintage, 1964.

Keynes, Geoffrey, ed. *The Letters of Rupert Brooke*. New York: Harcourt, Brace and World, 1968.

Keynes, John Maynard. *Two Memoirs*. London: Rupert Hart-Davis, 1949.

Krishnamurthi, M. G. *D. H. Lawrence: Tale as Medium*. Mysore, India: Rao and Raghavan, 1970.

Langbaum, Robert. "Lords of Life, Kings in Exile: Identity and Sexuality in D. H. Lawrence." *American Scholar* 45 (Winter 1975/76): 807–15.

Laslett, Peter. *The World We Have Lost: England before the Industrial Age*. New York: Scribner's, 1973.

Laquer, Walter, and Mosse, George L., eds. *Literature and Politics in the Twentieth Century*. Journal of Contemporary History #5. New York: Harper Torchbooks, 1967.

Lavrin, Janko. *Aspects of Modernism: From Wilde to Pirandello*. Freeport, N.Y.: Books for Libraries Press, 1968 (1935).

Lawrence, D. H. *Aaron's Rod*. New York: Viking, 1971.

———. *Apocalypse*. Introduction by Richard Aldington. New York: Viking, 1967.

———. *The Complete Poems of D. H. Lawrence*. Collected and Edited with an Introduction and Notes by Vivian de Sola Pinto and Warren Roberts. New York: Viking, 1973.

———. *The Complete Short Stories*. 3 vols. New York: Viking, 1968.

———. *D. H. Lawrence and Italy*. Introduction by Anthony Burgess. New York: Viking, 1972.

———. "England, My England." *The English Review* 21 (October 1915): 238–52.

———. *Four Short Novels of D. H. Lawrence*. New York: Viking, 1972.

———. *Lady Chatterley's Lover*. Introduction by Mark Schorer. New York: Grove Press, 1957.

———. *The Lost Girl*. New York: Viking, 1968.

———. *Movements in European History*. London: Oxford University Press, 1971.

————. *Phoenix: The Posthumous Papers of D. H. Lawrence* (1936). Edited and with an Introduction by Edward McDonald. New York: Viking, 1972.

————. *Phoenix II: Uncollected, Unpublished, and Other Prose Works by D. H. Lawrence.* Collected and Edited with an Introduction and Notes by Warren Roberts and Harry T. Moore. New York: Viking, 1971.

————. *The Plumed Serpent.* New York: Knopf, 1951.

————. *Psychoanalysis and the Unconscious and Fantasia of the Unconscious.* Introduction by Philip Rieff. New York: Viking, 1972.

————. *The Rainbow.* New York: Viking, 1969.

————. *St. Mawr together with "The Princess."* London: Martin Secker, 1925.

————. *Selected Poems.* Introduction by Kenneth Rexroth. New York: Viking, 1961.

————. *Sex, Literature and Censorship.* Edited by Harry T. Moore. New York: Viking, 1969.

————. *Sons and Lovers.* New York: Viking, 1964.

————. *Studies in Classic American Literature.* New York: Viking, 1968.

————. *The Trespasser.* London: Heinemann, 1955.

————. *The White Peacock.* Carbondale, Ill.: Southern Illinois University Press, 1966.

————. *Women in Love.* New York: Modern Library, 1950.

Lawrence, Frieda. *"Not I, but the Wind . . ."* New York: Viking, 1934.

Leavis, F. R. *D. H. Lawrence: Novelist.* New York: Clarion, 1969.

————. "Keynes, Lawrence and Cambridge." *Scrutiny* 16 (September 1949): 242–46.

————. "Mr. Eliot and Lawrence." *Scrutiny* 18 (June 1951): 66–73.

————. *New Bearings in English Poetry: A Study of the Contemporary Situation.* London: Chatto and Windus, 1932.

Lehmann, John. *In My Own Time: Memoirs of a Literary Life.* Boston: Little, Brown, 1969.

————. *A Nest of Tigers: The Sitwells in Their Times.* Boston: Little, Brown, 1968.

Lehmann, John, and Parker, Derek, eds. *The Selected Letters of Edith Sitwell.* London: Macmillan, 1970.

Lester, John. *Journey through Despair, 1880–1914: Transformations in British Literary Culture.* Princeton: Princeton University Press, 1968.

Lewis, Wyndham. *Time and Western Man.* Boston: Beacon, 1957.

Lowell, Amy, ed. *Some Imagist Poets: An Anthology.* Boston and New York: Houghton Mifflin, 1915.

Lubbock, Percy, ed. *Letters of Henry James.* 2 vols. New York: Scribner's, 1920.

Lucas, Barbara. "Apropos of 'England, My England.'" *Twentieth Century* 169 (March 1961): 288–93.

Lucas, Robert. *Frieda Lawrence: The Story of Frieda von Richthofen and D. H. Lawrence.* Translated by Geoffrey Skelton. New York: Viking, 1973.

Ludwig, Richard M., ed. *Letters of Ford Madox Ford.* Princeton, N.J.: Princeton Universty Press, 1965.

Maas, Henry, ed. *The Letters of A. E. Housman.* Cambridge, Mass.: Harvard University Press, 1971.

MacCarthy, Desmond. *Criticism.* London: Putnam, 1932.

Mack, Maynard, and Gregor, Ian, eds. *Imagined Worlds: Essays on Some English Novels and Novelists in Honour of John Butt.* London: Methuen, 1968.

Mackenzie, Compton. *Carnival.* London: Martin Secker, 1929.

———. *Literature in My Time.* Freeport, N.Y.: Books for Libraries Press, 1967.

Mackenzie, Norman and Jeanne. *H. G. Wells.* New York: Touchstone, 1973.

Mannheim, Karl. *Diagnosis of Our Time.* New York: Oxford University Press, 1944.

Mansfield, Katherine. *Journal of Katherine Mansfield.* Edited with Introduction and Notes by John Middleton Murry. New York: McGraw-Hill, 1964.

Marcus, Geoffrey. *Before the Lamps Went Out.* Boston and Toronto: Little, Brown, 1965.

Marinetti, Filippo Tommaso. *Marinetti: Selected Writings.* Edited by R. W. Flint. Translated by Flint and Arthur A. Coppotelli. New York: Farrer, Straus and Giroux, 1972.

Marrot, H. V., ed. *Life and Letters of John Galsworthy.* New York: Scribner's, 1936.

Marsh, Edward. *A Number of People.* New York and London: Harper and Bros., 1939.

———. *Rupert Brooke: A Memoir.* New York: John Lane, 1918.

———, ed. *Georgian Poetry 1911–1912.* London: The Poetry Bookshop, 1912.

———, ed. *Georgian Poetry 1913–1915.* London: The Poetry Bookshop, 1916.

Marshall, Tom. *The Psychic Mariner.* New York: Viking, 1970.

Martin, Marianne W. *Futurist Art and Theory, 1900–1915.* Oxford: Clarendon Press, 1968.

Martin, Wallace. *The New Age under Orage: Chapters in English Cultural History*. Manchester: Manchester University Press, 1967.

————, ed. *Orage as Critic*. London: Routledge and Kegan Paul, 1974.

Marwick, Arthur. *The Deluge: British Society and the First World War*. London: The Bodley Head, 1965.

Masefield, John. *The Everlasting Mercy*. New York: Macmillan, 1917.

————. *So Long to Learn*. New York: Macmillan, 1952.

Masterman, C. F. G. *The Condition of England*. Edited with an Introduction by J. T. Boulton. London: Methuen, 1960.

————. *England after War*. New York: Harcourt, Brace, 1923.

————. *In Peril of Change*. London: T. Fisher Unwin, 1905.

Materer, Timothy. "The English Vortex: Modern Literature and the 'Pattern of Hope.'" *Journal of Modern Literature* 3 (July 1974): 1123–39.

Matthews, T. S. *Great Tom: Notes Towards the Definition of T. S. Eliot*. New York: Harper and Row, 1974.

Maugham, W. Somerset. *The Summing Up*. Garden City, N.Y.: Doubleday, Doran, 1939.

May, Rollo, ed. *Symbolism in Religion and Literature*. New York: George Braziller, 1960.

Merivale, Patricia. *Pan the Goat-God: His Myth in Modern Times*. Cambridge, Mass.: Harvard University Press, 1969.

Meyer, Leonard B. *Music, the Arts, and Ideas: Patterns and Predictions in Twentieth-Century Culture*. Chicago: University of Chicago Press, 1967.

Meynell, Viola, ed. *Letters of J. M. Barrie*. New York: Scribner's, 1947.

Miles, Kathleen. *The Hellish Meaning*. Carbondale, Ill.: Southern Illinois University Press, 1969.

Miller, J. Hillis. *Poets of Reality: Six Twentieth-Century Writers*. New York: Atheneum, 1969.

Mirsky, Dmitri. *The Intelligentsia of Great Britain*. Translated by Alec Brown. London: Gollancz, 1935.

Mizener, Arthur. *The Saddest Story: A Biography of Ford Madox Ford*. New York and Cleveland: World, 1971.

Monro, Harold. *Some Contemporary Poets (1920)*. London: Leonard Parsons, 1920.

Monroe, Harriet. *A Poet's Life: Seventy Years in a Changing World*. New York: Macmillan, 1938.

Moore, Harry T. *The Priest of Love: The Life of D. H. Lawrence*. Rev. ed. New York: Farrar, Straus and Giroux, 1974.

————, and Schorer, Mark. *Poste Restante*. Berkeley and Los Angeles: University of California Press, 1956.

Moore, Harry T., ed. *The Collected Letters of D. H. Lawrence.* 2 vols. New York: Viking, 1962.

————, ed. *A D. H. Lawrence Miscellany.* Carbondale, Ill.: Southern Illinois University Press 1959.

————, ed. *D. H. Lawrence's Letters to Bertrand Russell.* New York: Gotham Book Mart, 1948.

Morrell, Ottoline. *Ottoline at Garsington: Memoirs of Lady Ottoline Morrell 1915–1918.* Edited by Robert Gathorne-Hardy. London: Faber and Faber, 1974.

————. *Ottoline: The Early Memoirs of Lady Ottoline Morrell.* Edited by Robert Gathorne-Hardy. London: Faber and Faber, 1963.

Moynahan, Julian. *The Deed of Life: The Novels and Tales of D. H. Lawrence.* Princeton, N.J.: Princeton University Press, 1966.

Muir, Edwin. *Latitudes.* New York: Huebsch, 1924.

————. *One Foot in Eden.* London: Faber and Faber, 1956.

————. *Transition.* London: Hogarth Press, 1926.

Mumford, Lewis. *The City in History: Its Origins, Its Transformations, and Its Prospects.* New York: Harbinger, 1961.

Murry, John Middleton. *Between Two Worlds: An Autobiography.* London: Jonathan Cape, 1935.

————. *Reminiscences of D. H. Lawrence.* New York: Henry Holt, 1933.

Myers, Neil. "Lawrence and the War." *Criticism* 4 (Winter 1962): 44–59.

Nehls, Edward, ed. *D. H. Lawrence: A Composite Biography.* 3 vols. Madison, Wis.: University of Wisconsin Press, 1957.

Nicolson, Nigel, and Trautmann, Joanne, eds. *The Letters of Virginia Woolf.* 6 vols. New York and London: Harcourt Brace Jovanovich, 1975–80.

Nietzsche, Friedrich. *The Use and Abuse of History.* Translated by Adrian Collins. Indianapolis and New York: The Library of Liberal Arts, Bobbs-Merrill, 1957.

Norman, Charles. *Ezra Pound.* Rev. ed. New York: Minerva Press, 1960.

Oates, Joyce Carol. *The Hostile Sun: The Poetry of D. H. Lawrence.* Los Angeles: Black Sparrow Press, 1974.

Orwell, George. *A Collection of Essays.* Garden City, N.Y.: Doubleday Anchor, 1954.

————. *The Road to Wigan Pier.* New York: Berkeley Medallion, 1967.

Owen, Harold, and Bell, John, eds. *The Collected Letters of Wilfred Owen.* London: Oxford University Press, 1967.

Owen, Wilfred. *The Collected Poems of Wilfred Owen.* Edited with Introduction and Notes by C. Day Lewis, and with a Memoir by Edmund Blunden. New York: New Directions, 1965.

Ozenfant, Amédée. *Foundations of Modern Art*. New American edition, augmented. New York: Dover, 1952.

Paige, D. D., ed. *The Letters of Ezra Pound 1907–1941*. New York: Harvest, 1950.

Palmer, Herbert. *Post-Victorian Poetry*. London: J. M. Dent and Sons, 1938.

Panichas, George A. "D. H. Lawrence's War Letters." *Texas Studies in Literature and Language* 5 (Autumn 1963): 398–409.

———. *The Reverent Discipline*. Knoxville, Tenn.: University of Tennessee Press, 1974.

Pater, Walter. *Studies in the History of the Renaissance*. London: Macmillan, 1873.

Patmore, Brigit. "Conversations with Lawrence." *London Magazine* 4 (June 1957): 31–45.

Paz, Octavio. *Alternating Current*. Translated by Helen R. Lane. New York: Viking, 1973.

———. *Children of the Mire: Modern Poetry from Romanticism to the Avant-Garde*. Translated by Rachel Phillips. Cambridge, Mass.: Harvard University Press, 1974.

Perkins, David. *A History of Modern Poetry: From the 1890's to the High Modernist Mode*. Cambridge, Mass.: Harvard University Press, 1976.

Phelps, Gilbert. *The Russian Novel in English Fiction*. London: Hutchinson's University Library, 1956.

Plumb, J. H. *The Death of the Past*. Boston: Sentry, 1970.

Pound, Ezra. *Gaudier-Brzeska: A Memoir*. New York: New Directions, 1970.

———. *Guide to Kulchur*. New York: New Directions, 1968.

———. *Literary Essays of Ezra Pound*. Edited with an Introduction by T. S. Eliot. New York: New Directions, 1968.

———. *Pavannes and Divagations*. New York: New Directions, 1974.

———. *Personae: The Collected Shorter Poems of Ezra Pound*. New York: New Directions, 1971.

———. *Selected Prose 1909–1965*. Edited with an introduction by William Cookson. New York: New Directions, 1975.

Pratt, William, ed. *The Imagist Poem*. New York: Dutton, 1963.

Pritchard, R. E. *D. H. Lawrence: Body of Darkness*. London: Hutchinson's University Library, 1971.

Pritchard, William H. "Wyndham Lewis and Lawrence." *Iowa Review* 2 (September 1971): 91–96.

Read, Herbert. *Art and Society*. New York: Macmillan, 1937.

Reck, Michael. *Ezra Pound: A Close-Up*. New York: McGraw-Hill, 1967.

Rexroth, Kenneth. *Assays*. New York: New Directions, 1961.

————. *Bird in the Bush*. New York: New Directions, 1959.

Rhys, Ernest. *Everyman Remembers*. New York: Cosmopolitan Book Corporation, 1931.

Richards, I. A., et al., eds. *Essays on Wyndham Lewis*. N.p.: Folcroft Library Editions, 1971.

Rieff, Philip. *The Triumph of the Therapeutic: Uses of Faith after Freud*. New York: Harper and Row, 1966.

Rose, W. K., ed. *The Letters of Wyndham Lewis*. London: Methuen, 1963.

Rosenbaum, S. P., ed. *The Bloomsbury Group: A Collection of Memoirs, Commentary and Criticism*. Toronto: University of Toronto Press, 1975.

————, ed. *English Literature and British Philosophy*. Chicago: University of Chicago Press, 1971.

Ross, Robert H. *The Georgian Revolt: Rise and Fall of a Poetic Ideal, 1910–1922*. London: Faber and Faber, 1967.

Russell, Bertrand. *Portraits from Memory and Other Essays*. New York: Clarion, 1969.

Sackville-West, Vita. *The Edwardians*. London: Hogarth Press, 1930.

Sagar, Keith. *The Art of D. H. Lawrence*. London: Cambridge University Press, 1966.

Sale, Roger. "D. H. L., 1912–1916." *The Massachusetts Review* 6 (Spring–Summer 1965): 467–80.

————. *Modern Heroism: Essays on D. H. Lawrence, William Empson and J. R. R. Tolkien*. Berkeley and Los Angeles: University of California Press, 1973.

Salter, Elizabeth. *The Last Years of a Rebel: A Memoir of Edith Sitwell*. Boston: Houghton Mifflin, 1967.

Sanders, Scott. *D. H. Lawrence: The World of the Five Major Novels*. New York: Viking, 1974.

Sassoon, Siegfried. *Memoirs of an Infantry Officer*. London: Faber and Faber, 1931.

Savage, Henry, ed. *Richard Middleton's Letters to Henry Savage*. London: Mandrake, 1929.

Saxena, H. S. "D. H. Lawrence and Impressionist Technique." *The Indian Journal of English Studies* 3 (1962): 145–52.

Scholes, Robert, ed. *Papers of the Midwest Modern Language Association #1*. Iowa City, Ia.: Midwest Modern Language Association, 1969.

Selgādo, R. G. M. "Review of *Complete Poems*." *The Critical Quarterly* 7 (Winter 1965): 389–92.

Seligman, Herbert. *D. H. Lawrence: An American Interpretation*. New York: Seltzer, 1924.

Sharpe, Michael C. "The Genesis of D. H. Lawrence's *The Trespasser*." *Essays in Criticism* 11 (January 1961): 34–39.

Shattuck, Roger. *The Banquet Years: The Origins of the Avant-Garde in France 1885 to World War I*. Rev. ed. New York: Vintage, 1968.

Shaw, George Bernard. *Heartbreak House*. Harmondsworth, Middlesex: Penguin, 1967.

Silkin, Jon. *Out of Battle: The Poetry of the Great War*. London: Oxford University Press, 1972.

Simon, Myron. *The Georgian Poetic*. Berkeley: University of California Publications: Occasional Papers #8: Literature, 1975.

Sitwell, Edith. *Taken Care Of*. New York: Atheneum, 1965.

Sitwell, Osbert. *Noble Essences*. New York: Grosset and Dunlap, 1950.

Spears, Monroe K. *Space Against Time in Modern Poetry*. Prefatory note by Betsey Colquitt. Fort Worth, Tex.: Texas Christian University Press, 1972.

Spender, Stephen. *The Destructive Element*. Boston and New York: Houghton Mifflin, 1936.

———. *Love-Hate Relations: English and American Sensibilities*. New York: Vintage, 1975.

———. *The Struggle of the Modern*. Berkeley and Los Angeles: University of California Press, 1965.

———. *World Within World*. Berkeley and Los Angeles: University of California Press, 1966.

Spilka, Mark, ed. *D. H. Lawrence: A Collection of Critical Essays*. Englewood Cliffs, N.J.: Prentice-Hall, 1963.

Squires, Michael. *The Pastoral Novel: Studies in George Eliot, Thomas Hardy, and D. H. Lawrence*. Charlottesville, Va.: University Press of Virginia, 1974.

Stallybrass, Oliver, ed. *Aspects of E. M. Forster*. New York: Harcourt, Brace and World, 1969.

Stead, C. K. *The New Poetic: Yeats to Eliot*. New York: Harper Torchbooks, 1964.

Stevens, Wallace. *Opus Posthumous*. Edited by Samuel French Morse. New York: Knopf, 1957.

Stock, Noel. *The Life of Ezra Pound*. New York: Pantheon, 1970.

Stoll, John. *The Novels of D. H. Lawrence: A Search for Integration*. Columbia, Mo.: University of Missouri Press, 1971.

Stone, Wilfred. *The Cave and the Mountain: A Study of E. M. Forster*. Palo Alto, Calif.: Stanford University Press, 1966.

Stonesifer, Richard J. *W. H. Davies: A Critical Biography*. London: Jonathan Cape, 1963.

Strachey, Lytton. *Eminent Victorians*. New York: Putnam, 1918.

———. *Literary Essays*. New York: Harcourt, Brace and World, n.d.

———. *Lytton Strachey by Himself: A Self-portrait*. Edited with introduction by Michael Holroyd. New York: Holt, Rinehart and Winston, 1971.

———. *The Really Interesting Question and Other Papers*. Edited by Paul Levy. New York: Coward, McCann and Geoghegan, 1973.

Sussman, Herbert L. *Victorians and the Machine*. Cambridge, Mass.: Harvard University Press, 1968.

Swigg, Richard. *Lawrence, Hardy, and American Literature*. London: Oxford University Press, 1972.

Swinnerton, Frank. *Figures in the Foreground: Literary Reminiscences 1917–1940*. Garden City, N.Y.: Doubleday, 1964.

———. *The Georgian Scene: A Literary Panorama*. New York: Farrar and Rinehart, 1934.

———. *Swinnerton: An Autobiography*. Garden City, N.Y.: Doubleday, Doran, 1936.

Sypher, Wylie. *Loss of the Self in Modern Literature and Art*. New York: Vintage, 1963.

Tate, Allen. *The Forlorn Demon: Didactic and Critical Essays*. Freeport, N.Y.: Books for Libraries Press, 1969.

Thomas, Edward. *Cloud Castle*. New York: Dutton, 1922.

———. *Collected Poems*. London: Faber and Faber, 1961.

Toliver, Harold E. *Marvell's Ironic Vision*. New Haven, Conn.: Yale University Press, 1965.

Townsend, J. Benjamin. *John Davidson: Poet of Armageddon*. New Haven, Conn.: Yale University Press, 1961.

Trilling, Lionel. *Freud and the Crisis of Our Culture*. Mid-Century Essays #1. Boston: Beacon, 1955.

———. *Sincerity and Authenticity*. Cambridge, Mass.: Harvard University Press, 1973.

Tuchman, Barbara. *The Proud Tower*. New York: Macmillan, 1966.

Valéry, Paul. *The Outlook for Intelligence*. Translated by Denise Folliot and Jackson Mathews. New York: Harper Torchbooks, 1963.

Vickery, John. *The Literary Impact of the Golden Bough*. Princeton, N.J.: Princeton University Press, 1973.

Wade, Allan, ed. *The Letters of W. B. Yeats*. New York: Macmillan, 1955.

Wagner, Geoffrey. *Wyndham Lewis*. New Haven, Conn.: Yale University Press, 1957.

Ward, Maisie. *Gilbert Keith Chesterton*. New York: Sheed and Ward, 1943.

Wasson, Richard. "Comedy and History in *The Rainbow*." *Modern Fiction Studies* 13 (1967–1968): 465–77.

Waugh, Arthur. *Tradition and Change: Studies in Contemporary Literature*. London: Chapman and Hall, 1919.

Waugh, Evelyn. *A Little Learning: An Autobiography*. Boston: Little, Brown, 1964.

Wees, William. "England's Avant-Garde: The Futurist-Vorticist Phase." *Western Humanities Review* 21 (Spring 1967): 117–28.

————. *Vorticism and the English Avant-Garde*. Toronto: University of Toronto Press, 1972.

Weil, Simone. *The Need for Roots*. Translated by Arthur Wills, with a Preface by T. S. Eliot. New York: Harper Colophon, 1971.

Wells, H. G. *Ann Veronica*. Harmondsworth, Middlesex: Penguin, 1968.

————. *Experiment in Autobiography*. New York: Macmillan, 1934.

————. *Mind at the End of Its Tether*. New York: Didier, 1946.

————. *Tono-Bungay*. Boston: Houghton Mifflin, 1966.

West, Paul. *The Wine of Absurdity*. University Park, Pa.: Pennsylvania State University Press, 1966.

West, Rebecca. *D. H. Lawrence*. London: Martin Secker, 1930.

————. *The Strange Necessity: Essays by Rebecca West*. Garden City, N.Y.: Doubleday, Doran, 1928.

White, William Hale [Mark Rutherford]. *The Autobiography of Mark Rutherford*. London: Oxford University Press, 1936.

Widmer, Kingsley. *The Art of Perversity: D. H. Lawrence's Shorter Fictions*. Seattle: University of Washington Press, 1962.

Wildi, Max. "The Birth of Expressionism in the Work of D. H. Lawrence." *English Studies* 19 (December 1937): 241–59.

Williams, Raymond. *The Country and the City*. New York: Oxford University Press, 1973.

————. *Culture and Society 1780/1950*. New York: Harper Torchbooks, 1958.

————. *The English Novel from Dickens to Lawrence*. New York: Oxford University Press, 1970.

Williams, William Carlos. *Autobiography*. New York: Random House, 1951.

Wilson, Angus. *Anglo-Saxon Attitudes*. New York: Viking, 1956.

————. *The Wild Garden*. London: Secker and Warburg, 1963.

Wind, Edgar. *Art and Anarchy*. New York: Vintage, 1969.

Woodeson, John. *Mark Gertler: Biography of a Painter, 1891–1939*. To-ronto: University of Toronto Press, 1973.

Woodruff, Douglas, ed. *For Hilaire Belloc: Essays in Honor of His 71st Birth-day*. New York: Sheed and Ward, 1942.

Woolf, Leonard. *Beginning Again: An Autobiography of the Years 1911 to 1918*. New York: Harcourt Brace Jovanovich, 1964.

Woolf, Leonard, and Strachey, James, eds. *Virginia Woolf and Lytton Strachey: Letters*. London: Hogarth, 1956.

Woolf, Virginia. *The Captain's Death Bed and Other Essays*. New York: Harcourt, Brace, 1950.

———. *Collected Essays*. 4 vols. London: Hogarth, 1966.

———. *Roger Fry: A Biography*. New York: Harcourt, Brace, 1940.

Yeats, W. B., ed. *The Oxford Book of Modern Verse, 1892–1935*. New York: Oxford University Press, 1936.

Young, Jessica Brett. *Francis Brett Young: A Biography*. London: Heine-man, 1962.

Zolla, Elémire. *The Eclipse of the Intellectual*. Translated by Raymond Ro-senthal. New York: Funk and Wagnalls, 1968.

Zytaruk, George J., ed. *The Quest for Rananim: D. H. Lawrence's Letters to S. S. Koteliansky*. London: McGill-Queen's University Press, 1970.

Index

A. E. *See* Russell, George William
Aaron's Rod (D. H. Lawrence), 29
Abercrombie, Lascelles, 15, 41, 47, 49, 52, 55, 57, 98, 107, 113, 115, 116, 117, 118–19, 130, 175
Aldington, Richard, 18, 29, 61, 128, 143, 148, 151, 152, 153, 154, 156
Angelico, Fra, 138
Anglo-Saxon Attitudes (A. Wilson), 120
Ann Veronica (Wells), 18, 34
Anna of the Five Towns (Bennett), 39
Asquith, Cynthia, 109, 111
Attitudes toward History (K. Burke), 135–36
Austin, Alfred, 24

"Baby Movements" (D. H. Lawrence), 144–45
Baden-Powell, Robert, 26
Balla, Giacomo, 129
"Ballad of Another Ophelia" (D. H. Lawrence), 153
"Ballad of the Goodly Fere" (Pound), 61, 142
Bantock, G. H., 41
Barrie, James, 33, 34
Beardsley, Aubrey, 26
Bell, Clive, 15
Bell, John, 161
Bell, Quentin, 175–76, 178
Bell, Vanessa, 15
Bellamy, William, 28
Belloc, Hilaire, 27
Bennett, Arnold, 16, 27, 28, 31, 33, 34, 39, 42, 44
Bentham, Jeremy, 174
Bersani, Leo, 124–25
Bid Me to Live (H. D.), 154–55

Birds, Beasts, and Flowers (D. H. Lawrence), 75
Blackmur, R. P., 109
Blake, William, 174, 181
BLAST, 125
"Blind Man, The" (D. H. Lawrence), 178
Bloomsbury group, 15, 19, 20, 23, 44, 138, 172–49
Blue Bird, The (Maeterlinck), 72
Blunden, Edmund, 15, 161
Blunt, Wilfrid Scawen, 145
Boccioni, Umberto, 129
Borrow, George, 72
Bottomley, Gordon, 15, 52, 58–59, 72, 116, 151
Boulton, James T., 184
Bourne, George, 72
Bradbury, Malcolm, 17
Breaking Point, The (E. Garnett), 34
Brett, Dorothy, 17
Brewster, Earl and Achsah, 17
Brooke, Rupert, 45, 46, 47, 48, 49, 50, 52, 55–56, 57, 60, 61, 63, 66–67, 101–2, 103, 104, 108, 111, 112, 158–62, 167, 170
Burke, Kenneth, 127, 135–36
Burne-Jones, Edward, 82
Burrow, Trigant, 90
Burrows, Louie, 143, 184
Buzzi, Paolo, 129
Bynner, Witter, 17
Byron, Lord, 50, 106

Call, A (F. M. Ford), 34
Cambridge, 23, 172–79
Campbell, Gordon, 135, 160
Cannan, Gilbert, 31

Carlyle, Thomas, 34
Carnival (C. Mackenzie), 84
Carpenter, Edward, 72
Carra, Carlo D., 129
Carswell, Catherine, 17, 156, 171
Chambers, Jessie, 17, 57, 141
Chambers of Imagery, First Series (G. Bottomley), 58–59
Chambers of Imagery, Second Series (G. Bottomley), 58–59
"Channel-Passage" (R. Brooke), 50
Chapple, J. A. V., 17
Chesteron, G. K., 22, 27, 84
"Child and the Mariner, The" (Davies), 57
Cholmondeley, Mary, 141
Churchill, Winston, 158, 170
Cioran, E. M., 103
Coffman, Stanley, 153
Collected Letters of Wilfred Owen, The (eds. H. Owen and J. Bell), 161
Complete Poetical Works (Hulme), 140
Condition of England, The (Masterman), 37
Conrad, Joseph, 15, 27, 31, 34, 39, 126, 162
Cooper, James Fenimore, 90
Corke, Helen, 32–33
Country House, A (Galsworthy), 34
"Country of the Blind, The" (Wells), 119
Cran, Marion, 61
Crock of Gold, The (J. Stephens), 72, 106
Croquet Player, The (Wells), 162
"Cruelty and Love" (D. H. Lawrence), 54

D. H. Lawrence (Kermode), 17
D. H. Lawrence: A Composite Biography (Nehls), 183
D. H. Lawrence's Nightmare (Delaney), 22
Daiches, David, 52–53
Daleski, H. M., 132
Dangerfield, George, 43, 46, 47
D'Annunzio, Gabriele, 136
Davidson, John, 25, 34, 183–85
Davies, W. H., 15, 48, 52, 57, 64, 100, 111, 116, 118, 160
de la Mare, Walter, 57, 64, 106
de Sola Pinto, Vivian, 27

"Dead, The" (Brooke), 159
Delany, Paul, 16, 22, 173, 175–76
Delavenay, Emile, 16
Demoiselles d'Avignon, Les (Picasso), 103
Des Imagistes, 144, 147, 148, 156
Diaghilev, Serge, 45
Dickens, Charles, 34
Dickinson, Goldsworthy Lowes, 167
"Dining-Room Tea" (R. Brooke), 57
[D]oolittle, [H]ildad, 61, 143, 148, 152, 153–55
Dostoevsky, Fyodor, 45–46, 131
Dowson, Ernest, 26
Doyle, Arthur Conan, 183
"Dreams Old and Nascent: Old" (D. H. Lawrence), 57
Drinkwater, John, 15, 48, 50, 52, 57, 63, 116, 170

Edwardian Turn of Mind, The (Hynes), 26
Eagleton, Terry, 91–92
Edel, Leon, 178
Edward VII (king of England), 41, 42, 51, 98
Eliot, George, 34
Eliot, T. S., 15, 21, 27, 49, 60, 64, 115, 120, 123, 124, 126, 145, 146–47
"End of the World" (Abercrombie), 116, 118–19, 130, 175
"England, My England" (D. H. Lawrence), 75–76, 104, 158–71, 186–87
English Review, 28, 34, 53, 57, 144, 145, 186–87
Everlasting Mercy, The (Masefield), 47, 57, 63
Everyman Remembers (E. Rhys), 183, 184
Ezra Pound (C. Norman), 183

Fantasia of the Unconscious (D. H. Lawrence), 133
"Fires of God, The" (Drinkwater), 57
Figaro, Le, 127
Flaubert, Gustave, 39, 51
Flecker, James Elroy, 53, 109
Fletcher, John Gould, 103, 150, 152
Flint, F. S., 61, 152
Ford, Ford Madox, 25, 28, 29, 34, 50, 115, 121, 141, 142, 146, 148, 183–85
Ford, George H., 16, 77, 98
Forster, E. M., 15, 18, 20, 27, 34, 37,

38, 67–71, 75, 83, 124, 126, 159, 160, 163, 176, 178

Forsyte Saga, The (Galsworthy), 31

Fraser, G. S., 17

Freeman, Mary, 135–36

Fry, Roger, 15, 44

Russell, Paul, 19, 159

Future for Astyanax, A (Bersani), 124–25

Futurist Art and Theory (M. Martin), 127–28

Gajdusek, Robert, 78

Galsworthy, John, 27, 28, 30, 31, 33, 36, 42, 120

Garnett, Constance, 45

Garnett, David, 15, 17, 32, 138, 176, 177

Garnett, Edward, 29, 30, 31, 33, 34, 64, 107, 121, 122, 131, 132, 134, 148

Garsington, 36

"Gates of Damascus" (Flecker), 53

Gaudier-Brzeska, Henri, 148

Gauguin, Paul, 101

George, W. L., 33

Georgians, 56–59; use of dramatic narrative in poetry, 57; attitude toward industrialization, 57–59; attitude toward the reading public, 64–65; use of landscape in work, 73–86, 92–95, 117–18; reaction against Georgians, 92–93, 99, 100–107, 115–19, 158–71; attitudes about poetic technique, 106–15, 155–56; and Wyndham Lewis, 120–21, 125; and Vorticism, 121–26; ideas about the novel, 121–23, 125, 131–35, 180–81; and Ezra Pound, 123–25, 140–48, 183–85; and Futurism, 127–40; and Imagism, 140–57; and Ford Madox Ford, 141–42; 146, 148, 183–85; and "Amygism," 147–54; and H. D., 154–55; and World War I, 160–62, 167–71, 172, 186–87; and Cambridge-Bloomsbury milieu, 172–79; and Bertrand Russell, 172–75, 178; and Virginia Woolf, 177–78, 181. Works: *Aaron's Rod*, 29; "Baby Movements," 144–45; "Ballad of Another Ophelia," 153; *Birds, Beasts and Flowers*, 75; "Blind Man, The," 178; "Cruelty and Love," 54; "Dreams Old and Nascent: Old," 57; "England, My England," 75–76, 104, 158–71; *Fantasia of the Unconscious*, 133; "Green," 153; "Grief," 113; *Kangaroo*, 29, 33, 168; *Lady Chatterley's Lover*, 29, 124–25, 138–39, 178; *Lost Girl, The*, 18, 104; *Love Poems and Others*, 57, 59, 146, 147; *New Poems*, 57; "Night Songs," 145; "North Country, The," 57, 58; "Note to 'The Crown,'" 138; "Nottingham and the Mining Country," 89; *Plumed Serpent, The*, 29, 178; "Poetry of the Present," 155–56; *Rainbow, The*, 22, 29, 30, 32, 35, 52, 65, 73, 75, 76, 86, 89, 91–99, 105, 117, 122, 125, 126, 130, 135, 162, 170, 173, 180; "Review of *Georgian Poetry 1911–1912*," 50–53, 87, 100, 108; *St. Mawr*, 18, 76, 91, 178; "Schoolmaster, The," 57; *Sisters, The*, 110; "Snapdragon," 53–56, 57, 64, 109; *Sons and Lovers*, 22, 29, 30, 31–32, 33, 58, 65, 86, 87–89, 91, 93, 108, 113, 119, 122; *Studies in Classic American Literature*, 90; "Study of Thomas Hardy," 92–93, 116, 117, 130, 133–34; "Surgery for the Novel—or a Bomb," 180; "Thomas Mann," 107–8; *Trespasser, The*, 29, 33, 53, 58, 73–74, 87, 93, 136; *Twilight in Italy*, 136, 137; *Virgin and the Gipsy, The*, 33; "Wedding Morn," 153; *Wedding Ring, The*, 131; *White Peacock, The*, 22, 29, 32–33, 35, 37, 53, 58, 65, 74, 76–86, 87, 89, 93, 136, 162; *Women in Love*, 23, 29, 35, 36, 86, 89–90, 97, 98, 104, 105, 124–25, 126, 130, 135, 137–38, 140, 164, 168–69, 173, 178, 180

Georgian Poetry 1911–1912, 50–53, 54, 57, 59, 61, 63, 64, 66, 87, 99, 100, 108, 109

Georgian Poetry 1913–1915, 57, 116, 118

Gertler, Mark, 176

Ghiselinm, Brewster, 21

Gibson, W. W., 49, 52, 57, 63, 113, 116, 118, 119, 146

Gilbert, Sandra, 54–55, 144

"Golden Journey to Samarkand, The" (Flecker), 109, 112

Goldring, Douglas, 123
Goodheart, Eugene, 16, 86, 91, 107
Gosse, Edmund, 18, 48
Gould, Jean, 148, 153
Grahame, Kenneth, 72
Grant, Duncan, 15, 138
Graves, Robert, 161
Gray, Cecil, 154
"Green" (D. H. Lawrence), 153
Green, Martin, 16
Gregory, Horace, 100
"Grief" (D. H. Lawrence), 113

Hahn, Emily, 17
Hardy, Thomas, 25, 511, 76, 99, 130, 133, 137, 157, 162
"Hare, The" (W. W. Gibson), 57
Hassall, Christopher, 113, 175
Heart of Darkness (Conrad), 126
Henley, W. E., 25
Hochman, Baruch, 78
Hodgson, Ralph, 111, 118
Holroyd, Michael, 178
Hough, Graham, 62, 86
Housman, A. E., 72
Howards End (Forster), 34, 68–71, 72, 81, 160
Hudson, W. H., 31, 72, 103
Hughes, Glenn, 143
Hulme, T. E., 27, 46, 60, 61, 62, 115, 123, 140, 151, 155, 156
Huneker, James Gibbons, 128
Hunt, Violet, 32, 141, 183–85
Huxley, Aldous, 15, 16, 75
Hynes, Samuel, 19, 25, 26, 27, 44, 46, 47

Ibsen, Henrik, 51
Image, Selwyn, 61
"In Romney Marsh" (Davidson), 183
Inness, Kenneth, 81
"Inside the Whale" (Orwell), 60
"Iron-Founders and Others" (Bottomley), 59
Irving, Henry, 142

James, Henry, 28, 31, 32, 105
Jefferies, Richard, 72
Jerrold, Douglas, 27

Joad, C. E. M., 134
John Davidson: Poet of Armageddon (Townsend), 183
Johnson, Lionel, 26
Jones, Alun R., 61
Joyce, James, 15, 46, 49, 120, 157, 180

Kangaroo (D. H. Lawrence), 29, 33, 168
Keats, John, 151
Kenner, Hugh, 17, 18, 124
Kermode, Frank, 17, 132
Keynes, Geoffrey, 101
Keynes, John Maynard, 15, 172–77
"King Lear's Wife" (Bottomley), 116, 119
Kingsmill, Hugh, 17
Kinkead-Weekes, Mark, 130
Kipling, Rudyard, 15, 25, 62
Kipps (Wells), 34
Koteliansky, S. S., 171, 176

Lady Chatterley's Lover (D. H. Lawrence), 29, 124–25, 138–39, 178
Lamartine, A. M. de, 110
Last Judgment, The (Fra Angelico), 138
Lawrence, David Herbert: difficulty of "placing," 16–18; early intention, 21–23, 157; conflicting impulses between community and society, 22–23, 86–92; and Edwardians, 24–38; and H. G. Wells, 29–30; and John Galsworthy, 30–31; and Henry James, 31–32; and Edward Garnett, 33; and Arnold Bennett, 33–34, 39; reading during 1908–14, 34; and *Tono-Bungay*, 34–36, 73; early attitude toward Georgians, 39–40, 59, 61, 98; opinion of *Georgian Poetry 1911–1912*, 50–52, 64; and Edward Marsh, 53–54, 64, 106–15, 118–19; and Rupert Brooke, 54–56, 160–62, 167, 170; pastoral emphasis in work, 56, 80–85, 87
Lawrence, Frieda, 104, 106, 110, 143, 154, 157, 174
Lawrence in Love: Letters to Louis Burrows (Boulton), 184
Leavis, F. R., 16, 71, 97–98, 164
Lehmann, John, 15–16

Lester, John, 17, 126
Letters from America (Brooke), 101, 159–60
Lewis, Wyndham, 19, 27, 46, 120, 123–26, 148
Longest Journey, The (Forster), 20
Lord Jim (Conrad), 34
Lorenzo (Hahn), 17
Lost Girl, The (D. H. Lawrence), 18, 104
Love and Mr. Lewisham (Wells), 34
Love Poems and Others (D. H. Lawrence), 57, 59, 146, 147
"Love Song of J. Alfred Prufrock, The" (T. S. Eliot), 126
Low, Ivy, 32
Lowell, Amy, 147, 148–54
Lowell, James Russell, 154
Lucas, Madeleine, 171
Lucas, Percy, 171
Luhan, Mabel Dodge, 17
Lunacy and Letters (Chesterton), 84

MacCarthy, Desmond, 15, 44
Mackenzie, Compton, 31, 32, 84
McLeod, A. W., 122, 129, 131, 134, 154
Maeterlinck, Maurice, 72, 130
Mann, Thomas, 107–8, 118
Mansfield, Katharine, 50, 176
"Marble and the Statue, The" (Kinkead-Weekes), 130
Margaret Ogilvy (Barrie), 34
Marinetti, F. T., 121, 127–32, 134, 135, 138, 140
Marsh, Edward, 15, 39, 45, 47–48, 53, 56–57, 60, 61, 63, 64, 106–15, 118, 119, 128, 140, 150, 155, 156, 157, 158, 175
Marshall, Tom, 58
Martin, Marianne W., 127–28
Martindale, Elizabeth, 141
"Mary and the Bramble" (Abercrombie), 119
Masefield, John, 47, 52, 57, 63, 106, 119, 146
Masterman, C. F. G., 26, 34, 37, 38, 74
Matisse, Henri, 45
Maugham, W. Somerset, 101–2, 103, 104
Memoirs of an Infantry Officer (Sassoon), 161

Meredith, George, 25, 42, 65, 119
Merivale, Patricia, 72
Middleton, Richard, 33
Mirrors of Illusion (Storer), 114–15
Mizener, Arthur, 183
Monro, Harold, 15, 18–19, 46, 47, 61, 63, 70–71, 127
Monroe, Harriet, 144, 147, 152, 154, 156
Moore, G. E., 172, 175
Moore, George, 31
Moore, Harry T., 16, 154, 183
Moore, T. Sturge, 57, 61, 113
Morrell, Ottoline, 36, 138, 172, 176, 177
Mortimer, Raymond, 15
Mottram, R. H., 33
"Mr. Bennett and Mrs. Brown" (V. Woolf), 28
Muir, Edwin, 56
Murry, John Middleton, 17, 50, 134, 176, 178
Myers, Neil, 168

Nature Poems (Davies), 100
Nehls, Edward, 16, 183
Nest of Tigers, A (J. Lehmann), 15–16
Nevinson, C. R. W., 123
New Age, The, 34, 41–42, 43, 44, 46
Newbolt, Henry, 62, 145
New Numbers, 118
New Poems (D. H. Lawrence), 57
Nichols, Robert, 15, 108, 161
Nicolson, Nigel, 178
Nietzsche, Friedrich, 22, 46, 51, 59, 181
"Night Songs" (D. H. Lawrence), 145
Norman, Charles, 183
"North Country, The" (D. H. Lawrence), 57, 58
"Note to 'The Crown'" (D. H. Lawrence), 136
"Nottingham and the Mining Country" (D. H. Lawrence), 89
Noyes, Alfred, 24, 62

Old Wives' Tale, The (Bennett), 34
Orage, A. R., 42–43
Orwell, George, 60
Owen, Harold, 161
Owen, Wilfred, 161

Ozenfant, Amédée, 124

Palmer, Herbert, 53
Pan the Goat-God (Merivale), 72
Paradise Lost (Milton), 119
Passage to India, A (Forster), 18, 124, 126
Pater, Walter, 125
Paz, Octavio, 103
"Peace" (Brooke), 159
Perkins, David, 152
Plumed Serpent, The (D. H. Lawrence), 29, 178
Phillips, Stephen, 24
Picasso, Pablo, 103
Pinker, J. B., ,30
Poetry Bookshop, 61, 164
Poetry (Chicago), 147, 154
"Poetry of Cities, The" (Chesterton), 84
"Poetry of the Present" (D. H. Lawrence), 155–56
Portrait of a Genius, But . . . (Aldington), 29
Pound Eza, The (Kenner), 17
Pound, Ezra, 19, 21, 41, 48, 49, 50, 60, 61, 62–63, 64, 115, 117, 120, 123, 124, 125, 126, 140–57, 183, 185
"Preludes" (T. S. Eliot), 145
Priest of Love, The (H. T. Moore), 183
Priestley, J. B., 15
Pritchard, R. E., 132
Proust, Marcel, 157, 180

Rainbow, The (D. H. Lawrence), 22, 29, 30, 32, 35, 52, 65, 73, 75, 76, 86, 89, 91–99, 105, 117, 122, 125, 126, 130, 135, 162, 170, 173, 180
Rananim, 22, 86, 173
"Retrospect, A" (Pound), 149
"Review of Georgian Poetry 1911–1912" (D. H. Lawrence), 50–53, 87, 100, 108
Rhys, Ernest, 141–43, 183–85
Rhys, Grace (Mrs. Ernest), 184
Rhythm, 50
Richardson, Dorothy, 180
"Romanticism and Classicism" (Hulme), 156
Rosenbaum, S. P., 178
Ross, Robert H., 49, 116
Ross, Ronald, 61

Russell, Bertrand, 172–78
Russell, George William [pseud. A. E.], 15
Russian Ballet, 45, 128

Sackville, Margaret, 61
Sacre du printemps, Le (Stravinsky), 103
Saddest Story, The (Mizener), 183
St. Mawr (D. H. Lawrence), 18, 76, 91, 178
"Sale of Saint Thomas, The" (Abercrombie), 57, 115, 119
Sanders, Scott, 16
Sargant, Edmund Beale, 52
Savage, Henry, 110, 122
Sassoon, Siegfried, 161
"Schoolmaster, The" (D. H. Lawrence), 57
Schorer, Mark, 16, 92
Selgādo, R. G. N., 57
Sentimental Tommy (Barrie), 34
"Serious Artist, The" (Pound), 117
Severini, Gino, 129
Shakespeare, William, 47, 67
Shanks, Edward, 15
Sharp, Cecil, 72
Shaw, George Bernard, 15, 27, 28, 34, 42, 67, 120
"Sicilian Idyll, A" (T. Sturge Moore), 57
Simon, Myron, 66, 175
Simpson, Henry, 61
Sinzelle, Claude M., 76
Sisters, The (D. H. Lawrence), 110
Sitwell family (Edith, Osbert, Sacheverell), 15, 19
"Snap-dragon" (D. H. Lawrence), 53–56, 57, 64, 109
Soffici, Ardengo, 129
Some Imagist Poets, 152, 153
"Song of Honour" (Hodgson), 111
Sons and Lovers (D. H. Lawrence), 22, 29, 30, 31–32, 33, 58, 65, 86, 87–89, 91, 93, 108, 113, 119, 122
Spectator, The, 48
Spender, Stephen, 20
Squire, John, 15, 116–17
Stead, C. K., 50, 63
Stephens, James, 15, 72, 106
Stevens, Wallace, 157

Stevenson, Robert Louis, 101
Storer, Edward, 114–15
Strachey, Lytton, 15, 28, 177
Stravinsky, Igor, 103
Strindberg, August, 121
Strong, L. A. G., 71
Studies in Classic American Literature (D. H. Lawrence), 90
"Study of Thomas Hardy," 92–93, 116, 117, 130, 133–34
"Surgery for the Novel—or a Bomb" (D. H. Lawrence), 180
Swinburne, Algernon, 25, 42, 145
Synge, J. M., 103

Tancred, F. W., 61
"Technical Manifesto of Futurist Literature" (Marinetti), 134
Tennyson, Alfred, 26
Terriss, Ellaline, 141
Theocritus, 73
Thomas, Edward, 46, 161
"Thomas Mann" (D. H. Lawrence), 107–8
Times Literary Supplement, 48
Times (London), 44, 45
To the Lighthouse (Woolf), 124
Tolstoy, Leo, 34, 131
Tono-Bungay (Wells), 34, 35, 73
"Town and Country" (Brooke), 55–56
Townsend, J. Benjamin, 183
Trespasser, The (D. H. Lawrence), 29, 33, 53, 58, 73–74, 87, 93, 136
Trevelyan, R. C., 113
Trilling, Lionel, 105
Turgenev, Ivan, 131
Twilight in Italy (D. H. Lawrence), 136, 137

Ulysses (Joyce), 124
Upward, Allen, 40, 98

"Viaduct, The" (Bottomley), 58–59
Victoria (queen of England), 26, 42
Virgin and the Gipsy, The (D. H. Lawrence), 33
Vivas, Eliseo, 109

Wagner, Richard, 74
Wain, John, 46, 47
Walpole, Hugh, 15, 31
War of the Worlds, The (Wells), 26, 31
Watson, William, 24, 62
Waugh, Arthur, 48–50
Waugh, Evelyn, 48
"Wedding Morn" (D. H. Lawrence), 153
Wedding Ring, The (D. H. Lawrence), 131
Wells, H. G., 15, 18, 19, 25, 26, 27, 28, 29, 30, 31, 32, 34, 35, 36, 38, 42, 49, 66, 73, 119, 120, 162
West, Rebecca, 27
Westminster Gazette, The, 47
Wharton, Edith, 113
White Peacock, The (D. H. Lawrence), 22, 29, 32–33, 35, 37, 53, 58, 65, 74, 76–86, 87, 89, 93, 136, 162
Whitman, Walt, 63, 68
Widmer, Kingsley, 169
Wilde, Oscar, 26
Wildi, Max, 120–21
Williams, Raymond, 17, 23, 88–89, 118
Williams, Vaughan, 72
Wilson, Angus, 120, 121
Wind, Edgar, 115
Wind in the Willows, The (K. Grahame), 72
"Winter Dusk," 57
Women in Love (D. H. Lawrence), 23, 29, 35, 36, 86, 89–90, 97, 98, 104, 105, 124–25, 126, 130, 135, 137–38, 140, 164, 168–69, 173, 178, 180
Woodruff, Douglas, 27
Woolf, Leonard, 15, 41
Woolf, Virginia, 15, 28, 42, 43, 44, 45, 72, 124, 177, 178, 181
Wordsworth, William, 57, 72, 75, 151–52
Working Men's College Journal, The, 67

Yeats, W. B., 15, 26, 34, 46, 124, 141, 142
"Younger Generation, The" (James), 31